Ontology Management
Semantic Web, Semantic Web Services, and Business Applications

SEMANTIC WEB AND BEYOND
Computing for Human Experience

Series Editors:

Ramesh Jain
University of California, Irvine
http://ngs.ics.uci.edu/

Amit Sheth
University of Georgia
http://lsdis.cs.uga.edu/~amit

As computing becomes ubiquitous and pervasive, computing is increasingly becoming an extension of human, modifying or enhancing human experience. Today's car reacts to human perception of danger with a series of computers participating in how to handle the vehicle for human command and environmental conditions. Proliferating sensors help with observations, decision making as well as sensory modifications. The emergent semantic web will lead to machine understanding of data and help exploit heterogeneous, multi-source digital media. Emerging applications in situation monitoring and entertainment applications are resulting in development of experiential environments.

SEMANTIC WEB AND BEYOND
Computing for Human Experience
addresses the following goals:
- ➤ brings together forward looking research and technology that will shape our world more intimately than ever before as computing becomes an extension of human experience;
- ➤ covers all aspects of computing that is very closely tied to human perception, understanding and experience;
- ➤ brings together computing that deal with semantics, perception and experience;
- ➤ serves as the platform for exchange of both practical technologies and far reaching research.

Additional information about this series can be obtained from
http://www.springer.com   ISSN: 1559-7474

AdditionalTitles in the Series:
The Semantic Web:Real-World Applications from Industry edited by Jorge Cardoso, Martin Hepp, Miltiadis Lytras; ISBN: 978-0-387-48530-0
Social Networks and the Semantic Web by Peter Mika; ISBN: 978-0-387-71000-6
Ontology Alignment: Bridging the Semantic Gap by Marc Ehrig, ISBN: 0-387-32805-X
Semantic Web Services: Processes and Applications edited by Jorge Cardoso, Amit P. Sheth, ISBN 0-387-30239-5
Canadian Semantic Web edited by Mamadou T. Koné., Daniel Lemire; ISBN 0-387-29815-0
Semantic Management of Middleware by Daniel Oberle; ISBN: 0-387-27630-0

Ontology Management
Semantic Web, Semantic Web Services, and Business Applications

edited by

Martin Hepp
University of Innsbruck
Austria

Pieter De Leenheer
Vrije Universiteit Brussel
Belgium

Aldo de Moor
CommunitySense
The Netherlands

York Sure
University of Karlsruhe
Germany

 Springer

Martin Hepp
University of Innsbruck
Digital Enterprise Research Institute
Technikerstr. 21a
A-6020 INNSBRUCK
AUSTRIA
mhepp@computer.org

Pieter De Leenheer
Vrije Universiteit Brussel
Pleinlaan 2
B-1050 BRUSSELS 5
BELGIUM
pieter.de.leenheer@vub.ac.be

Aldo de Moor
CommunitySense
Cavaleriestraat 2
NL-5017 ET TILBURG
THE NETHERLANDS
ademoor@communitysense.nl

York Sure
SAP Research
Vincenz-Priessnitz-Str. 1
D-76131 KARLSRUHE
GERMANY
york.sure@sap.com

Library of Congress Control Number: 2007935999

Ontology Management: Semantic Web, Semantic Web Services, and Business Applications
Edited by Martin Hepp, Pieter De Leenheer, Aldo de Moor, York Sure

ISBN 978-0-387-69899-1   e-ISBN 978-0-387-69900-4

Printed on acid-free paper.

9 8 7 6 5 4 3 2 1

springer.com

Dedications

To Susanne and Matthis
Martin Hepp

To my parents
Pieter De Leenheer

To Mishko
Aldo de Moor

To my family
York Sure

TABLE OF CONTENTS

Foreword ix

Acknowledgements xiii

List of Reviewers xv

List of Authors xvii

I. OVERVIEW

1   Ontologies: State of the Art, Business Potential,
    and Grand Challenges 3

    Martin Hepp

II. INFRASTRUCTURE

2   Engineering and Customizing Ontologies 25
    The Human-Computer Challenge in Ontology Engineering

    Martin Dzbor and Enrico Motta

3   Ontology Management Infrastructures 59

    Walter Waterfeld, Moritz Weiten, and Peter Haase

4   Ontology Reasoning with Large Data Repositories 89

    *Stijn Heymans, Li Ma, Darko Anicic, Zhilei Ma, Nathalie Steinmetz,
    Yue Pan, Jing Mei, Achille Fokoue, Aditya Kalyanpur, Aaron
    Kershenbaum, Edith Schonberg, Kavitha Srinivas, Cristina Feier,
    Graham Hench, Branimir Wetzstein, and Uwe Keller*

III. EVOLUTION, ALIGNMENT, AND THE BUSINESS PERSPECTIVE

5   Ontology Evolution 131
    State of the Art and Future Directions

    Pieter De Leenheer and Tom Mens

6   Ontology Alignments 177
     An Ontology Management Perspective

     Jérôme Euzenat, Adrian Mocan, and François Scharffe

7   The Business View: Ontology Engineering Costs 207
     Elena Simperl and York Sure

IV. EXPERIENCES

8   Ontology Management in e-Banking Applications................... 229
     Integrating Third-Party Applications within an e-Banking Infrastructure

     *José-Manuel López-Cobo, Silvestre Losada, Laurent Cicurel, José
     Luis Bas, Sergio Bellido, and Richard Benjamins*

9   Ontology-Based Knowledge Management in
     Automotive Engineering Scenarios.. 245

     Jürgen Angele, Michael Erdmann, and Dirk Wenke

10   Ontologising Competencies in an
     Interorganisational Setting 265

     *Stijn Christiaens, Pieter De Leenheer, Aldo de Moor, and Robert
     Meersman*

     About the Editors 289

     Index.. 291

FOREWORD

Dieter Fensel
DERI, University of Innsbruck

About fifteen years ago, the word "ontologies" started to gain popularity in computer science research. The term was initially borrowed from philosophy but quickly established as a handy word for a novel approach of creating the abstractions needed when using computers for real-world problems. It was novel in at least three senses: First, *taking well-studied philosophical distinctions as the foundation for defining conceptual elements;* this helps create more lasting data and object models and eases interoperability. Second, using *formal semantics for an approximate description of what a conceptual element's intended meaning is.* This helps avoid unintended interpretations and, consequently, unintended usages of a conceptual element. It also allows using a computer for reasoning about implicit facts. And, last but not least, this improves the interoperability of data and services alike. Third, ontologies are meant to be *consensual abstractions of a relevant field* of interest, i.e., they are shared and accepted by a large audience. Even though the extreme stage of consensus in the form of a "true" representation of the domain is impossible to reach, a key goal is a widely accepted model of reality; accepted by many people, applicable for many tasks, and manifested in many different software systems.

It comes as no surprise that the idea of ontologies became quickly very popular, since what they promise was and is utterly needed: *a shared and common understanding of a domain that can be communicated between people and application systems.* It is utterly needed, because the amount of data and services which we are dealing with everyday is beyond of what traditional techniques and tools empower us to handle. The World Wide Web alone has kept on growing exponentially for several years, and the number of corporate Web services is vast and growing, too.

However, the initial excitement about ontologies in the late 1990s in academia did not show the expected impact in real-world applications; nor did ontologies actually mitigate interoperability problems at a large scale.

Quite obviously, early research had underestimated the complexity of building and using ontologies. In particular, an important duality[1] had been widely ignored:

1. Ontologies define a *formal* semantics for information allowing information processing by a computer.
2. Ontologies define a *real-world semantics* allowing to link machine processable content with meaning for humans based on *consensual* terminologies.

The first part of this duality can fairly easily be addressed by technology: by defining formalisms for expressing logical statements about conceptual elements and by providing infrastructure that can process it. The second part is much more difficult to solve: We have to produce models of relevant domains that reflect a consensual view of the respective domain, as perceived and comprehended by a wide audience of relevant human actors. It is this alignment with reality that makes building and using ontologies complex and difficult, since producing an ontology is not a finite research problem of having the inner structures of the world analyzed by a single clever individual or a small set of highly skilled researchers, but it is an ongoing, never ending social process.

It is thus pretty clear that there will never be such a thing as *the* ontology to which everybody simply subscribes. Much more, ontologies arise as pre-requisite and result of cooperation in certain areas reflecting task, domain, and sociological boundaries. In the same way as the Web weaves billions of people together to support them in their information needs, ontologies can only be thought of as a network of interweaved ontologies. This network of ontologies may have overlapping and excluding pieces, and it must be as dynamic in nature as the dynamics of the underlying process. In other words, ontologies are *dynamic networks of formally represented meaning*.

Ontology management is the challenging task of producing and maintaining consistency between formal semantics and real-world semantics. This book provides an excellent summary of the core challenges and the state of the art in research and tooling support for mastering this task. It also summarizes important lessons learned in the application of ontologies in several use cases.

The work presented in this book is to a large degree the outcome of European research projects, carried out in cooperation between enterprises and leading research institutions, in particular the projects DIP (FP6-507483), Knowledge Web (FP6-507482), SEKT (FP6-027705), and

---

[1] D. Fensel, *"Ontologies: Dynamic networks of formally represented meaning,"* available at http://sw-portal.deri.at/papers/publications/network.pdf

SUPER (FP6-026850). From early on, the European Commission had realized the enormous potential of ontologies for handling the interoperability problems in European business, research, and culture, which are caused by our rich cultural diversity. It is now that ontology management is ready for large, real-world challenges, thanks to this visionary and continuous support.

Innsbruck, August 2007   Prof. Dr. Dieter Fensel
                                          Director
                                          Digital Enterprise Research Institute
                                          University of Innsbruck

ACKNOWLEDGEMENTS

The editors would like to thank all authors for their contributions and their willingness to work hard on integrating numerous suggestions from the reviews, all reviewers for their thorough and constructive reviews, Damien Trog for his help in editing several chapters, Sharon Palleschi and Susan Lagerstrom-Fife from Springer for their excellent support, and Doug Wilcox from WordSmith Digital Document Services for the careful compilation and final layouting of the book.

This book was supported by the European Commission under the project DIP (FP6-507483) in the 6th Framework Programme for research and technological development.

LIST OF REVIEWERS

The following individuals supported this book as reviewers and provided numerous detailed and constructive reviews on previous versions of the papers included in this volume:

Jürgen Angele
Alessio Bosca
Jeen Broekstra
Andy Bytheway
Jorge Cardoso
Roberta Cuel
Harry S. Delugach
Alicia Díaz
Martin Dzbor
Dragan Gašević
Domenico Gendarmi
Stephan Grimm
Marko Grobelnik
Kristina Groth
Peter Haase
Andreas Harth
Stijn S.J.B.A Hoppenbrouwers
Mick Kerrigan
Michel Klein
Pia Koskenoja
Pär Lannerö
Ivan Launders
Holger Lausen

Juhnyoung Lee
Li Ma
Lyndon Nixon
Natasha Noy
Daniel Oberle
Eyal Oren
Simon Polovina
Laura Anna Ripamonti
Eli Rohn
Pavel Shvaiko
Elena Simperl
Katharina Siorpaes
Antonio Lucas Soares
Lucia Specia
Ljiljana Stojanovic
Heiner Stuckenschmidt
Tania Tudorache
Denny Vrandecic
Walter Waterfeld
Hans Weigand
Moritz Weiten
Bosse Westerlund

LIST OF AUTHORS

Darko Anicic
Digital Enterprise Research Institute (DERI), University of Innsbruck, Technikerstrasse 21a, A-6020 Innsbruck, Austria

Jürgen Angele
Ontoprise GmbH, Amalienbadstr. 36, D-76227 Karlsruhe, Germany

José Luis Bas
Bankinter, Paseo de la Castellana 29, E-28046, Madrid, Spain

Sergio Bellido
Bankinter, Pasco de la Castellana 29, E-28046, Madrid, Spain

Richard Benjamins
Telefónica Investigación y Desarrollo SAU, Emilio Vargas 6, E-28029, Madrid, Spain

Stijn Christiaens
Semantics Technology & Applications Research Laboratory (STARLab), Vrije Universiteit Brussel, Pleinlaan 2, B-1050 Brussel 5, Belgium

Laurent Cicurel
Intelligent Software Components S.A., C/ Pedro de Valdivia 10, E-28006, Madrid, Spain

Pieter De Leenheer
Semantics Technology & Applications Research Laboratory (STARLab), Vrije Universiteit Brussel, Pleinlaan 2, B-1050 Brussel 5, Belgium

Aldo de Moor
CommunitySense, Cavaleriestraat 2, NL-5017 ET Tilburg, The Netherlands

Martin Dzbor
Knowledge Media Institute, The Open University, Milton Keynes, MK7 6AA, UK

Michael Erdmann
Ontoprise GmbH, Amalienbadstr. 36, D-76227 Karlsruhe, Germany

Jérôme Euzenat
INRIA Rhône-Alpes & LIG, 655 avenue de l'Europe, F-38330 Montbonnot Saint-Martin, France

Cristina Feier
Digital Enterprise Research Institute (DERI), University of Innsbruck, Technikerstrasse 21a,
A-6020 Innsbruck, Austria

Achille Fokoue
IBM Watson Research Center, P.O. Box 704, Yorktown Heights, NY 10598, USA

Peter Haase
AIFB, Universität Karlsruhe (TH), Englerstr. 28, D-76128 Karlsruhe, Germany

Graham Hench
Digital Enterprise Research Institute (DERI), University of Innsbruck, Technikerstrasse 21a,
A-6020 Innsbruck, Austria

Martin Hepp
Digital Enterprise Research Institute, University of Innsbruck, Technikerstrasse 21a, A-6020
Innsbruck, Austria

Stijn Heymans
Digital Enterprise Research Institute (DERI), University of Innsbruck, Technikerstrasse 21a,
A-6020 Innsbruck, Austria

Aditya Kalyanpur
IBM Watson Research Center, P.O. Box 704, Yorktown Heights, NY 10598, USA

Uwe Keller
Digital Enterprise Research Institute (DERI), University of Innsbruck, Technikerstrasse 21a,
A-6020 Innsbruck, Austria

Aaron Kershenbaum
IBM Watson Research Center, P.O. Box 704, Yorktown Heights, NY 10598, USA

José-Manuel López-Cobo
Intelligent Software Components S.A., C/ Pedro de Valdivia 10, E-28006, Madrid, Spain

Silvestre Losada
Intelligent Software Components S.A., C/ Pedro de Valdivia 10, E-28006, Madrid, Spain

Li Ma
IBM China Research Lab, Building 19 Zhongguancun Software Park, Beijing 100094, China

Zhilei Ma
Institute of Architecture of Application Systems (IAAS), University of Stuttgart,
Universitätsstraße 38, D-70569 Stuttgart, Germany

Robert Meersman
Semantics Technology & Applications Research Laboratory (STARLab), Vrije Universiteit
Brussel, Pleinlaan 2, B-1050 Brussel 5, Belgium

Jing Mei
IBM China Research Lab, Building 19 Zhongguancun Software Park, Beijing 100094, China

Tom Mens
University of Mons-Hainaut (U.M.H.), Software Engineering Lab, 6, Avenue du Champ de Mars, B-7000 Mons, Belgium

Adrian Mocan
Digital Enterprise Research Institute (DERI), University of Innsbruck, Technikerstrasse 21a, A-6020 Innsbruck, Austria

Enrico Motta
Knowledge Media Institute, The Open University, Milton Keynes, MK7 6AA, UK

Yue Pan
IBM China Research Lab, Building 19 Zhongguancun Software Park, Beijing 100094, China

François Scharffe
Digital Enterprise Research Institute (DERI), University of Innsbruck, Technikerstrasse 21a, A-6020 Innsbruck, Austria

Edith Schonberg
IBM Watson Research Center, P.O. Box 704, Yorktown Heights, NY 10598, USA

Elena Simperl
Digital Enterprise Research Institute (DERI), University of Innsbruck, Technikerstrasse 21a, A-6020 Innsbruck, Austria

Kavitha Srinivas
IBM Watson Research Center, P.O. Box 704, Yorktown Heights, NY 10598, USA

Nathalie Steinmetz
Digital Enterprise Research Institute (DERI), University of Innsbruck, Technikerstrasse 21a, A-6020 Innsbruck, Austria

York Sure
SAP Research, Vincenz-Priessnitz-Str. 1, D-76131 Karlsruhe, Germany

Walter Waterfeld
Software AG, Uhlandstr. 12, D-64289 Darmstadt, Germany

Moritz Weiten
Ontoprise GmbH, Amalienbadstr. 36, D-76227 Karlsruhe, Germany

Dirk Wenke
Ontoprise GmbH, Amalienbadstr. 36, D-76227 Karlsruhe, Germany

Branimir Wetzstein
Institute of Architecture of Application Systems (IAAS), University of Stuttgart, Universitätsstraße 38, D-70569 Stuttgart, Germany

I. OVERVIEW

Chapter 1

ONTOLOGIES: STATE OF THE ART, BUSINESS POTENTIAL, AND GRAND CHALLENGES

Martin Hepp

Digital Enterprise Research Institute, University of Innsbruck, Technikerstraße 21a, A-6020 Innsbruck, Austria, mhepp@computer.org

Abstract: In this chapter, we give an overview of what ontologies are and how they can be used. We discuss the impact of the expressiveness, the number of domain elements, the community size, the conceptual dynamics, and other variables on the feasibility of an ontology project. Then, we break down the general promise of ontologies of facilitating the exchange and usage of knowledge to six distinct technical advancements that ontologies actually provide, and discuss how this should influence design choices in ontology projects. Finally, we summarize the main challenges of ontology management in real-world applications, and explain which expectations from practitioners can be met as of today.

Keywords: conceptual dynamics; conceptual modeling; costs and benefits; information systems; knowledge representation; ontologies; ontology management; scalability; Semantic Web

1. ONTOLOGIES IN COMPUTER SCIENCE AND INFORMATION SYSTEMS

Within less than twenty years, the term "ontology," originally borrowed from philosophy, has gained substantial popularity in computer science and information systems. This popularity is likely because the promise of ontologies targets one of the core difficulties of using computers for human purposes: Achieving interoperability between multiple representations of reality (e.g. data or business process models) residing inside computer systems, and between such representations and reality, namely human users and their perception of reality. Surprisingly, people from various research communities often use the term ontology with different, partly incompatible meanings in mind. In fact, it is a kind of paradox that the seed term of a novel field of research, which aims at reducing ambiguity about the intended meaning of symbols, is understood and used so inconsistently.

In this chapter, we try to provide a clear understanding of the term and relate ontologies to knowledge bases, XML schemas, and knowledge organization systems (KOS) like classifications. In addition, we break down the overall promise of increased interoperability to six distinct technical contributions of ontologies, and discuss a set of variables that can be used to classify ontology projects.

1.1   Different notions of the term ontology

Already in the early years of ontology research, Guarino and Giaretta (1995) raised concerns that the term "ontology" was used inconsistently. They found at least seven different notions assigned to the term: "…

1. *Ontology as a philosophical discipline*
2. *Ontology as a an informal conceptual system*
3. *Ontology as a formal semantic account*
4. *Ontology as a specification of a conceptualization*
5. *Ontology as a representation of a conceptual system via a logical theory*
   5.1 characterized by specific formal properties
   5.2 characterized only by its specific purposes
6. *Ontology as the vocabulary used by a logical theory*
7. *Ontology as a (meta-level) specification of a logical theory"* (from Guarino & Giaretta, 1995).

As the result of their analysis, they suggested to weaken the popular — but often misunderstood and mis-cited — definition of "a specification of a conceptualization" by Tom Gruber (Gruber, 1993) to "a logical theory which gives an explicit, partial account of a conceptualization" (Guarino & Giaretta, 1995). Partial account in here means that the formal content of an ontology cannot completely specify the intended meaning of a conceptual element but only approximate it — mostly, by making unwanted interpretations logical contradictions.

Although this early paper had already pointed to the possible misunderstandings, even as of today there is still a lot of inconsistency in the usage of the term, in particular at the border between computer science and information systems research.

The following three aspects of ontologies are common roots of disagreement about what an ontology is and what its constituting properties are:

Truth vs. consensus: Early ontology research was very much driven by the idea of producing models of reality that reflect the "true" structures and that are thus valid independent of subjective judgment and context. Other researchers, namely Fensel (Fensel, 2001), have stressed that it is not possible to produce such "true" models and that instead consensual, shared human judgments must be the core of ontologies.

Formal logic vs. other modalities: For a large fraction of ontology researchers, formal logic as a means (i.e., modality) for expressing the semantic account is a constituting characteristic of an ontology. For those researchers, neither a flat vocabulary with a set of attributes specified in natural language nor a conceptual model of a domain specified using an UML class diagram is an ontology. This is closely related to the question on whether the ontological commitment is only the logical account of the ontology or whether it also includes the additional account in textual definitions of its elements. In our opinion, it is highly arguable whether formal logic is the only or even the most appropriate modality for specifying the semantics of a conceptual element in an ontology.

Specification vs. conceptual system: There is also some argument on whether an ontology is the *conceptual system* or its specification. For some researchers, an ontology is an abstraction over a domain of interest in terms of its conceptual entities and their relationships. For others, it is the explicit (approximate) *specification of such an abstraction* in some formalism, e.g. in OWL, WSML, or F-Logic. In our opinion, the more popular notion is reading an ontology as the *specification* of the conceptual system in the form of a machine-readable artifact.

These differences are not mere academic battles over terminology; they are the roots of severe misunderstandings between research in computer science and research in information systems, and between academic research and practitioners. In computer science, researchers assume that they can define the conceptual entities in ontologies mainly by formal means — for example, by using axioms to specify the intended meaning of domain elements. In contrast, in information systems, researchers discussing ontologies are more concerned with understanding conceptual elements and their relationships, and often specify their ontologies using only informal means, such as UML class diagrams, entity-relationship models, semantic nets, or even natural language. In such contexts, a collection of named conceptual entities with a natural language definition — that is, a controlled vocabulary — would count as an ontology.

Also, we think it is important to stress that ontologies are not just formal representations of a domain, but *community contracts* about such representations. Given that a discourse is a dynamic, social process during which participants often modify or discard previous propositions or introduce new topics, such a community contract cannot be static, but must evolve. Also, the respective community must be technically and skill-wise able to build or commit to the ontology (Hepp, 2007). For example, one cannot expect an individual or a legal entity to authorize the semantic account of an ontology without understanding what they commit to by doing so.

1.2   Ontologies vs. knowledge bases, XML schemas, and knowledge organization systems

In this section, we try to differentiate ontologies from knowledge bases, XML schemas, and knowledge organization systems (KOS) as related terminology.

Knowledge bases: Sometimes, ontologies are confused with knowledge bases, in particular because the same languages (OWL, RDF-S, WSML, etc.) and the same tools and infrastructure can be used both for creating ontologies and for creating knowledge bases. There is, however, a clear distinction: Ontologies are the *vocabulary* and the formal specification of the vocabulary only, which can be *used for* expressing a knowledge base. It should be stressed that one initial motivation for ontologies was achieving interoperability between multiple knowledge bases. So, in practice, an ontology may specify the concepts "man" and "woman" and express that both are mutually exclusive — but the individuals Peter, Paul, and Marry are normally not part of the ontology. Consequently, not every OWL file is an ontology, since OWL files can also be used for representing a knowledge base.

This distinction is insofar difficult as individuals (instances) sometimes belong to the ontology and sometimes do not. Only those individuals that are part of the specification of the domain and not pure facts within that domain belong to the ontology. Sometimes it depends on the scope and purpose of an ontology which individuals belong to it, and which are mere data. For example, the city of Innsbruck as an instance of the class "city" would belong to a tourism ontology, but a particular train connection would not.

We suggest speaking of *ontological individuals* and *data individuals*. With ontological individuals we mean such that are part of the specification of a domain, and with data individuals, we mean such being part of a knowledge base within that domain.

XML schemas are also not ontologies, for three reasons:

1. They define a single representation syntax for a particular problem domain but not the semantics of domain elements.
2. They define the sequence and hierarchical ordering of fields in a valid document instance, but do not specify the semantics of this ordering. For example, there is no explicit semantics of nesting elements.
3. They do not aim at carving out re-usable, context-independent categories of things — e.g. whether a data element "student" refers to the human *being* or the *role* of being as student. Quite the opposite, we can often observe that XML schema definitions tangle very different categories in their element definitions, which hampers the reuse of respective XML data in new contexts.

Knowledge organization systems (KOS) are means for structuring the storage of knowledge assets for better retrieval and use. Popular types of KOS are classifications and controlled vocabularies for indexing documents. There is a long tradition of KOS research and applications, in particular in library science.

The main difference between traditional KOS and ontologies is that the former often tangle the dimension of search paths with the actual domain representation. In particular do classical KOS mostly lack a clear notion of what it means to be an instance or a subclass of a category. For example, the directory structure on our personal computer is a KOS, but not an ontology — since we mostly put a file into exactly one single folder, we try to make our folder structure match our typical search paths, and not to intersubjective, context-independent, and abstract categories of things.

In contrast, one key property of an ontology is a context-independent notion of what it means to be an instance or a subclass of a given concept. So while in a closed corporate KOS, one can put an invoice for batteries for a portable radio in the "Radio and TV" folder, ontologies make sense only if we clearly distinguish things, related things, parts and component of those things, documents describing those things, and similar objects that are held together mainly by being somehow related to a joint topic.

This tangling between search path and conceptualization in traditional KOS was caused by past technical limitations of knowledge access. For example, libraries must often sort books by one single identifier only, and maintaining extra indices was extremely labor-intensive and error-prone. Thus, the core challenge in designing traditional KOS was to partition an area of interest in a way compatible with popular search paths instead of carving out the true categories of existence guided by philosophical notions.

This does not mean that designing KOS is a lesser art than ontology engineering — it is just that traditional KOS had to deal with the technical limitation of a single, consensual search path, which is now less relevant. One of the most striking examples of mastering the design of a KOS is the science of using fingerprints for forensic purposes back in the 1920s: The major achievement was not spotting that fingerprints are unique and suitable for identifying a human being. Instead, the true achievement was to construct a suitable KOS so that traces found at a crime scene could be quickly compared with a large set of registered fingerprints — without visually comparing every single registered print, see e.g. Heindl (1927).

So while ontology engineering can learn a lot from KOS research, it is not the same, because intersubjective, context-neutral categories of objects are key for successful ontology design. Without such "clean" categories of objects, the potential of ontologies for improved data interoperability cannot materialize (see also section 2.1).

1.3   Six characteristic variables of an ontology project

There exist several approaches of classifying types of ontologies, namely by Lassila and McGuinness (Lassila & McGuinness, 2001) and by Oberle (Oberle, 2006, pp. 43–47). Lassila and McGuinness did order ontologies by increasing degree of formal semantics, while Oberle introduced the idea of combining multiple dimensions. On the basis of these two approaches, we suggest classifying ontology projects using the following six characteristics:

Expressiveness: The expressiveness of the formalism used for specifying the ontology. This can range from a flat frame-based vocabulary to a richly axiomatized ontology in higher order logic. A higher expressiveness allows more sophisticated reasoning and excludes more unwanted interpretations, but also requires much more effort for producing the ontology. Also, it is more difficult for users to understand an expressive ontology, because it requires a better education in logic and more time. Lastly, expressiveness increases the computational costs of reasoning.

Size of the relevant community: Ontologies that are targeted at a large audience must have different properties than those intended for a small group of individuals only. For a large relevant community, an ontology must be easy to understand, well documented, and of limited size. Also, the consensus finding mechanism in broad audiences must be less subtle. For an in-depth discussion of this, see (Hepp, 2007). The important number in here is the number of human actors that are expected to commit to the ontology.

Conceptual dynamics in the domain, i.e., the amount of new conceptual elements and changes in meaning to existing ones per period of time: Most domains undergo some conceptual dynamics, i.e., new categories of things become relevant, the definition of existing ones changes, etc. The amount of conceptual dynamics in the domain of interest determines the necessary versioning strategy and also limits the feasible amount of detail of the ontology — the more dynamics there is in a given domain, the harder it gets to maintain a richly axiomatized ontology.

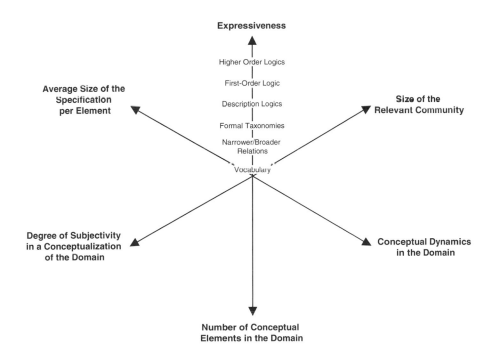

Figure 1-1. The six characteristic variables of an ontology project

Number of conceptual elements in the domain: How large will the ontology be? A large ontology is much harder to visualize properly, and takes more effort to review. Also, large ontologies can be unfeasible for use with reasoners that require an in-memory model of the ontology. Often, smaller ontologies are adopted more quickly and gain a greater popularity than large ones (Hepp, 2007).

Degree of subjectivity in a conceptualization of the respective domain: To which degree are the notions of a concept different between actors? For example, domains like religion, culture, and food are likely much more prone to subjective judgments than natural sciences and engineering. The degree of subjectivity determines the appropriate type of consensus-finding mechanisms, and it also limits the feasible specificity per element (i.e., the richness of the ontological commitment). The latter is because the likelihood of disagreement increases the more specific our definitions get.

Average size of the specification per element: How comprehensive is the specification of an average element? For example, are we expecting two attributes per concept only, or fifty first-order logic axioms? This variable influences the effort needed for achieving consensus, for coding the ontology, and for reviewing the ontological commitment before adopting the respective ontology.

Figure 1-1 presents the six variables in the form of a radar graph. By adding scales to the axes, one can use this to quickly characterize ontology projects.

2.   SIX EFFECTS OF ONTOLOGIES

The promises of what ontologies can solve are broad, but as a matter of fact, ontologies are not good for every problem. Since ontologies are not everlasting assets but have a lifespan and require maintenance, there are situations in which building the ontologies required for a specific task is more difficult or more costly that solving the task without ontologies.

In this section, we will analyze the actual contribution of ontologies to improved access and use of knowledge resources and identify six core parts of this contribution. This is insofar relevant as the various contributions differ heavily in how they depend on the formal account of an ontology. In particular, we will show that several claims of what ontologies can do depend not mainly on a rich formalization, but are materialized by clean conceptual modeling based on philosophical notions and by well-thought lexical enrichment (e.g. a human-readable documentation or synonym sets per cach element). This also explains why ontologies are much more useful for new information systems as compared to problems related to legacy systems. Ontologies, for example, can provide little help if old source systems provide data in a poorly structured way.

The uses of ontologies have been summarized by Gruninger and Lee as follows (Gruninger & Lee, 2002, p. 40): "...

- *for communication*
  - o   *between implemented computational systems*
  - o   *between humans*
  - o   *between humans and implemented computational systems*
- *for computational inference*
  - o   *for internally representing plans and manipulating plans and planning information*
  - o   *for analyzing the internal structures, algorithms, inputs and outputs of implemented systems in theoretical and conceptual terms*
- *for reuse (and organization) of knowledge*

    o *for structuring or organizing libraries or repositories of plans and planning and domain information."*

Note that ontologies provide more than the basis for computational inference on data, but are also helpful in improving the interaction between multiple human actors and between humans and implemented computer systems.

Whenever computer science meets practical problems, there is a trade-off problem between human intelligence and computational intelligence. Consequently, it is important to understand what ontologies are not good for and what is difficult. For example, people from outside the field often hope for support in problems like unit conversion (inches to centimeters, dollars to Euro, net prices to gross prices, etc.) or different reference points for quantitative attributes, while current ontology technology is not suited for handling functional conversions and arithmetics in general.

Also, it was often said that integrating e-business product data and catalogs would benefit from ontologies, see e.g. the respective challenge of mapping UNSPSC and eCl@ss (Schulten et al., 2001). While there were academic prototypes and success stories (Corcho & Gómez-Pérez, 2001), the practical impact is small, since the conceptual modeling quality of the two standards is limited, which constrains the efficiency of possible mappings. For example, assume that we have two classification systems A and B, and that system A includes a category "TV Sets and Accessories" and system B a related one "TV Sets and Antennas." Now, the only possible mapping is that "TV Sets and Antennas" is a subclass of "TV Sets and Accessories." This provides zero help for reclassifying source data stored using system A into system B. Also, those two classifications undergo substantial change over time, and a main challenge for users is to classify new, unstructured data sets using semi-automatic tools. In general, for any problem where the source representation is weakly structured, the actual contribution of ontologies is limited, because the main problem is then lifting that source data to a more structured conceptual level — something for which machine learning and natural language technologies can contribute more than ontologies can.

Fortunately, there are now more and more successful examples of ontology usage, e.g. matching patients to clinical trials (Patel et al., 2007) and the three uses cases in chapters 8, 9, and 10 of this book. Additional use cases are described in Cardoso, Hepp, & Lytras (2007). It must be said, though, that the broad promises of the early wave of ontology research were too optimistic, because the advocates had ignored the technical difficulties of (1) providing ontologies of sufficient quality and currency, (2) of annotating source data, and (3) of creating complete, current, and correct mappings — and did mostly not compare the costs and benefits of ontologies over their lifespan. Two notable exceptions are Menzies in 1999 (Menzies, 1999) and recently Oberle (Oberle, 2006, in particular pp. 242–243).

In the following, we trace back the general advancement that ontologies provide to six distinct technical effects.

2.1   Using philosophical notions as guidance for identifying stable and reusable conceptual elements

One core part of ontological engineering is the art and science of producing clean, lasting, and reusable conceptual models. With clean we mean conceptual modeling choices that are based on philosophically well-founded distinctions and that hold independent of the application context. The most prominent contribution in this field is the OntoClean methodology, see (Guarino & Welty, 2002) and (Guarino & Welty, 2004).

A practical example is the distinction between actors and their roles, e.g. that being a student is not a subclass of being a human, but a role — or that a particular make and model of a commodity is not a subclass of a particular type of good, but a conceptual entity in its own right.

Such untangling of objects increases the likelihood of interoperability of data, because it is the precision and subtleness of the source representation that always determines the degree of automation in the usage and access to knowledge representations. Also, maintaining attributes for types of objects is much easier if the hierarchy of objects is designed in this way.

In other words: The cleaner our conceptual distinctions are, the more likely it is that we are not putting into one category objects that need to be kept apart in other usages of the same data — in future applications and in novel contexts.

So ontology engineering is also a school of thinking that leads to better conceptual models.

2.2   Unique identifiers for conceptual elements

Exactly 20 years ago, Furnas and colleagues have shown that the likelihood that two individuals choose the same word for the same thing in human-system communication is less than 20% (Furnas, Landauer, Gomez, & Dumais, 1987). They have basically proven that there is "no good access term for most objects" (Furnas, Landauer, Gomez, & Dumais, 1987, p. 967). They also studied the likelihood that two people using the same term refer to the same referent, with only slightly better results; as a cure, they suggested the heavy use of synonyms.

Ontologies provide unique identifiers for conceptual elements, often in the form of a URI. We call this the "controlled vocabulary effect" of ontologies. This effect is an important contribution, and the use of ontologies is often motivated by problems caused by homonyms and synonyms in natural languages.

However, we should note that this vocabulary effect does not require the specification of domain elements by formal means. Well-thought vocabularies with carefully chosen terminology and synonym sets can serve the same purpose. Much more, we do not know of any quantitative evidence that the formal semantics of any available ontology surpasses such well-designed vocabularies in efficiency. At the same time, formal content raises the bar for user participation.

2.3 Excluding unwanted interpretations by means of informal semantics

Besides providing unique identifiers only, ontologies can be augmented by well-thought textual definitions, synonym sets, and multi-media elements like illustrations. In fact, the intended semantics of an ontology element cannot be conveyed by the formal specification only but requires a human-readable documentation. In practice, we need ontologies that define elements with a narrow, real-world meaning. For example, we may need ontologies with classes like

$$\texttt{Portable Color TV} \subseteq \texttt{TV Set} \subseteq \texttt{Media Device}$$

In such cases, the intended semantics goes way beyond

$$\texttt{A} \subseteq \texttt{B} \subseteq \texttt{C}$$

Instead, we will have to exclude unwanted interpretations by carefully chosen labels and textual definitions. There exists a lot of experience in the field of terminology research that could help ontology engineers in this task, namely the seminal work by Eugen Wüster, dating back to the 1930s on how we should construct technical vocabularies in order to mitigate interoperability problems in technology and trade in a world of high semantic specificity (Wüster, 1991). His findings and guidelines on how to create consensual, standardized multi-lingual vocabularies for technological domains are by far more specific and more in-depth than the simplistic examples of ontologies for e-commerce in the early euphoria about ontologies in the late 1990.

This "linguistic grounding" of ontology projects is a major challenge — at the same time, such proper textual definitions can often already keep a large share of what ontologies promise. In particular when it comes to attributes and relations, specifying their intended semantics by axioms is difficult and often unfeasible, while properly chosen textual definitions are in practice sufficient for communicating the intended meaning. eCl@ss (eClass e.V., 2006) and eClassOWL (Hepp, 2006a) and (Hepp, 2006b) for example, specify the intended meaning of the attribute "height" (property BAA020001) as follows:

"With objects with [a] preferred position of use, the dimension which is generally measured oriented to gravity and generally measured perpendicular to the supporting surface."

It is noteworthy that the RosettaNet Technical Dictionary, a standardized vocabulary for describing electronic components (RosettaNet, 2004) does not include any hierarchy, because the participating entities could not reach consensus on that. Instead, it consists just of about 800 flat classes augmented by about 3000 datatype properties but was still practically useful.

This subsection should tell two things: First, that matching the state of the art in terminology research is key for the informal part of an ontology project. Second, that a large share of the promise of ontologies can be achieved solely by the three technical effects described so far, which do not require the specification of ontology elements by axioms and neither a reasoner at run-time.

2.4   Excluding unwanted interpretations by means of formal semantics

As we have already discussed, a large part of ontology research deals with the formal account of ontologies, i.e., specifying an approximate conceptualization of a domain by means of logic. For example, we may say that two classes are disjoint, that one class is a subclass of another, or that being an instance of a certain class implies certain properties. For some researchers, this formal account of an ontology is even the only relevant aspect of ontologies.

The axiomatic specification of conceptual elements has several advantages. First of all, formal logic provides a precise, unambiguous formalism — compared to the blurriness of e.g. many graphical notations. In contrast, it took quite some time until Brachman described in his seminal paper that the blurriness of is-a relations in semantic nets is very problematic, teaching us in particular to make a clear distinction between sublassOf and instanceOf (Brachman, 1983).

In a nutshell, logical axioms about the element of an ontology constrain the interpretation of this element. The more statements are made about a conceptual element by means of axioms, the less can we err on what is meant, because some interpretations would lead to logical contradictions. For an in-depth discussion on whether aximatization is effective as "the main tool used to characterize the object of inquiry," see Ferrario (2006). Also, we highly recommend John Sowa's "Fads and Fallacies of Logic" (Sowa, 2007).

It is definitely not a mistake to use a rock-solid formal ground for specifying what needs to be specified in an ontology, because it eliminates subjective judgment and differences in the interpretation of the language for specifying an ontology. Many graphical notations, including the popular entity-relationship diagrams (ERDs) have suffered from being used by different people with a different meaning in mind, hampering exchange and reuse of models.

However, this does not mean that full axiomatization is the most important aspect of building an ontology. Whether an ontology should be heavyweight or lightweight in terms of its formal account depends on the trade-off between what one gains by a richer axiomatization vs. what efforts are necessary to produce this. Note that producing in here means not only writing down an axiomatic definition of a conceptual element, but also to achieve consensus with all stakeholders about this axiomatic definition.

2.5   Inferring implicit facts automatically

The axiomatic definition of conceptual elements as described in the previous section also empowers computational inferences, i.e., the use of a reasoner component to deduce new, implicit facts. An important contribution of this property is that it reduces redundancy in the representation of a knowledge base and thus eases its maintenance, because we do not need to assert explicitly what is already specified in the ontology.

However, it is sometimes assumed that being able to infer new facts from the axiomatization using a reasoner is the main gain of an ontology, and that without it, an ontology would not be "machine-readable." That is not correct, because the unique identifiers, provided for the conceptual elements, alone improve the machine-readability of data. For example, simply using a specific URI for expressing the relationship "knows" between two individuals empowers a computer to find, aggregate, and present any such statement in any Fried-of-a-Friend document. Same holds for the rich libraries of datatype properties contained in eClassOWL (Hepp, 2006a)— their formal semantics is constrained to what kind of datatype a value used in a respective statement is, but their informal content is very rich.

In short, the ability to use computers to deduce additional facts based on the axiomatic content of an ontology can be valuable and is interesting from a research perspective. However, it is only one of at least six positive effects of ontologies, and its share on improved interoperability has, to our knowledge, so far not been quantitatively analyzed.

2.6   Spotting logical inconsistencies

A side effect on the axiomatic specification of conceptual elements in an ontology is that it increases the likelihood that modeling errors can be spotted, because an inference engine is empowered to find logical inconsistencies. Again, this is a potentially valuable contribution, but its effect on more consistent conceptual models of domains still needs quantitative evidence. Also, it must be stressed that only logical inconsistencies can be spotted this way, while other types of modeling errors remain undetected.

3.   GRAND CHALLENGES OF ONTOLOGY CONSTRUCTION AND USE

The main goal of ontology engineering is to produce useful, consensual, rich, current, complete, and interoperable ontologies. In the following, we discuss six fundamental problems of building and using ontologies in real-world applications.

3.1   Interaction with human minds

Since ontologies are not for machines only, but are the glue between human perception of reality and models of that reality in computers, it is crucial that humans can understand an ontology specification, both at design time and when using an ontology to annotate data or to express queries. This problem has two major branches:

HCI challenge and visualization: It is difficult to develop suitable visualization techniques for ontologies. For example, it has been investigated to reuse popular modeling notations, namely from conceptual modeling, like ERM, UML class diagrams, and ORM (Jarrar, Demey, & Meersman, 2003). The advantage of this approach is a higher degree of familiarity, but there is a danger that human users underestimate the differences between data modeling and ontology engineering. In general, the larger the ontology and the more expressive the underlying formalism, the more difficult is it to provide a suitable ontology visualization. Chapter 2 discusses this problem and current solutions in more detail.

Interplay between human languages and ontologies: Human language is likely the most comprehensive phenomenon in which human thought, including our abstractions, subjective judgments, and categories of thinking manifest. Unfortunately, a large share of ontology researchers avoid natural language both as a resource to be harvested when creating ontologies and as a modality for expressing the semantics (see also section 2.3). For successful ontology projects, however, a tight integration with human language is crucial. This is for example taken into account by the DOGMA-MESS approach with a strong lexical component in the development process (de Moor, De Leenheer, & Meersman, 2006). Also, ontology learning as the attempt to deduce conceptual structures from lexical resources is getting more and more attention, and respective expertise is gaining relevance. For an overview of the field, see e.g. (Buitelaar, Cimiano, & Magnini, 2005).

3.2   Integration with existing knowledge organization systems

A lot of existing knowledge is stored using traditional systems of knowledge organization, for example, standardized hierarchical classifications like eCl@ss[1] and UNSPSC[2] in the e-commerce domain or the "International Classification of Diseases" (ICD-10)[3] in the medical sector. If we want to use ontology technology for increasing interoperability between multiple such representations or increased access to existing data, we need to build ontologies that are linked to those existing knowledge organization systems (KOS). Also, reusing existing resources and consensus from those systems can reduce the effort for building ontologies.

Several researchers have analyzed the complexity of deriving ontologies from existing consensus in the form of informal thesauri and classifications, e.g. thesauri to SKOS (van Assem, Malaisé, Miles, & Schreiber, 2006), classifications into lightweight ontologies (Giunchiglia, Marchese, & Zaihrayeu, 2006) and (Hepp & de Bruijn, 2007), or products and services classification standards to OWL ontologies (Hepp, 2006b).

3.3   Managing dynamic networks of formal meaning

As ontologies are not static conceptual models of "eternal" truth, but artifacts reflecting our gradual understanding of reality, we face the difficulty of managing such dynamic networks of meaning (Fensel, 2001). This creates at least three branches of problems:

Ontology evolution, i.e., dealing with change: We need to make sure that ontologies are continuously updated so that they reflect the current state of the respective domain. For example, product innovation leads to new types of products and services, and advancement in research to new classes

---

[1] http://www.eclass.de
[2] http://www.unspsc.org
[3] http://www.who.int/classifications/icd/en/

of diseases and symptoms. For quickly evolving domains, it is an open research question whether we can we build ontologies fast enough to reflect those domains properly. See Chapter 5 for more on ontology evolution.

Interoperability between ontologies: If we have more than one single ontology, the problem of data interoperability turns into a problem of interoperability between multiple ontologies. Such is achieved by alignments between ontologies, e.g. sets of statements of semantic relationships. Those alignments are ontological commitments themselves, and there can be multiple sets of statements of semantic relationships for different purposes. See Chapter 6 for more on ontology alignments.

Integration of ontology construction and ontology usage: Due to their high level of abstraction, ontologies mostly suffer from a very disadvantageous decoupling between their construction and their usage. It is very desirable that using ontologies for annotating instances and for expressing queries is much more tightly integrated with the evolution of the ontologies. For example, users spotting the need for a new element while expressing a query should be able to do so. The current state is similar to developing a dictionary without speaking the respective language, i.e., without continuously probing our assumptions about the semantics and usage of words by communicating.

3.4   Scalable infrastructure

While relational database management systems (RDBMS) have reached a high level of maturity and provide high performance and scalability even on desktop computers, ontology repositories still fall short in those terms. In fact, it is only recently that ontology repositories with some degree of reasoning support have been released that can deal with larger ontologies or large sets of instance data. However, quite clearly, users will not accept falling behind the state of the art in scalability and performance when adopting semantic technology.

There are two main branches of research in this field: First, determining fragments of existing ontology languages that provide an attractive combination of expressiveness and computational costs. The main idea is that e.g. RDF-S is a too limited ontology language, while OWL DL reasoning is too complex for many large-scale contexts.

The second is trying to combine reasoners with relational databases so that the existing achievements in terms of scalability and performance can be built on.

Chapter 4 summarizes the state of the art in this field.

3.5   Economic and legal constraints

So far, research has mainly addressed the technical problems of ontology usage, but largely ignored the economic and legal constraints. However, the large deployment of ontology technology will require answers to those questions, too.

Resource consumption: Does the gain in automation that the ontology provides justify the resources needed to develop it? From another perspective, do the technical problems that the ontology can help us solve outweigh the problems we must master to create it? A first approach in that direction is the work on cost estimation models for ontologies, see Chapter 7.

Incentive conflicts and network externalities: Is the incentive structure for relevant actors in the process compatible with the required contributions? For example, are those who must dedicate time and resources benefiting from the ontologies? Moreover, ontologies exhibit *positive network effects*, such that their perceived utility increases with the number of people who commit to them (Hepp, 2007). This implies that convincing individuals to invest effort into building or using ontologies is particularly difficult while the user base associated with it is small or nonexistent.

Intellectual property rights: For many applications, we need ontologies that represent existing standards. However, standards are often subject to intellectual property rights (Samuelson, 2006). Establishing the legal framework for deriving ontologies from relevant standards is thus nontrivial.

A more detailed discussion of these problems is in Hepp (2007).

3.6   Experience

Since ontologies are a rather new technology outside of academia, one inhibitor to their wide usage is the lack of experiences from their application. Such successful use cases can provide best practices and experiences, and help assess the costs and benefits of new projects.

In this book, we present the collected experiences from three application domains, see Chapters 8, 9, and 10. Also, there is another compilation of use cases of semantic technology in the book Cardoso, Hepp, & Lytras (2007).

4.   CONCLUSION

Managing ontologies and annotated data throughout their lifecycles is at the core of semantic systems of all kinds. This begins with establishing a consensual conceptualization of a domain and includes, often iteratively, a wealth of operations on (or on the basis of) the resulting ontologies, and creates challenges in the elicitation, storage, versioning, retrieval, and application. All such operations must support collaboration and may require the involvement of the individuals defining and using the ontologies (i.e., the committing communities), where human interpretation and negotiation of the elicited knowledge is indispensable.

This eventually makes managing ontologies in large-scale applications very difficult. While a lot of foundational research results have been achieved and published in the past years, mostly in academia, the true complexity of ontology management is still a major research challenge.

With this book, we aim at presenting a current summary of the state of the art in the field. Part II of the book will discuss the infrastructure for ontology management and related tools. Part III addresses the evolution of ontologies and how alignments between multiple ontologies can be produced. It concludes with a section that presents a cost estimation model for ontology projects. Part IV summarizes the practical experiences from ontology engineering and ontology management in three selected use cases in e-banking, engineering in the automotive sector, and managing competencies in the Dutch bakery domain.

ACKNOWLEDGEMENTS

The overall work on this book has been supported by the European Commission under the project DIP (FP6-507483). This chapter was written with partial support from the European Commission under the projects SUPER (FP6-026850) and MUSING (FP6-027097), and from the Austrian BMVIT/FFG under the FIT-IT project myOntology (grant no. 812515/9284). Martin Hepp has also support from a Young Researcher's Grant (Nachwuchsförderung 2005–2006) from the Leopold-Franzens-Universität Innsbruck, which is thankfully acknowledged.

REFERENCES

v. Assem, M., Malaisé, V., Miles, A., & Schreiber, G. (2006). *A Method to Convert Thesauri to SKOS*. Proceedings of the 3rd European Semantic Web Conference (ESWC 2006), Budva, Montenegro, pp. 95–109.

Brachman, R. J. (1983). What IS-A Is and Isn't: An Analysis of Taxonomic Links in Semantic Networks. *IEEE Computer, 16*(10), pp. 30–36.

Buitelaar, P., Cimiano, P., & Magnini, B. (2005). *Ontology Learning from Text: Methods, Evaluation and Applications* (Vol. 123). Amsterdam, The Netherlands: IOS Press.

Cardoso, J., Hepp, M., & Lytras, M. (Eds.). (2007). *The Semantic Web. Real-World Applications from Industry*. Berlin etc.: Springer.

Corcho, O., & Gómez-Pérez, A. (2001). *Solving Integration Problems of E-commerce Standards and Initiatives through Ontological Mappings.* Proceedings of the Workshop on E-Business and Intelligent Web at the Seventeenth International Joint Conference on Artificial Intelligence (IJCAI-2001), Seattle, USA, pp. 1–10.

eClass e.V. (2006). eCl@ss: Standardized Material and Service Classification, http://www.eclass-online.com/

Fensel, D. (2001). Ontologies: Dynamic networks of formally represented meaning, http://sw-portal.deri.at/papers/publications/network.pdf

Ferrario, R. (2006). Who Cares about Axiomatization? Representation, Invariance, and Formal Ontologies. *Epistemologia, Special Issue on the Philosophy of Patrick Suppes, 2,* (forthcoming).

Furnas, G. W., Landauer, T. K., Gomez, L. M., & Dumais, S. T. (1987). The Vocabulary Problem in Human-System Communication. *Communications of the ACM, 30*(11), pp. 964–971.

Giunchiglia, F., Marchese, M., & Zaihrayeu, I. (2006). *Encoding Classifications into Lightweight Ontologies.* Proceedings of the 3rd European Semantic Web Conference (ESWC 2006), Budva, Montenegro, pp. 80–94.

Gruber, T. R. (1993). A Translation Approach to Portable Ontology Specifications. *Knowledge Acquisition, 5*(2), pp. 199–220.

Gruninger, M., & Lee, J. (2002). Ontology Applications and Design. *Communications of the ACM, 45*(2), pp. 39–41.

Guarino, N., & Giaretta, P. (1995). Ontologies and Knowledge Bases. Towards a Terminological Clarification. In N. Mars (Ed.), *Towards Very Large Knowledge Bases: Knowledge Building and Knowledge Sharing* (pp. 25–32). Amsterdam: IOS Press.

Guarino, N., & Welty, C. A. (2002). Evaluating Ontological Decisions with OntoClean. *Communications of the ACM, 45*(2), pp. 61–65.

Guarino, N., & Welty, C. A. (2004). An Overview of OntoClean. In S. Staab & R. Studer (Eds.), *The Handbook on Ontologies* (pp. 151–172). Berlin: Springer.

Heindl, R. (1927). System und Praxis der Daktyloskopie und der sonstigen technischen Methoden der Kriminalpolizei (3rd ed.). Berlin: Walter de Gruyter & Co.

Hepp, M. (2006a). eCl@ssOWL. The Products and Services Ontology, http://www.heppnetz.de/eclassowl/

Hepp, M. (2006b). Products and Services Ontologies: A Methodology for Deriving OWL Ontologies from Industrial Categorization Standards. *Int'l Journal on Semantic Web and Information Systems (IJSWIS), 2*(1), pp. 72–99.

Hepp, M. (2007). Possible Ontologies: How Reality Constrains the Development of Relevant Ontologies. *IEEE Internet Computing, 11*(7), pp. 90–96.

Hepp, M., & de Bruijn, J. (2007). GenTax: A Generic Methodology for Deriving OWL and RDF-S Ontologies from Hierarchical Classifications, Thesauri, and Inconsistent Taxonomies. Proceedings of the 4th European Semantic Web Conference (ESWC 2007), Innsbruck, Austria, pp. 129–144.

Jarrar, M., Demey, J., & Meersman, R. (2003). On Using Conceptual Data Modeling for Ontology Engineering. *Journal on Data Semantics, LNCS 2800*(I), pp. 185–207.

Lassila, O., & McGuinness, D. L. (2001). The Role of Frame-Based Representation on the Semantic Web. *Linköping Electronic Articles in Computer and Information Science, Vol. 6 (2001), No. 005,* http://www.ep.liu.se/ea/cis/2001/005/

Menzies, T. (1999). Cost Benefits of Ontologies. *intelligence, 10*(3), pp. 26–32.

de Moor, A., De Leenheer, P., and Meersman, R. (2006). *DOGMA-MESS: A meaning evolution support system for interorganizational ontology engineering.* Proceedings of the 14th International Conference on Conceptual Structures, Aalborg, Denmark, pp. 189–203.

Oberle, D. (2006). *Semantic Management of Middleware*. New York: Springer.

Patel, C., Cimino, J., Dolby, J., Fokoue, A., Kalyanpur, A., Kershenbaum, A., et al. (2007). *Matching Patient Records to Clinical Trials Using Ontologies* (IBM Research Report No. RC24265 (W0705-111)). Almaden etc.: IBM Research.

RosettaNet. (2004). RosettaNet Technical Dictionary, http://www.rosettanet.org/technicaldictionary

Samuelson, P. (2006). Copyrighting Standards. *Communications of the ACM, 49*(6), pp. 27–31.

Schulten, E., Akkermans, H., Botquin, G., Dörr, M., Guarino, N., Lopes, N., et al. (2001). The E-Commerce Product Classification Challenge. *IEEE Intelligent Systems, 16*(4), pp. 86–89.

Sowa, J. (2007). Fads and Fallacies about Logic. *IEEE Intelligent Systems, 22*(2), pp. 84–87.

Wüster, E. (1991). Einführung in die allgemeine Terminologielehre und terminologische Lexikographie (3rd ed.). Bonn: Romanistischer Verlag.

II. INFRASTRUCTURE

Chapter 2

ENGINEERING AND CUSTOMIZING ONTOLOGIES

The Human-Computer Challenge in Ontology Engineering

Martin Dzbor and Enrico Motta

Knowledge Media Institute, The Open University, UK, {M.Dzbor, E.Motta}@open.ac.uk, Tel. +44-1908-653-800; Fax +44-1908-653-169

Abstract: In this chapter we introduce and then discuss the broad and rather complex area of human-ontology interaction. After reviewing generic tenets of HCI and their relevance to ontology management, we give an empirical evidence of some HCI challenges for ontology engineering tools and the shortcomings in some existing tools from this viewpoint. We highlight several functional opportunities that seem to be missing in the existing tools, and then look at three areas that may help rectifying the identified gaps. We relate methods from user profiling, large data set navigation and ontology customization into a "triple stack," which may bring tools for engineering ontologies from the level of niche products targeting highly trained specialists to the 'mainstream' level suitable for practitioners and ordinary users. The work presented in this chapter is based on the authors' research together with other colleagues in the context of the "NeOn: Lifecycle Support for Networked Ontologies" project.

Keywords: HCI; human-ontology interaction; NeOn; networked ontologies; ontology customization; user study of ontology engineering tools

1. INTRODUCTION

Human-computer interaction (HCI) is a well-established and rich subject that has an impact not only on those who develop computational systems, but also on the users of such systems, the vendors, maintainers, and many more stakeholders who are normally involved in designing and delivering software and computer-based tools. At the centre of HCI as a science is the core of its investigation: *interactions*. Note that this emphasis on an abstract notion "interaction" does not reduce the importance of the users or push them into a background.

On the contrary, the term "interaction" is broader, and in general, involves three constituting parts: *the user, the technology,* and *the way they work together.* One can then study such phenomena as how the users work with a particular technology, what the users prefer, how the technology addresses given issues, etc. The purpose of this chapter is not to delve into generic HCI issues applicable to any technology. We want to expand the views of HCI to cover what we label as human-ontology interaction.

Human-ontology interaction can be seen as a subset of HCI issues that apply to specific tasks and specific technologies. Our aim is to investigate how users interact with the ontologies, in general, and with *networked* ontologies, in particular, and how they do it in a realistic ontology lifecycle scenario. While HCI is a subject almost as old as the computer science, the specifics of interacting with ontologies were not considered in much depth. Tools supporting ontological engineering are considered to be primarily software tools, and thus, it is presumed that general findings of the HCI practitioners also apply to ontologies.

To some extent, this is true; however, design, engineering and subsequently maintenance of ontologies are indeed specific ways to interact with the technology. In other words, the change in the activity implies a change in the entire interaction. Thus, an action that may look similarly to other software systems (e.g. opening a file) may acquire semantically very specific meaning in the context of a particular activity (in our case, ontology engineering).

In this chapter, we look at several different aspects of how a user may interact with ontologies in a varied sort of ways. The first part of the chapter is concerned with a user study that we carried out in order to improve our understanding of the level of user support provided by current ontology engineering tools in the context envisaged by the NeOn project[1]. That is, in a scenario when ontology engineers are developing complex ontologies by reuse, i.e., by integrating existing semantic resources.

While the existing empirical work on exploring HCI aspects of the ontology engineering tools points to several problems and challenges, we decided to conduct a new study, because none of the studies reviewed in section 2.1 provided sufficient data to drive the development of the ontology engineering tools addressing the NeOn scenario. In particular, the use of tools by ordinary users, the emphasis on ontology reuse and the embedment of the study in a real-world engineering task.

A complementary view to this empirical user study is presented in the latter part of the chapter: exploring the HCI challenge with more analytic

---

[1] "NeOn: Lifecycle support for networked ontologies" is a large-scale integrated project co-funded by the European Commission by grant no. IST-2005-027595; more information on its focus, outcomes and achievements so far can be found on http://NeOn-project.org.

lenses, and focusing on a variety of tools that were specifically designed to support ontological engineering, or could be reused with ontologies in a serendipitous manner. With this view in mind we consider several approaches, technologies, and tools to illustrate various aspects of where user interaction with ontologies becomes somewhat specific and different from using other software systems and tools.

Before going more in depth, let us introduce the basic terminology first. In order to work in a structured manner, we separate the terms that traditionally come from the HCI domain from the terms that are typical for ontology engineering.

1.1 Terms frequently used in HCI

In this section we present common and established meanings of terms and issues that are usually mentioned in connection with user interaction in general. The purpose of this brief glossary is twofold: (i) to introduce terms that are used in the subsequent sections of this chapter to those practitioners with less background in traditional HCI, and (ii) to differentiate between terms that are often used interchangeably by lay persons. We are not defining here any terms related to ontology engineering in general, as these have a broader scope of validity than the chapter on HCI challenges, and are covered elsewhere in the book.

- **Accessibility**: In general, this term reflects the degree to which a given system is usable by different users. It can be expressed in terms of ease with which to access certain features or functions of the system, together with the possible benefits such access may bring to the user. Often this term is interpreted in the sense of 'enabling people who are physically disabled to interact with the system.' This is a slightly unfortunate emphasis on one specific motivation for pursuing accessibility. In a non-disabled sense, accessibility may include aspects like appropriate language, jargon, level of detail, choice of action, etc.
- **Customization**: In the computer science this term refers to the capability of users to modify or otherwise alter the layout, appearance and/or content of information with which they want to interact. This term is often used together with personalization (see also explanation of term 'profile' below). In this deliverable we shall see customization as an ability to adapt user interfaces and tools so that they fit a particular user's needs and accessibility constraints (see also term 'accessibility' above for some objective, explicit criteria that may be customized).
- **End user**: Popularly used to describe an abstract group of persons who ultimately operate or otherwise use a system — in computing, where this

term is most popular, the system corresponds to a piece of software. The abstraction is expressed in terms of a relevant sub-set of a user's characteristics (e.g. his/her technical expertise, prior knowledge, task, objective, skill, etc.) — leading to such user categories as knowledge engineers, developers, administrators, etc.

- **Graphical User Interface (GUI)**: GUI is a type of user interface that came to prominence in computer science in the 1980s. The hallmark of this type is the use of graphical images (so called widgets), texts and their managed appearance on the computer screen to represent the information and actions available to the user. Another hallmark is that the user's actions are performed by directly manipulating the graphical elements (widgets) on the screen. GUI is often defined in contrast with command-based, text-only or terminal-based user interfaces.

- **Localization**: In the context of computing and HCI, localization is seen as the adaptation of an object or a system to a particular locality. A typical example is where a locality is defined in terms of different languages (e.g. English, Spanish, etc.), and the system is expected to translate messages and other aspects of its UI into the language suitable for or selected by the user. Thus, localization may be seen as a customization of a tool for a specific country, region or language group. In some literature, this term is used jointly with term 'internationalization.' However, language is only one (albeit most visible) aspect of the system UI that can be translated to the local customs. Other aspects that may need amendments include issues like time and date formatting, decimal number formatting, phone and postcode formatting, and locally used units of measure (e.g. feet, meters, etc.) Less common adaptations are in the use of colors, layouts and imaging appropriate to a particular locality.

- **Modality (of user interface)**: A path or communication channel employed by the user interface to accomplish required inputs, outputs and other activities. Common modalities include e.g. keyboard, mouse, monitor, etc.

- **(User) Preference**: This term represents a real or imagined choice between alternatives and a capability to rank the alternatives according to some criterion. In computer science, this term is typically used in the sense that users choose among alternative user interactions, user interface components and/or paths. In computing, user preferences are often based on the utility (value) of the available alternatives to the particular user, in a particular situation or task.

- **(User) Profile**: a term seen in the context of computing as a way to describe some user properties that are relevant for a particular task and can help in tailoring information delivery to the specific user. Note that 'user' may mean a concrete individual person as well as an abstract user (e.g. a group or type).

- **Usability**: A degree to which the design of a particular user interface takes into account human needs defined in terms of psychology or physiology of the users. Usability looks at how effective, efficient and satisfying the user interface (and the underlying application) is.
- **User experience**: Broadly, this term describes an overall experience, satisfaction and/or attitude a user has when using a particular system. In computing, this term is often used interchangeably with terms like usability and sometimes accessibility.

1.2   About ontological engineering

In the early 1990's, a group of Artificial Intelligence (AI) and database (DB) researchers got together to define a standard architecture stack for allowing intelligent systems to interoperate over a knowledge channel and share data, models, and other knowledge without sharing data schema or formats. This group comprised Tom Gruber — the person who is widely credited with clarifying a definition of ontology for the AI community and for promoting the vision of ontologies as enabling technology:

> *"In the context of knowledge sharing, I use the term ontology to mean a specification of a conceptualization. That is, an ontology is a description (like a formal specification of a program) of the concepts and relationships that can exist for an agent or a community of agents. This definition is consistent with the usage of ontology as set-of-concept-definitions, but more general."* (Gruber 1993a; Gruber 1993b)

Ontologies are designed artifacts, similar to cars, desks or computers. As such, they always have a purpose, they are *engineered for something*. In the original vision of Tom Gruber, ontologies were artifacts facilitating sharing and interchange of knowledge, or making commitments to particular meanings. While an ontology may be in principle an abstract conceptual structure, from the practical perspective, it makes sense to express it in some selected *formal language* to realize the intended shareable meaning.

Such formal languages then enable the negotiation of formal vocabularies, which, in turn, may be shared among parties in the knowledge sharing interaction without being dependent on either the user/agent or its context. One example of such a vocabulary may be description logic that allows us to make statements holding for some or all entities in a given world satisfying a given condition.

From the point of view of this book (and chapter), we often align the ontology management and engineering with the actual design, creation and overall interaction with such formal vocabularies. If we take the Web Ontology Language (OWL[2]) as the current preferred formal vocabulary, then ontology engineering is often seen as a synonym to designing and coding conceptual commitment about the world or a particular problem in this language. Thus, for the purpose of this chapter, user challenge in engineering OWL ontologies is broadly definable as a user interaction with a particular software product, code, OWL model, OWL-based tool, technique, etc.

2.   USERS IN ONTOLOGICAL ENGINEERING

In order to illustrate and ground the issues users are facing during the process of ontology design, engineering and management, this section includes extracts from a larger user study that has been conducted in the context of gathering and analyzing requirements in the NeOn project. The following sub-sections are based on our earlier workshop publication (Dzbor, Motta *et al.* 2006).

The existing empirical work on exploring HCI aspects of the ontology engineering tools highlights several problems with ontology engineering tools. However, at the beginning of the NeOn project we felt that there was a need to conduct a novel study, as none of the studies mentioned in section 2.1 provided the kind of data that can be used as a baseline to inform the development of the next generation ontology engineering tools.

2.1   Motivation and background

Some work on evaluating tools for ontology engineering has been done in the past. For example, Duineveld, Stoter *et al.* (2000) observed that the tools available in the time of their study (around 1999) were little more than research prototypes with significant problems in their user interfaces. These included too many options for visualizing ontologies, which tended to confuse the user and hinder navigation. Moreover, the systems' feedback was found to be poor, which meant a steep learning curve for non-expert users. Finally, most tools provided little support for raising the level of abstraction in the modelling process and expected the user to be proficient in low-level formalisms.

Pinto, Peralta *et al.* (2002) evaluated Protégé, one of the leading ontology engineering tools currently in use (Noy, Sintek *et al.* 2001), in several tasks, from the perspective of a power user. The authors found the system intuitive for expert knowledge engineers, as long as the operations were triggered by

---

[2] Specification of OWL as a W3C recommendation is on http://w3.org/TR/owl-ref

them (e.g. knowledge re-arrangement). However, difficulties arose when assistance from the tool was expected; e.g. in inference or consistency checks. Weak performance was also noted in language interoperability. In another survey, Fensel and Gómez-Pérez (2002) also noted issues with tool support for operations on ontologies beyond mere editing (e.g. integration or re-use). In particular, the authors emphasized the limited 'intelligence' of current tools — e.g. no possibility to re-use previously used processes in current design. Tools expected the user to drive the interaction, with the tool imposing constraints rather than adapting itself to users' needs.

Yet another study by Storey, Lintern *et al.* (2004) focused on a fairly narrow aspect of visualization support in Protégé and its customization models are too complex and do not reflect users' models of what they would normally want to see. Similar observations were made of the users having difficulties with description logic based formalisms in general (Kalyanpur, Parsia *et al.* 2005). Again, tools expected detailed knowledge of intricate language and logic details, and this often led to modelling errors.

As we mentioned earlier in the introduction, the existing empirical work on exploring HCI aspects of the ontology engineering tools highlighted several problems with ontology engineering tools. We conducted a new study, because none of the studies mentioned above provided the kind of data that can be used to inform the development of the ontology engineering tools envisaged by NeOn. Specifically, the studies did not satisfactorily address the following key concerns:

- **"Normal" users vs. "Power" users**. As ontologies become an established technology, it makes less sense to focus only on highly skilled knowledge engineers. There are so many organizations developing ontologies that it seems safe to assert that indeed most ontologies are currently built by people with no formal training in knowledge representation and ontology engineering. Therefore, it is essential to conduct studies, which focus on "normal users," i.e., people with some knowledge of ontologies, but who are not classified as "power users."

- **Emphasis on ontology reuse.** We adopt the view that ontologies will be networked, dynamically changing, shared by many applications and strongly dependent on the context in which they were developed or are used. In such scenario it would be prohibitively expensive to develop ontologies from scratch, and the re-use of existing, possibly imperfect, ontologies becomes the key engineering task. Thus, it makes sense to study the re-use task for OWL ontologies, rather than focusing only on a narrow activity (e.g. ontology visualization or consistency checking).

- **Evaluating formal ontology engineering tasks.** Studies reported earlier focused on generic tool functionalities, rather than specifically assessing performance on concrete ontology engineering tasks. This creates two problems: (i) the results are tool-centric, i.e., it is difficult to go beyond a specific tool and draw generic lessons in terms of HCI on how people do ontology engineering tasks; (ii) by assessing the performance of our users on concrete tasks using OWL ontologies, we acquire robust, benchmark-like data, which (for example) can be used as a baseline to assess the support provided by other tools (including those planned in NeOn).

2.2   Overview of the observational user study

We conducted an observational study rather than an experiment to capture user needs and gaps in the tool support, rather than merely compare different tools. As mentioned earlier, NeOn is concerned with several facets of networked ontologies, and many of these facets are currently supported to a very limited extent. This lack of tools and techniques makes it difficult to assess the actual user performance in any of these tasks. However, it enables us to acquire generic requirements and insights on a broader ontology engineering task or process.

Ontology is, by definition, a shared artefact integrating views of different parties (Gruber 1993a). One form of integration used in this study was temporal, where an agent re-used previously agreed ontologies, perhaps from different domains. All studied ontologies were public; all were results of principled engineering processes and knowledge acquisition, and they all modelled domains comprehensible to a 'normal user.' The table shows some statistical information on the OWL ontologies included in the study.

Table 2-1. Descriptive features of the ontologies used in the evaluation study: numbers of primitives classified as **Cl**(asses), **Pr**(operties), and **Re**(strictions)

Ontology	Cl	Pr	Re	Notes
Copyright	85	49	128	Mostly cardinality & value type restrictions, some properties untyped [http://rhizomik.net/2006/01/copyrightontology.owl]
AKT Support	14	15	n/a	All properties fully typed, no axioms [http://www.aktors.org/ontology/support]
AKT Portal	162	122	130	10 classes defined by equivalence/enumeration, most properties untyped [http://www.aktors.org/ontology/portal]

Two environments were used — Protégé from Stanford University[3] and TopBraid Composer from TopQuandrant[4] — these satisfied the initial

[3] Extensive details on the Protégé project and tool are available to an interested reader on
   http://protege.stanford.edu

requirements from ontologies (e.g. on OWL fragment or visualization features). We worked with 28 participants from 4 institutions (both academic and industrial). Participants were mixed in terms of different experience levels with designing ontologies and with different tools. Each person worked individually, but was facilitated by a member of the study team. Participants were expected to have knowledge of basic OWL (e.g. sub-classing or restrictions), while not necessarily being 'power users.' They were recorded with screen capture software Camtasia, and at the end they filled in a questionnaire about their experiences with ontology integration.

2.2.1   Evaluation methodology

In our investigation of the ontology engineering environments, we opted for a formative evaluation (Scriven 1991). This choice was made mainly to inform design of new OWL engineering tools in the context of NeOn. Two constraints were observed: (i) gathered data shall not be tool-specific (it was not our objective to prove which one tool was best); and (ii) while generic tool usability was considered important, measures were expected not to be solely usability-centric. In terms of what was analyzed, we selected the following levels of analysis (Kirkpatrick 1994): (i) user's satisfaction with a tool, (ii) effectiveness of a tool in achieving goals, and (iii) behavioural efficiency. In our study, these categories took the form of questions exploring usability, effectiveness, and efficiency categories, to which we added a generic functional assessment category.

Our questionnaire reflected situations that typically appear in the literature correlated with enhancing or reducing effectiveness, efficiency, usability or user satisfaction (Shneiderman and Plaisant 2004), and covered these situations by 36 questions. The remaining 17 questions inquired about various functional aspects considered relevant to the NeOn vision; including ontology re-use, visualization, contextualization, mapping, reasoning, etc.

The questionnaire included both open and closed (evaluative) questions. The former asked for opinions; the latter used a Likert scale ranging from very useful (+1) to very poor (−1). Each question was then expressed frequencies and counts — largely in the context of open, qualitative items and observations. Positively and negatively stated questionnaire items were interspersed to avoid the tendency of people to agree with statements rather than disagree (Colman 2001). Nevertheless, this tendency towards agreeing appeared during analysis; as was discussed in our preliminary report (Dzbor, Motta *et al.* 2006).

---

[4] More about TopBraid Composer can be found on http://www.topbraidcomposer.com/

2.2.2   User tasks

Participants were given three tasks considering different ways of integrating ontologies into a network. In Task 1, they were told that the *Copyright* ontology did not formalize temporal aspects, and had to be augmented with the relevant definitions from other ontologies (e.g. AKT Support). The objective was to review the three given ontologies, locate the relevant classes (i.e. *CreationProcess* and *Temporal-Thing*), import ontologies as needed, and assert that *CreationProcess* is a subclass of *Temporal-Thing*.

Task 2 was motivated by pointing to a western-centric notion of any right being associated only with a person, which excluded collective rights. Participants were asked to review concept copyright:Person, and replace its use with deeper conceptualizations from the AKT Portal and AKT Support ontologies. In principle, the task asked people to express two types of restrictions on property ranges:

- **simple**: e.g. for concept *Economic-Rights* introduce statement
  rangeOf (agent , Legal-Agent);
- **composite**: e.g. state that
  *rangeOf (recipient , (Generic-*Agent AND ($\neg$ *Geo-Political*))).

Task 3 asked people to re-define concept *copyright:Collective* so that formal statements could match an informal description. Participants were told to make amendments in the base — *Copyright* ontology, rather than to the other two. We expected they would first create new local sub-classes for the concept *copyright:Collective*, and then make them equivalent to the actual AKT classes. Task 3 also comprised a definition of a new property (e.g. *copyright:hasMember*) with appropriate domain and range, together with its restriction for class *copyright:Collective*, so that a collective is defined as containing min. 2 *persons*.

2.3   Findings from the user study

This section summarizes some findings from our study. For selected categories of measures we give a general summary of observations across the whole population, followed by commenting on differences (if any) between two common denominators of user performance in knowledge-intensive tasks — the choice of and the expertise with the tool. Particularly interesting is to look at how efficient people felt in different tasks, how they were assisted by the help system or tool tips, how the tools helped to navigate the ontologies or how easy it was to follow the formalisms used in definitions. Table 2-2 shows general observations, and Table 2-3 compares features where differences between tools were observed.

The efficiency of the two tools was approximately the same. When asked about efficient handling of ontology dependencies and navigating through them, Protégé users thought they were significantly less efficient. Many users were not happy with the abstract syntax of the axiom formulae, which was not helped by the inability to edit more complex restrictions in the same windows and wizards as the simple ones.

Table 2-2. Selection of a few general observations across population

Measure/question	−1	0	+1	Total	Mean
providing sufficient information about ontologies	32%	55%	13%	29	−0.172
support provided by documentation, help	60%	40%	0%	16	−0.500
usefulness of the tool tips, hints, ...	50%	46%	4%	27	−0.423
subjective time taken for task 2	25%	55%	20%	31	−0.065
subjective time taken for task 3	6%	56%	38%	31	+0.300

Table 2-3. Comparison of attitudes between tools and expertise groups (TB: TopBraid, Pr: Protégé, Be: less experienced, Ex: expert); significance threshold: χ^2=5.99 at p=0.05

Measure/question	Type	Outcome	χ^2	Sign
help with handling ontology dependencies	tools	TB (0.0) vs. Pr (−0.37)	7.65	yes
useful visualization & ontology navigation facilities	tools	TB (−0.33) vs. Pr (−0.63)	6.00	yes
handling ontology syntax / abstract syntax	tools	TB (+0.40) vs. Pr (−0.07)	2.33	no
ease/speed of carrying out integrations	experience	Le (−0.21) vs. Ex (+0.27)	9.75	yes
level of visualization and navigation support	experience	Le (−0.69) vs. Ex (−0.40)	2.40	no
ontology representation languages, abstract syntax, etc.	experience	Le (−0.22) vs. Ex (+0.23)	3.64	no

One qualitative feature in both tools concerns the depth of an operation in the user interface. Subjectively, 32% participants felt they had an explicit problem with finding an operation in a menu or workspace. The main 'offenders' were the import function (expected to be in File → Import... menu option) and the in-ontology search (which was different from the search dialog from Edit → Find... menu option).

Expertise seemed to have minimal effect on the assessment of the efficiency dimension. Both groups concurred that while a lot of information was available about concepts, this was not very useful, and the GUI often seemed cluttered. They missed a clearer access to 'hidden' functions such as defining equivalence or importing ontology. Non-experts saw themselves inefficient due to lack of visualization and navigation support, and also due to the notation of abstract DL-like formalism. Experts were at ease with the formats; non-experts considered support for this aspect not very good.

The overwhelming demand was for complying with common and established metaphors of user interaction. A quote from one participant sums this potential source contributing to inefficiency: *"More standard compliance and consistency. The search works differently ... usual keyboard commands ... don't always work..."*

In addition to the efficiency of the existing ontology management tools, two aspects were evaluated with respect to user experiences: (i) *usability* of the tool (which included accessibility and usefulness), and (ii) overall user *satisfaction* with the tool. The latter included comments regarding user interface intuitiveness, acceptability, customization, and so on.

As Table 2-4 shows, responses in this category are generally negative; participants considered the existing support as "very low" or "not very good." Almost invariably, they were dissatisfied with the role of documentation, help system, tool tips, and various other tool-initiated hints. Support for tool customization — i.e. either its user interface or functionality — was also inadequate. A common justification of the low scores was (among others) the lack of opportunity to automate some actions, lack of support for keyboard-centric interaction, lack of support for more visual interactions. As can be seen from these examples, the reasons were quite diverse, and to some extent depended on the user's preferred style.

Table 2-4. Selection of a few general observations across population

Measure/question	−1	0	+1	Total	Mean
usability/helpfulness of the tooltips, hints, ...	50%	46%	4%	27	−0.423
usability of tool's help system	60%	40%	0%	16	−0.500
support for customization of the tool, its GUI or functionality	48%	44%	8%	25	−0.400
usability of handling ontology dependency support	31%	66%	3%	27	−0.259
visualization of imports, constraints & dependencies	58%	39%	3%	28	−0.536
support for [partial] ontology import	62%	14%	4%	29	−0.739
useful tool interventions in establishing integrations	48%	52%	0%	26	−0.480

One emerging trend on the tools' usability was that too many actions and options were available at any given point during the integration tasks. On the one hand, this refers to the amount of information displayed and the number of window segments needed to accommodate it. An example of this type of usability shortcoming is the (permanent) presence of all properties on screen. On the other hand, while constant presence can be accepted, it was seen as too rigid — e.g. no filtering of only the properties related to a concept was possible. In fact 32% claimed that unclear indication of inheritance and selection was a major issue, and further 14% reported being unable to find all uses of a term (e.g., property or concept label) in a particular ontology. Other comments related to usability are summarized below:

- *unclear error messages and hints* (e.g. red boundary around an incorrect axiom was mostly missed);

- *proprietary user interface conventions* (e.g. icons looked differently, search icon was not obvious, some menu labels were misleading);
- *lack of intuitiveness* (e.g. finding an operation, flagging a concept in the ontology so that it does not disappear, full- vs. random-text search);
- *inconsistent editing* & amending of terms (e.g. while "subClassOf" was visible at the top level of the editor, "equivalentTo" was hidden)

Table 2-5. Comparison of attitudes between tools and expertise groups (TB: TopBraid, Pr: Protégé, Be: less experienced, Ex: expert); significance threshold: χ^2=5.99 at p=0.05

Measure/question	Type	Outcome	χ^2	Sign.
level of overall satisfaction with the tools	tools	TB (+0.10) vs. Pr (–0.19)	2.67	no
overall satisfaction with tool's GUI environment	tools	TB (+0.10) vs. Pr (–0.24)	3.14	no
satisfaction with handling dependencies in ontologies	tools	TB (0.0) vs. Pr (–0.37)	7.65	yes
satisfaction with visualization and navigation support	tools	TB (–0.33) vs. Pr (–0.63)	6.00	yes
ease/speed of carrying out integrations	tools	TB (+0.50) vs. Pr (+0.10)	5.85	no
effort to get acquainted with the tool	experience	Be (–0.27) vs. Ex (+0.12)	3.02	no
satisfaction with support for interpreting inferences	experience	Le (0.0) vs. Ex (+0.07)	2.40	no
support for multiple ontology representation formats	experience	Le (–0.22) vs. Ex (+0.23)	3.64	no

As shown in Table 2-5, a significant difference of opinion was in the overall satisfaction with the tools, their design and intuitiveness, where it was more likely that people complained about Protégé than TopBraid. In this context, people tended to be more positive in the abstract than in the specific. Responses to specific queries were negative (between –0.500 and –0.100), yet overall experiences oscillate between –0.111 and +0.100. As we mentioned, the overall satisfaction with the TopBraid environment was more positive (some possible reasons were discussed above).

One case where experience weighed strongly on less experienced users is the tool intuitiveness. Probably the key contributing factors were the aforementioned non-standard icons, lack of standard keyboard shortcuts, ambiguous operation labels, and an overall depth of key operations in the tool. Less experienced users also had issues with basic features — e.g. namespaces and their acronyms, or ontology definition formalisms. The issue with formalisms is partly due to the inability of the tools to move from an OWL- and DL-based syntax to alternative views, which might be easier in specific circumstances (such as modification of ranges in Task 2). Experienced users missed functionalities such as version management — here less experienced users were probably not clear in how versioning might actually work in this particular case.

2.4   Lessons learned from the user study

Technology (such as OWL), no matter how good it is, does not guarantee that the application for its development would support users in the right tasks or that the user needs in performing tasks are taken on board. At a certain stage, each successful tool must balance the technology with user experience and functional features (Norman 1998). This paper explored some persevering issues with OWL engineering tools that reduce the appeal and adoption of otherwise successful (OWL) technology by the practitioners.

Although the tools made a great progress since the evaluations reported in section 2.1, issues with user interaction remain remarkably resilient. The effort was spent to make the formalisms more expressive and robust, yet they are not any easier to use, unless one is proficient in the low-level languages and frameworks (incl. DL in general and OWL's DL syntax in particular). Existing tools provide little help with the user-centric tasks — a classic example is visualization: There are many visualization techniques; most of them are variations of the same, low-level metaphor of a graph. And they are often too generic to be useful in the users' problems (e.g. seeing ontology dependencies or term occurrences in an ontology).

Table 2-6 highlights a few gaps between what the current tools provide and what people see as useful for framing problems in a more user-centric way. Some 'wishes' (white rows) already exist; e.g. Prompt (Noy and Musen 2003) for version comparison, but perhaps our findings may further improve design of the existing OWL engineering tools.

For instance, identification of frequently used operations and their correlations with errors and mistakes may provide us with opportunities to target the support towards most visible sources of user dissatisfaction. The most frequent steps in OWL development are the actual coding of definitions and import of ontologies (unsurprisingly), but, surprisingly, also search (71% users), re-conceptualization of restrictions and editing of logical expressions (both 54%), and locating terms in ontologies (46%). Compare these operations with the situations requiring assistance from facilitators (in Table 2-7).

Table 2-6. User attitudes to some functional features missing in existing tools (grey rows) and to some proposed extensions (white rows)

Current presence (grey) vs. wished-for feature	User attitude
Existing support for ontology re-use	–0.097 (not very good)
Support for partial re-use of ontologies	–0.739 (very poor)
→ flag chunks of ontologies or concept worked with	+0.519 (would be very useful)
→ hide selected (irrelevant?) parts of ontologies	+0.357 (would be useful)
Existing support for mappings, esp. with contextual boundaries	–0.065 (not very good)
Management and assistance with any mappings –0.480	(not very good / poor)
→ query ontology for items (instead search/browse)	+0.433 (would be useful)
→ compose testing queries to try out consequences of mappings	+0.045 (would be possibly useful)
Existing support for versioning, parallel versions/alternatives	–0.200 (not very good)
Existing visualizing capabilities & their adaptation	–0.536 (very poor)
→ mechanism to propagate changes between alternative versions	+0.519 (would be very useful)
⟩ compare/visualize different interpretations/versions	+0.700 (would be very useful)
→ visualize also on the level of ontologies (not just concepts)	+0.357 (would be useful)

Table 2-7. Observations of issues with OWL engineering and user interaction

Observation	Frequency	% affected	Examples
Syntactic axiom check → user not alerted or not noticing	21x	64.3%	Buttons/icons after axioms misleading; Single/double clicks to select, edit, etc
Testing & understanding (Inference, meaning)	26x	64.3%	Which inference is the right one?; How to check the intended meaning(s)?
Translate/compose logical operation (e.g. equivalence)	37x	60.7%	How to start complex axiom?; Stepwise definition?
Dialogs, buttons,... (confusion, inconsistency,...)	43x	89.1%	Buttons/icons after axioms misleading; Single/double clicks to select, edit, etc.
Searching for the class (partial text search on labels)	25x	64.3%	Label starts with X different from label contains X; namespaces in search?
Functionality unclear (drag&drop, error indication, alphabetic view)	26x	60.7%	Am I in the edit mode?; Where is it alerting me about error?

One example we identified is the correlation between an incorrect logical conceptualization and confusion caused by ambiguous labels or dialogs. Other correlations were between problems with importing an ontology and absence or semantic ambiguity of appropriate widgets in the workspace, and between difficulties with definitions and the failure of tools to alert users about automatic syntactic checks (e.g. on brackets). The translation of a conceptual model of a restriction into DL-style formalism was a separate issue: 70% were observed to stumble during such definitions. From our data, we suggest considering multiple ways for defining and editing axioms (to a limited extent this partly exists in Protégé). Any way, DL may be good for reasoning, but it is by no means the preferred "medium for thinking" (even among ontology designers). This is not a novel finding, similar observations were made for other formalisms and their relationship to informal thought generation (Goel 1995).

Another issue is the gap between the language of users and language of tools; a high number of users was surprised by syntactically incorrect statements. In 64.3% sessions at least one issue due to syntax (e.g. of complex restrictions) was observed. Because of these minor issues they had to be alerted to by a facilitator, people tended to doubt results of other operations (e.g. search or classification) if these differed from what they expected. Lack of trust is problematic because it puts the tool solely in the role of a plain editor, which further reduces tool's initiative. In an attempt to restore 'user trust,' some tools (e.g. SWOOP) move towards trying to justify their results (Kalyanpur, Parsia *et al.* 2005).

The extensive use of features in the tools is also an issue increasing complexity of user interaction. Both tested tools showed most of possibly relevant information on screen at all times. There was little possibility to filter or customize this interaction. The granularity at which tools are customizable is set fairly high. For instance, one can add new visualization tabs into Protégé or use a different (DIG-compliant) reasoning tool, but one cannot modify or filter the components of user interaction.

Clearly, there is some way to go to provide the level of support needed by 'normal' users engineering OWL ontologies. Our analysis highlighted some shortcomings, especially the flexibility and adaptability of user interfaces and lifting the formal abstractions. With this study, we obtained a benchmark, which we plan to use to assess the support provided by our own future tools in 18–24 months. Obviously, we intend to include other OWL engineering tools (e.g. SWOOP or OntoStudio) to make the study robust.

3.   USER INTERACTION WITH ONTOLOGIES

In the previous section we mostly considered one particular category of the users with respect to ontologies; namely, those users who want to author, design and amend ontologies as a part of some integrative task. This is an important group of users; however, these are not necessarily the only users who may have a need to interact with networked ontologies. The issue of interacting with ontologies effectively and efficiently is much more pressing with less experienced users, who carry out an ad-hoc, occasional ontology-related task — as shown, to some extent by our study reported in section 2.

Therefore, in this section we explore the problem of user interaction with ontologies more in depth, from several angles.

3.1 Configurable user interfaces

One of the findings in the user study we briefly described in section 2.3 was pointing to the fact that the ontology engineering environments tend to be reasonably modular, but they are essentially built alongside "one size fits all" strategy. In reality, such a strategy is rare among the successful software products. As users within the corporate intranets or outside of companies take on different roles, they come across and emphasize different business needs from, in principle, the same information content. Subsequently, they typically expect the tools of their trade would somehow reflect those different business needs.

One of the most often mentioned features of a new software product is an easy customization of its user-facing components. We explore this theme in the second half of the chapter on HCI challenges in ontology engineering. The quote from a software company's catalogue (anonymized by the authors) below summarizes the point:

> *[Our product] provides an easy to configure user interface enabling you to meet diverse business needs across your enterprise, as well as support localization. [Among other functionalities, the product supports] menu localization and support for international languages, enabling and disabling functions for users based on their permissions, [...]*

Users involved in ontology-driven production of information and knowledge need to be equipped with a range of software configurations and diverse user interfaces to deliver the outcomes of their work as effectively and efficiently as possible. There are two broad strategies how one can match the tools to the needs:

1. different tools for different users and different purposes;
2. different configurations of one tool or toolkit for different users or purposes.

The two strategies are not mutually exclusive; very often we find that users rely on a limited range of tools, and then may have different, specialized configurations for some of those tools. Let us briefly consider the key advantages and disadvantages of the above approaches: In the former situation, tools are well defined but apparently independent of each other. This may lead to a proliferation of a large number of highly specialized tools, something that is overwhelming and unlikely to alleviate the user's confusion. Moreover, with specialized tools, there is an increasing risk of them being mutually less compatible or compatible on a rather cumbersome level (e.g. import/export mechanism of various graphical editors is a good example of this compatibility issue). The main advantage is that the user will only get to work with tools and interfaces s/he necessarily needs to carry out given tasks, and nothing more.

In the latter situation, we tend to see more complex and multi-functional tools that can exhibit a variety of user interfaces and user interaction components in different situations. In many tools of this type, we see an aggregation of functionalities and a fairly seamless switching between many tasks the user may carry out at some point. This is essentially a "one-stop shop" approach where the user has (almost) everything they may ever need already inside the tool, and only needs to activate different configurations. A typical example of this would be editors like Microsoft Word, and its 'rich document editor' face, as opposed to (say) 'content revision' face or 'mail merge and distribution' face.

Formally, these notions were explored by Shneiderman (2000) who introduced so-called *universal usability*. While this rather broad issue is clearly beyond the scope of this chapter, Shneiderman points to several factors that may affect the tool usability. These are factors that vary from one user to another, and hence trigger a degree of adaptation to the user interface. Importantly, Shneiderman highlights many common factors that are not always recognized as valid reasons for UI customization. For example, he talks about technological variety (i.e. the need to support a range of software and hardware platforms, networks, etc.), about gaps in user knowledge (what users know, what they should know, etc.), or about demographic differences (skills, literacy, income) or environmental effects (light, noise, etc.)

One approach to achieving more universal usability of a tool is to introduce user interface adaptation into the loop. The rationale is that while a standard UI may not fit the user completely, it might be tweaked so that it gets as closely as possible to the user needs. There are two distinct strategies of how UI adaptation may be accomplished. Since this differentiation may have impact on what is actually modified in the tool, we decided to include this brief detour to generic issues of adaptation. The two strategies distinguish between the following types (Kules 2000):

- **adaptive UI**: These are systems and user interfaces that are capable of monitoring its users, their activity patterns, and automatically adjust the user interface or content to accommodate these local differences in activity patterns (which may be due to user's skill, preference, etc.).
- **adaptable UI**: These are systems and user interfaces that allow the users to control and specify adjustments, and often come with the provision of some guidance or help.

According to the informal definitions, the difference is in the actor; who performs the adaptation act. In adaptive UI-s it is the tool, applications or the system that takes the active role; whereas in adaptable UI-s it is the human — typically the actual user of the system, but possibly another user (such as system administrator).

Why do we mention user interface adaptation in this context? Ontologies are highly structured, formalized artefacts that have sufficient expressiveness to describe the structure of a system, tool, or its user interface. Considering that such common tools as Web browsers make use of ontological formalisms to support customization and thus make life easier for the user, it is rather surprising that very little of a similar approach is used to improve the tools for interacting with ontologies.

4. USERS AND ONTOLOGY ENGINEERING

In this section we briefly sketch some of the existing approaches that have been developed mostly in the context of personalization and scalability (i.e. the capability to work with large data sets). This overview is intended to be informative rather than exhaustive; it is intentionally compiled on a level that abstracts from individual tools and method to approaches and strategies.

As ontologies become more and more complex and as they are integrated into networks of ontologies, it is reasonable to investigate the means, which would be capable of making a large network of complex ontologies more manageable. The customization and personalization of ontologies includes, in principle, two areas relevant to ontologies:

- customization of the view on an ontology, e.g. during exploring a network of ontologies. This customization is more or less ad-hoc and the results of the customization may be discarded once the user proceeds with exploring the ontology. This customization during exploring an ontology tries to reduce the complexity of an ontology and only shows parts which are relevant for the current user.
- customization for the purposes of reusing ontologies and integrating them into a network with other ontologies according to specific needs (e.g. during the ontology deployment, reasoning or design phases). Here the results of the customization will often be integrated into the edited ontology.

As one basis for the customization, we analyze and briefly overview user profiles and profiling work, followed by techniques for exploring and navigating in large data sets (including ontologies), and finally we touch on the role of algebraic operators to manipulate the topology or content of ontologies.

4.1   User profiling

User profiles are seen here as a way to describe some user properties or characteristics and thus as a representation of the context of a user. Such a profile may for example provide information about the role of a user, the domain of interest or the current task. This information about the context helps in a user-tailored information delivery, e.g. by offering personalized ontology views. When talking about the user, it is important to mention that we can decide to have an *abstract user*—this would be, in principle, corresponding to any member of a group of users in a particular situation.

A user profile can be constructed in different ways depending on the data it includes and the methods used for its construction, including manual, semi-automatic and automatic methods. Each of them has some advantages and disadvantages. For a review of specific user profile acquisition techniques, consider e.g. sources mentioned in (Dellschaft, Dzbor *et al.* 2006). Let us focus in this chapter on how such profiles might be deployed and used in the context of ontology management.

In principle we see the role of user profiles as twofold: (i) as a means allowing recommendations based on some typicality effects, and (ii) as a means having a predefined description on the actions to be applied by the system, depending on some predefined user profile characteristic.

In the former case, it is interesting to acquire information, e.g. about which ontology views a given category of users prefers, what level of detail they use in annotating documents using that ontology, or which partition of a larger ontology they mostly interact with (and for what purpose).

In the latter case, a user profile may act as a kind of task definition for the activity the user is expected to carry out — an example of such a situation might be provision of an ontology view that would be less suitable to editors but much more efficient to validators.

There are many profiling systems in existence; most of them developed in the context of user interaction with Web documents and Web browsing. One example is Lifestyle finder (Krulwich 1997)—a collaborative recommendation system as it groups similar users based on the similarity of their manually constructed user profiles. It recommends potentially interesting Web documents to the user based on the ratings of the documents provided by similar users. A similar example is NewsWeeder (Lang 1995), a system for electronic Usenet news alerts.

An example of the semi-automatic approach is OntoGen (Fortuna, Mladenic *et al.* 2006) that constructs a profile from a set of documents provided by the user, and then proposes a topic hierarchy (i.e. a simple ontological model of the user's interests) that can then be used e.g. to recommend navigational steps to the user (Fortuna, Mladenic *et al.* 2006) or to visualize a particular collection based on the hierarchy of user interests (Grcar, Mladenic *et al.* 2005).

User profiling is one of the important aspects for customizing human-ontology interaction. User profiles can be used to mesh different data sources, where the preferences for a data source are based on the user profile (initially manually, but possibly adjusted based on the user's activity). User profiling can also be used for providing a personalized view on an ontology based on the ontologies previously constructed by the same or a similar user. Such a personalized view can be seen as putting ontologies in a particular context, which is familiar to the user (and hence, simplifies his or her interpretation of the ontology).

4.2 Navigating in complex conceptual structures

Since ontologies are often formal artefacts, the need some transformation to be comprehensible to the ordinary users. This is rarely straightforward. First, ontological datasets are relatively large; they contain thousands of statements the user may need to interact with. For example, a fairly simple geographic ontology of regions in New York state[5] contains as many as 59,000 unique statements just about congressional districts in a single US state. Second, ontologies could be complex structures representing different types of relationships. If each of such potential relations is treated as a dimension in which allowed values could be depicted, then even a moderately complex ontology leads to a multi-dimensional space, which poses challenges for navigation and interaction — in particular, when human cognition naturally prefers (and is able of coping with) two or three dimensions.

Two strategies that may apply to ontologies are their *reduction* and *projection*. Where reduction is concerned with showing *less at a given point in time* (in our case, fewer concepts, entities or relationships), *projection* works by showing the same set of concepts, entities and relations differently. The two strategies are somewhat complementary.

4.2.1 Reducing complexity of navigation

One common reduction strategy has been implemented in a number of faceted browsers (but not in the context of ontologies). The key principle of this strategy is that large collections (e.g. libraries or galleries) have many dimensions according to which they can be viewed, browsed, searched or navigated. Thus, faceted navigation is an interaction style whereby users

---

[5] A serialization and a downloadable version of this ontology is available from:
http://www.daml.org/2003/02/fips55/NY.owl

filter an appropriate set of items by progressively, step-by-step selecting from valid dimensions of a particular classification. That classification can be created according to many principles (including ontology-derived).

Earlier representatives of this strategy include Flamenco — a portal for browsing fine arts collections (Hearst 2000; Yee, Swearingen *et al.* 2003) or mSpace — an access site to a repository about the computer science in the UK (Schraefel, Karam *et al.* 2003). More recent examples include e.g. Longwell and Fresnel (Pietriga, Bizer *et al.* 2006) from MIT's Simile project as representatives of generic frameworks and vocabularies (respectively) for faceted navigation through RDF collections and for specifying facets. Other recent examples include BrowseRDF (Oren, Delbru *et al.* 2006), a generic RDF browser, or /facet (Hildebrand, van Ossenbruggen *et al.* 2006), an RDF browser used in a manner similar to Flamenco, but in the context of the Dutch cultural heritage project. Nonetheless, most of the above tools focus on data rather than triple-level graph structures typical for ontological concepts and relations.

User interaction in faceted style usually starts with an overview of the browsed collection, which often yields a large number of possibly relevant matches. In the subsequent browsing steps, this 'relevant' set is structured according to selected categories (e.g. locations, styles, themes, etc.). Alternatively, the user may narrow the view down by referring to hierarchical classification (if available). The navigation may end with accessing a particular item from the collection. We use term 'may' because alongside the item the user always sees all other categories and metadata that provide bridges to alternative collections.

A slightly different view on the principle of faceted navigation is advocated by the authors of CS AKTive Space and the family of similar mSpace-based applications (Shadbolt, Gibbins *et al.* 2004). The faceted views for browsing the collections are fairly typical, but there is one pane that also uses a projection strategy — geographic data are shown naturally, i.e. on a map. A useful side effect of such projections is that they enable the user to express relations very succinctly (including fuzzy ones such as *near* or *in the South*). Unlike Flamenco, mSpace is more tightly linked to ontologies — they act as the primary classification of different facets that are available to the user.

To explore the role of spatial metaphors in navigating complex structures we point e.g. to work by Mancini (2005), who experimented with ways how the same content may yield different interpretation if presented (and navigated) in a spatially different manner. Nevertheless, the use of such techniques for ontology management needs further research, before we are able to link them to particular use case scenarios and requirements. More details on how faceted browsers may assist ontology management has been provided in (Dellschaft, Dzbor *et al.* 2006), which also formed the base for this section.

In general, what faceted browsers like Flamenco support rather well is the iterative formulation of the search queries or navigational goals. Key advantage of this technology is the step away from forcing the user to go through deep, complex hierarchies in order to find items they are interested in. Users only navigate to the next slice by following some conceptual clues (e.g. sub-categories or orthogonal views). Arguably, faceted navigation seems to be a more natural way of coping with messy, conceptually complex space, than a rigid, hierarchical tree-like structure.

Thus, the "divide and conquer" strategy also works in the context of complex conceptual spaces such as ontologies. What is hard to visualize at once because of variability and differences between different relationships, can be split into sequences of partial visualizations through which it is easier to move and which are also more comprehensible to the end user. On the other hand, faceted browsers suffer from the scaling issue; i.e. they work reasonably well with a few well-defined facets that can be arbitrarily combined by the end user. For instance, CS AKTive Space used only three key (i.e. navigable) dimensions (location, topic and institution). In Longwell, deployed for MIT OpenCourseWare, there are similarly three dimensions (level of study, teacher and keywords). An ongoing tension emerges between offering as many facets to the user as possible while simultaneously helping to reduce navigational complexity.

4.2.2   Projections for large ontological data sets

In addition to conceptual and relational complexity that has been tackled by the research into faceted navigation, another similarly hard task is to navigate through large datasets. A number of projections were proposed to tackle this. In particular, the fish-eye metaphor enables customizable navigation; it uses different properties of the objects in a knowledge base to create clusters of different granularity and of different semantics. For example, Komzak and Slavik (2003) illustrate this capability to handle large networks of diverse but conceptually related data in the context of visualizing the 200k strong student population of The Open University in the UK, which can be shown on a geographic, per-faculty, per-program or per-course basis.

The strategy relies on showing the *contextual fringe* of a part of the semantic network not corresponding to a particular user's query or intention using more coarse-grained clusters than the part that actually corresponds to the query and is currently *in focus*. The authors also open up the context-focus metaphor (Lamping, Rao *et al.* 1995), so that each particular focus (fine-grained view) can be embedded into an arbitrary context (coarse-grained view).

Another algorithm based on the focus-context metaphor is SpaceTree (Plaisant, Grosjean *et al.* 2002). SpaceTree is a tree browser to some extent similar to hyper trees (Lamping, Rao *et al.* 1995). It addresses one difficulty of the hyperbolic geometry; namely constant updating of the visual representation, which makes it hard for the user to create a mental map of the ontology, hierarchy or taxonomy. SpaceTree uses dynamic rescaling of tree branches to fit within a constrained space; miniature tree icons are used to indicate the depth, breadth and size of the sub-trees hidden behind a given node.

A different example for projecting ontologies is provided by the "crop circles" metaphor (Parsia, Wang *et al.* 2005). As with the fish-eye, this metaphor also shows some implicit topography in an overview mode. In CropCircles classes and partitions are represented as circles. One can hover over a particular node in the visualization to see the class it actually represents. By clicking on a class one can quickly highlight its immediate neighborhood (children, parents). Also, zooming in and out is easily supported in this view, and as the recent study from Wang and Parsia (2006) showed, the metaphor in some cases could outperform other visual techniques (especially in the context of viewing richly interlinked and deep ontologies).

On a more traditional level, ontologies are often perceived by many developers, researchers and users as predominantly hierarchies of subsumed concepts; i.e. structures where one concept is a kind of another concept (as in "Ford is a Car"). Hence a lot of effort was put into navigating these, so-called *isA* structures. Techniques like IsaViz[6] focus on the structurally dominant relationship in any ontology (subClassOf). Two key shortcomings of this approach are: (i) its usefulness rapidly falls with the depth of a hierarchy, and (ii) very few graphs actually have a neat hierarchical structure. The *isA* graphs make visually interesting demonstrations, but by definition, they do not contain various lateral or horizontal relations (Brusilovsky and Rizzo 2002).

Some of the more recent developments in the field of ontology visualization took an approach more centered on the user needs. A good example of this is Jambalaya (Ernst, Storey *et al.* 2003), a project that started with the aim to visualize rich ontology graphs and was initially driven by the technological needs. However, at the application re-design stage, the needs of real users were considered for particular audiences comprising the biologists in a large national research center. These requirements came from observing the actual users — biologists, and conjecturing potentially useful

---

[6] More information available from http://www.w3.org/2001/11/IsaViz

functional requirements from these observations. As a result, Jambalaya is more balanced in addressing a range of users needs on an ontology visualization package.

One the level of underlying technology, Jambalaya's visualization is still based on the metaphor of a graph, but allows more customization of what can be visually depicted. Particularly its FilmStrip metaphor (Ernst, Storey *et al.* 2003) suggests an interesting compromise between data overviews and its specific context. Yet, due to realizing this idea through showing the relevant information as nodes, the outcome is full of boxes and overlapping edges. These often achieve the opposite of a positive user experience, as the overlapping graph sub-structures may easily obscure much of the underlying semantic structure.

Many practical ontologies use a range of relationship; e.g. UK Ordnance Survey reports on their use of a range of ontological relationships that may easily create issues if inappropriately visualized (Dolbear, Hart *et al.* 2006). In particular, they highlight issues with fairly common geo-spatial relationships like *contained within*, *next to* or *surrounded by*. In each of the cases illustrated, merely showing two nodes from the low-level data representation linked with a declared or inferred labeled arc is not of much use. For instance, in some cases objects such as fields may be both *surrounded by* and *contained within* and be *inside* of a wall. However, if field F is *contained within* something else (e.g. wall), by definition *it cannot be next to* another field F,' since they would need to share the 'container.' However, to anybody visualizing a dataset containing fields F and F' it makes perfect sense to 'ignore' the dividing walls and talk just about the fields.

4.2.3   Benefits of navigational and visualization techniques

Cognitive studies, one of the recent examples is a study by Demian and Fruchter (2004), show that there are several mutually not fully compatible requirements on interacting through visual user interfaces:

- a need to find a particular item (e.g. knowing some of its properties),
- a need to explore the context in which an item is defined (e.g. what does it mean if we say that "Ford is a Car"), and
- a need to establish the difference between two or more items, which may include temporal differences due to evolution or various conceptual differences (e.g. "Ford Transit is a Ford, but not a Car, and this is because…")

The simple IsaViz and related techniques basically address only the second need identified above, and even that to a very small extent. The implications of the discussion in the above paragraphs are that there is unlikely to be one perfect method or technique for scaling up the navigation through structured datasets. What is more likely to work is reusing familiar metaphors, such as the FishEye projections or CropCircles. However, it seems equally important to use these metaphors at the right point during the process of navigating ontologies. Crop Circles, for instance, seem to fit best if one is interested in seeing broad relationships among several ontologies. Map-like FishEye projections, on the other hand, seem to show a finer level of granularity — e.g. when one wants to explore the relationship of networked ontologies to a particular concept in one ontology.

One approach that has not been mentioned so far, but which actually could combine the need of dealing with large-scale datasets with the need to simplify the ontological definitions, is inspired by maps and mapping metaphor. By definition, any map is essentially a projection of a particular world (most often a landscape) onto a paper (or screen). One can imagine creating such domain landscapes from several different perspectives. For instance, a landscape of research topics in Europe is likely to look somewhat differently from the landscape of UK's football or the landscape of great maritime voyages.

Assume we have several pre-computed landscapes available that show the key terms of a particular domain (an example is shown in Figure 2-1), their links, relationships, closeness, etc. When we take one or several ontologies, we can cover these domains with the given ontologies. In some cases, the coverage would be better and more precise than in others. Different ontologies would be positioned into different regions of the landscape — dependent on which landscape the user takes as a foundation for his or her navigation. Although we have given this example with ontologies in general, most of the current tools deal only with data (possibly annotated using ontologies). Hence, adaptations of the familiar techniques are needed to apply to ontologies as topological structures, not only as data sets.

Another interesting strategy is motivated by work done by Collins, Mulholland *et al.* (2005) on spotlight browsing. The principle of this navigation strategy is again based on a metaphor — a torch throwing a beam of light. The user selects a resource or a concept from a particular collection; then the collection is dynamically restructured so that it conveys interesting properties, clusters, etc. that may be relevant to the initial 'spot.' These additional items and concepts are then structured around the original spot by calculating their semantic closeness. The navigation is then equivalent to shedding a light beam (as shown in the mockup in *Figure 2-1*), which puts certain concepts into light (i.e. into navigable focus) and certain other items into shadow (i.e. into non-navigable periphery).

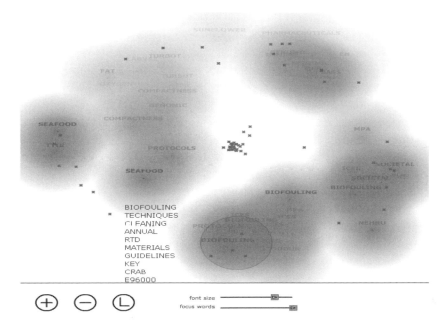

Figure 2-1 Mock-up of a 2D rendered landscape with two ontologies broadly covering and mapping different sections of it. Green areas roughly correspond to different ontologies and red crosses to selected terms whose distance/mutual positions depend on a particular corpus.

4.3   Customizing ontologies

One of the early works toward ontology customization came from Mitra and Wiederhold (2004), who proposed a modularized approach to creating ontologies as this would ease ontology reuse and would help breakdown the required effort into smaller, manageable pieces. To that goal, they describe a general idea of ontology customization operators that would support such a modularized approach and help combine the modules to larger ontologies. Examples of their operations include, e.g.:

- selection from an ontology (there are different criteria for this);
- intersection of several ontologies (i.e. a common denominator);
- union or extension of several ontologies;
- differentiation or discrimination between ontologies, etc.

In addition to the binary or n-ary operations, there is an important set of unary operations, those working on a single ontology. It is this particular set that is of interest in the context of our objective discussed in this chapter. For example, work by Jannink, Mitra *et al.* (1999) describes four binary and four unary operators. Among them are some interesting unary operators:

- *summarize* — centralizes the ontology into groups of similar concepts;
- *glossarize* — lists terms subordinate to a given concept without any of the recognition of the sub-structure;
- *filter* — extracts instances from ontology according to a given predicate;
- *extract* — reduces concepts and the possibly corresponding instances from the ontology according to a given predicate/condition.

Particularly useful operations, from the perspective of reducing ontology complexity, are the first two operations: summarization and glossarization. Both essentially drawing on the latter two operations, but providing useful interpretative viewpoints on a complex conceptual structure. In this chapter we are not going into more depth with regard to customization operations and how they may be realized, a brief overview of some tools and their support for this task is discussed, for instance, by Dellschaft, Dzbor *et al.* (2006).

Nonetheless, let us at least mention how the operators mentioned above might be related to section 4.1 (user profiles) and section 4.2 (ontology navigation). In both previous sections we relied on the fact that a part of the ontology is known, but we haven't really said how such parts might be obtained. For example, for the spotlight or fish-eye facility, we may need a central, in-focus portion of an ontology together with several summaries of the surrounding contextual fringes.

These requirements may be directly linked to the aforementioned operations for ontology customization — extraction (to get a focus area) and summarization (to obtain meaningful but brief summaries of what lies around the focal point). Hence, in general, the techniques described in this section may be seen as data feeds for the purpose of visualization and navigation methods, which in turn may act as points where the user may make choices, which could be captured in a specific profile.

Next we shall present how the three apparently independent areas may relate together in a kind of user support "stack."

4.4   Illustrative scenario — putting it all together

Imagine we work with several ontologies, which we want to navigate. Among others we have FishBase, AgroVoc, FIGIS, and other ontologies typically used by agricultural experts[7]. Let us assume our expert wants to edit parts of the ontology related to *Albacore* tuna. These need to be located,

---

[7] To learn more about these ontologies visit http://www.fao.org/fi

extracted, and presented appropriately, because the number of related terms is potentially exponentially large.

First, large ontologies may be reduced so that they contain the minimal number of concepts surrounding the albacore tuna, which are still ontologically complete and sound. This may be achieved by applying one of the ontology reduction/extraction operators mentioned in section 4.3. The extraction may find overlaps and possibly generalizations of term subsets, so that the diversity could be expressed using a smaller number of concepts.

Different alternative navigational paths can then be visually summarized in a manner following *Figure 2-1*. The initial position of the yellow "light beam" would reflect that exploratory path through the concept cloud that seems to be best covered by the existing fishery ontologies. The numbers in superscript in the figure may e.g. refer directly to the internal formal resources referring to a particular theme (e.g. FIGIS, AgroVoc, etc.). In addition, the weight of the terms is given by their ontological reliability and provenance — where our expert may quickly see that the fish species are particularly well conceptualized.

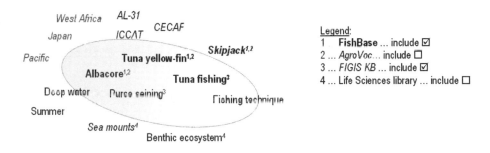

Figure 2-1. Mock-up of an ontology summary view showing concepts related to the focal term (*Albacore*) and ontologies covering these terms. Typefaces may reflect e.g. trustworthiness of terms against ontologies with same italic/bold typeface on the right.

In the shape as shown in Figure 2-1, an expert may easily see different dimensions corresponding to diverse ontological relationships around the concept of albacore tuna. Such a conceptual summary space may be easily reorganized without too much cognitive overhead on the part of our expert. For instance, re-pointing the beam towards the red section (which may denote some ontological inconsistency), it is possible to rapidly refine a particular type of ontological relationship. In our case, assume we target the locality and fish habitat relations. An outcome of such an action is sketched in Figure 2-2, where one sees more relevant ontologies, different concepts emerging in focus, and others fading into the fringe.

Thus, a typical use case applying the three layers of user-centred ontology management we discussed in this section, presents a mesh of several familiar techniques. The three areas we mentioned — user profiling, navigation and visualization techniques, and customization operators — can be seen as three layers of a stack, which influence each other in a variety of ways. For example, based on a user profile, one may prefer a particular navigational technique; such a technique may need to draw upon a specific customization operation. That, in turn, may help keep the profile up to date, etc. Hence, the three layers addressing complex user issues in our illustrative scenario are manifested in the following ways:

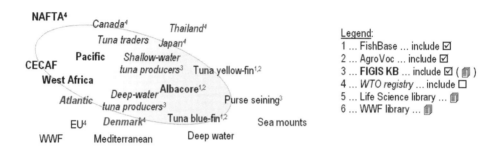

Figure 2-2. Mock-up of the repositioned focus of related terms and ontologies covering these terms

- User profiling techniques:
  o acquiring user and group profiles;
  o using machine learning to manage user profiles;
- Customized, abstract-level interaction with ontologies:
  o hiding the low-level aspects of several ontology engineering tasks;
  o making sense of links and relations within/between ontologies;
  o ontology visualization on the level of domain coverage;
  o spotlight browsing and other less common browsing extensions;
- Ontology customization operations:
  o reducing ontology complexity;
  o modularization and view customization based on user-selected criteria;
  o customization operations such as module reduction, compounding, differencing, etc.

5.   CONCLUSIONS

In this chapter we briefly covered the broad and rather complex area of human-ontology interaction. We started with reviewing generic tenets of HCI and their relevance to ontology management. We then presented some empirical evidence highlighting the fact that the existing ontology engineering tools are still at a very early developmental stage (from the software lifecycle point of view). We concluded this part with highlighting several functional opportunities that seem to be missing in the existing tools for ontology management, in particular for ontology engineering.

Then we offered an exploratory survey of some areas that are not commonly associated with ontological engineering, and considered what roles these techniques may play in making the human-ontology interaction more mainstream and more acceptable for so-called ordinary users. In particular, we started with user profiling, elaborated on the use of data visualization, navigation and exploration techniques, and briefly touched on the need to investigate ontology customization operations and methods, as the foundation of our triple stack of technologies that may make life of the user easier.

ADDITIONAL READING

Collins, T., Mulholland, P., *et al.* (2005). *Semantic Browsing of Digital Collections.* Proc. of the 4th Intl. Semantic Web Conf., Ireland, pp.127–141.

Dellschaft, K., Dzbor, M., *et al.* (2006). Review of methods and models for customizing/personalizing ontologies, NeOn project: From http://neon-project.org/web-content/index.php?option=com_weblinks&catid=17 &Itemid=35 (April 2007).

Duineveld, A. J., Stoter, R., *et al.* (2000). "WonderTools? A comparative study of ontological engineering tools." *Intl. Journal of Human-Computer Studies* **52**(6): pp.1111–1133.

Dzbor, M., Motta, E., *et al.* (2006). *Developing ontologies in OWL: An observational study.* OWL:Experiences & Directions wksp., Georgia, US.

Ernst, N. A., Storey, M. A., *et al.* (2003). *Addressing cognitive issues in knowledge engineering with Jambalaya.* Knowledge Capture Conference (K-Cap), Florida, US.

Norman, D. (1998). *The Invisible Computer.* Cambridge, MA, MIT Press.

Shneiderman, B. (2000). "Universal Usability: pushing human-computer interaction research to empower ever y citizen." *Communications of the ACM* **43**(5): pp.84–91.

Shneiderman, B. and Plaisant, C. (2004). *Designing the User Interface: Strategies for effective human-computer interaction*, Addison-Wesley, 672 pages.

Storey, M. A., Lintern, R., *et al.* (2004). *Visualization and Protégé.* 7th International Protégé Conference, Maryland, US.

REFERENCES

Brusilovsky, P. and Rizzo, R. (2002). "Map-Based Horizontal Navigation in Educational Hypertext." *Journal of Digital Information* **3**(1): pp.156.

Collins, T., Mulholland, P., *et al.* (2005). *Semantic Browsing of Digital Collections.* Proc. of the 4th Intl. Semantic Web Conf., Ireland, pp.127–141.

Colman, A. M. (2001). *A Dictionary of Psychology.* Oxford, Oxford University press, 864 pages.

Dellschaft, K., Dzbor, M., *et al.* (2006). Review of methods and models for customizing/personalizing ontologies, NeOn project: From http://www.neon-project.org/web-content/index.php?option=com_weblinks&catid=17&Itemid=35 (April 2007).

Demian, P. and Fruchter, R. (2004). CoMem: Evaluating Interaction Metaphors for Knowledge Reuse from a Corporate Memory. Stanford, Center for Integrated Facility Engineering, Stanford University: 47 pages.

Dolbear, C., Hart, G., *et al.* (2006). *What OWL has done for Geography and why we Don't Need it for Map Reading.* OWL:Experiences & Directions workshop, Georgia, US.

Duineveld, A. J., Stoter, R., *et al.* (2000). "WonderTools? A comparative study of ontological engineering tools." *Intl. Journal of Human-Computer Studies* **52**(6): pp.1111–1133.

Dzbor, M., Motta, E., *et al.* (2006). *Developing ontologies in OWL: An observational study.* OWL:Experiences & Directions wksp., Georgia, US.

Ernst, N. A., Storey, M. A., *et al.* (2003). *Addressing cognitive issues in knowledge engineering with Jambalaya.* Knowledge Capture Conference (K-Cap), Florida, US.

Fensel, D. and Gómez-Pérez, A. (2002). A survey on ontology tools, OntoWeb Project: http://www.aifb.uni-karlsruhe.de/WBS/ysu/publications/OntoWeb_Del_1-3.pdf (April 2007).

Fortuna, B., Mladenic, D., *et al.* (2006). *Semi-automatic data-driven ontology construction system.* Proc. of the 9th Multiconference on Information Society, pp.223–226.

Goel, V. (1995). *The Sketches of Thought.* Massachussets, US, MIT Press, 274 pages.

Grcar, M., Mladenic, D., *et al.* (2005). *User profiling for interest-focused browsing history.* Proc. of the 8th Multiconference on Information Society, pp.223–226.

Gruber, T. R. (1993a). "A Translation approach to Portable Ontology Specifications." *Knowledge Acquisition* **5**(2): pp.199–221.

Gruber, T. R. (1993b). "Towards principles for the design of ontologies used for knowledge sharing." *Intl. Journal of Human-Computer Studies* **43**(5/6): pp.907–928.

Hearst, M. (2000). "Next Generation Web Search: Setting Our Sites." *IEEE Data Engineering Bulletin* (Special issue on Next Generation Web Search, Luis Gravano (Ed.)).

Hildebrand, M., van Ossenbruggen, J., *et al.* (2006). */facet: A browser for heterogeneous semantic web repositories.* Proc. of the 5th Intl. Semantic Web Conf., Georgia, US, pp.272–285.

Jannink, J., Mitra, P., *et al.* (1999). *An algebra for semantic interoperation of semistructured data.* IEEE Knowledge and Data Engineering Exchange Workshop, Illinois, US.

Kalyanpur, A., Parsia, B., *et al.* (2005). "Debugging Unsatisfiable Classes in OWL Ontologies." *Journal of Web Semantics* **3**(4).

Kirkpatrick, D. L. (1994). *Evaluating Training Programs: the Four Levels.* San Francisco, Berrett-Koehler Publishers, 289 pages.

Komzak, J. and Slavik, P. (2003). *Scaleable GIS Data Transmission and Visualisation.* Intl. Conf. on Information Visualization (IV), UK.

Krulwich, B. (1997). "Lifestyle finder." *AI magazine* **18**(2): pp.37–46.

Kules, B. (2000). "User modeling for adaptive and adaptable software systems." *UUGuide: Practical design guidelines for Universal Usability,* From http://www.otal.umd.edu/UUGuide (April 2007).

Lamping, J., Rao, R., *et al.* (1995). *A focus-context technique based on hyperbolic geometry for visualizing large hierarchies.* Proc. of the Conf. on Human Factors in Computing Systems.

Lang, K. (1995). *News weeder : Learning to filter netnews.* Proc. of the 12th Intl. Conf. on Machine Learning.

Mancini, C. (2005). *Cinematic Hypertext: Investigating a New Paradigm.* Amsterdam, The Netherlands, IOS Press, 192 pages.

Mitra, P. and Wiederhold, G. (2004). An ontology composition algebra. *Handbook on Ontologies.* S. Staab and R. Studer. Heidelberg, Germany, Springer Verlag: pp.93–113.

Norman, D. (1998). *The Invisible Computer.* Cambridge, MA, MIT Press.

Noy, N. F. and Musen, M. A. (2003). "The PROMPT Suite: Interactive Tools For Ontology Merging And Mapping." *International Journal of Human-Computer Studies* **59**(6): pp.983–1024.

Noy, N. F., Sintek, M., *et al.* (2001). "Creating Semantic Web Contents with Protege 2000." *IEEE Intelligent Systems* **16**(2): pp. 60–71.

Oren, E., Delbru, R., *et al.* (2006). *Extending faceted navigation for RDF data.* Proc. of the 5th Intl. Semantic Web Conf., Georgia, US, pp.559–572.

Parsia, B., Wang, T., *et al.* (2005). *Visualizing Web Ontologies with CropCircles.* Proceedings of the ISWC 2005 Workshop on End User Semantic Web Interaction, Ireland.

Pietriga, E., Bizer, C., *et al.* (2006). *Fresnel: A browser-independent presentation vocabulary for RDF.* Proc. of the 5th Intl. Semantic Web Conf., Georgia, US, pp.158–171.

Pinto, S., Peralta, N., *et al.* (2002). *Using Protégé 2000 in Reuse Processes.* Evaluation of ontology-based tools (EON), pp.15–25.

Plaisant, C., Grosjean, J., *et al.* (2002). *Spacetree: Supporting exploration in large node link tree, design evolution and empirical evaluation.* Proc. of the Intl. Symposium on Information Visualization.

Shraefel, M C, Karam, M., *et al.* (2003). *mSpace: interaction design for user-determined, adaptable domain exploration in hypermedia.* Workshop on Adaptive Hypermedia and Adaptive Web Based Systems, UK, pp.217–235.

Scriven, M. (1991). Beyond Formative and Summative Evaluation. *Evaluation and Education: A Quarter Century.* M. W. McLaughlin and D. C. Phillips. Chicago, University of Chicago Press: pp.19–64.

Shadbolt, N. R., Gibbins, N., *et al.* (2004). "CS AKTive Space: or how we learned to stop worrying and love the Semantic Web." *IEEE Intelligent Systems* **19**(3): pp.41–47.

Shneiderman, B. (2000). "Universal Usability: pushing human-computer interaction research to empower every citizen." *Communications of the ACM* **43**(5): pp.84–91.

Shneiderman, B. and Plaisant, C. (2004). *Designing the User Interface: Strategies for effective human-computer interaction,* Addison-Wesley, 672 pages.

Storey, M. A., Lintern, R., *et al.* (2004). *Visualization and Protégé.* 7th International Protégé Conference, Maryland, US.

Wang, T. D. and Parsia, B. (2006). *CropCircles: Topology sensitive visualization of OWL class hierarchies.* Proc. of the 5th Intl. Semantic Web Conf., Georgia, US, pp.695–708.

Yee, P., Swearingen, K., *et al.* (2003). *Faceted Metadata for Image Search and Browsing.* Proc. of the ACM Conf. on Computer-Human Interaction (CHI).

Chapter 3

ONTOLOGY MANAGEMENT INFRASTRUCTURES

Walter Waterfeld[1], Moritz Weiten[2], Peter Haase[3]

[1]Software AG, Uhlandstr. 12, D-64289 Darmstadt, Germany,
Walter.Waterfeld@softwareag.com; [2]Ontoprise GmbH, Amalienbadstr. 36, D-76227
Karlsruhe, Germany, Weiten@ontoprise.com; [3]AIFB, Universität Karlsruhe(TH), Englerstr.
28, D-76128 Karlsruhe, Germany, pha@aifb.uni-karlsruhe.de

Abstract: In this chapter we examine tools for ontology management. A state of the art
analysis of the currently existing tools like editors, browsers and reasoners
shows a number of deficits like many isolated tools, which cover only a small
part of the lifecycle. Thus there is the need for an integrated environment for
ontology management. Based on these deficits we define for such an
integrated environment critical requirements, which cover the whole
engineering lifecycle of large scale ontologies in a distributed environment.
The NeOn architecture — a reference architecture for ontology management
tools — addresses these requirements through a layered and extensible
architecture. It enhances ontology management techniques with mechanisms
for large distributed semantic applications. It also opens traditional closed
ontology management tools with a service-based integration into scalable
standard infrastructures. The NeOn toolkit as the reference implementation of
the NeOn architecture resolves the deficits of these tools concerning the stated
requirements

Keywords: Ontology management; OWL; reasoner; registry; repository; rules

1.   INTRODUCTION AND MOTIVATION

Ontology management tools are needed for the development of semantic
applications especially in the growing corporate Semantic Web, which
comprises the application of semantic technologies in an enterprise
environment. The main infrastructure components needed are tools to
develop ontologies and reasoners to process these ontologies. The

functionality of development tools is currently mainly focussed on editing and browsing ontologies. A broad range of tools and a large common core of features have emerged in recent years. Opposite to that, reasoners as the other established ontology infrastructure, have quite small core functionality. Here the activities concentrate more in the area of the supported ontology languages and on efficient realisations of the reasoning process.

Analyzing the state-of-the-art ontology management tools, we observe that the evolution of semantic technologies has led to a number of concrete implementations to support specific ontology engineering activities and that in particular the initial development of single, static ontologies is well supported.

However, popular tools available today for ontology development are limited with respect to (i) lifecycle support, (ii) collaborative development of semantic applications, (iii) Web integration, and (iv) the cost-effective integration of heterogeneous components in large applications.

While typically today's environments are 'closed,' and focus on a single or a few individual aspects/phases of the lifecycle, we require an environment that adequately supports the developer user loop over the *lifecycle of networked* ontologies.

The NeOn project[1] addresses those aspects. NeOn is a large European Research project developing an infrastructure and tool for large-scale semantic applications in distributed organizations. Within NeOn, we aim at advancing the state of the art in ontology management by developing a reference architecture. Particularly, we aim at improving the capability to handle multiple networked ontologies that are created collaboratively, and might be highly dynamic and constantly evolving. This is achieved by providing — in a major integrative effort — an infrastructure for networked ontology management capable of suiting the community's needs. The heart of this infrastructure is the NeOn Toolkit[2] for engineering contextualized networked ontologies and semantic applications.

In this chapter, we will first provide an overview of the state-of-the-art in management tools in the subsequent Section 2. We then analyze requirements that modern ontology management tools must meet in order to support the lifecycle of ontologies in networked, distributed, and collaborative environments in Section 3. In Section 4 we present an overview of the NeOn reference architecture for ontology management in large-scale semantic applications. We conclude with a summary in Section 5.

---

[1] http://www.neon-project.org/

[2] http://www.neon-toolkit.org/

2.   STATE OF THE ART

In this section we provide an overview of state-of-the-art ontology management tools. We distinguish between development tools and infrastructure components.

2.1   Ontology infrastructures

In this section we provide an overview on state-of-the-art reasoners and repositories. Functionality-wise there is a clear distinction between reasoners and repositories.

While repositories aim at being able to efficiently store and retrieve large collections of data (i.e. managing explicit facts), reasoners focus on deduction procedures to derive implicit knowledge.

Thus independent reasoner and repository realisations can be normally integrated via defined interfaces. However for efficient large-scale ontology support, repository and reasoner realizations have often some of the other functionality. For example ontology repository realisations provide database-like functionalities with (typically limited) inferencing support. In turn, many reasoner realisations rely on an integrated repository.

In the following, we start with an overview on existing reasoners, where we discuss the supported ontology languages, their reasoning approaches, availability and interfaces. The overview is partially based on the Description Logic Reasoner site[3].

- Cerebra Engine is a commercially developed C++-based reasoner. It implements a tableau-based decision procedure for general TBoxes (subsumption, satisfiability, classification) and ABoxes (retrieval, tree-conjunctive query answering using an XQuery-like syntax). It supports the OWL-API and comes with numerous other features.
- FaCT++ is a free open-source C++-based reasoner for SHOIQ with simple data types (i.e., for OWL-DL with qualifying cardinality restrictions). It implements a tableau-based decision procedure for general TBoxes (subsumption, satisfiability, classification) and incomplete support of ABoxes (retrieval). It supports the Lisp-API and the DIG-API.
- KAON2 (Motik and Sattler, 2006) is a free (free for non-commercial usage) Java reasoner for SHIQ[4] extended with the DL-safe fragment of SWRL. It implements a resolution-based decision procedure for general

---

[3] http://www.cs.man.ac.uk/~sattler/reasoners.html

[4] That is a special description logic. For an overview see http://www.cs.man.ac.uk/~ezolin/logic/complexity.html.

TBoxes (subsumption, satisfiability, classification) and ABoxes (retrieval, conjunctive query answering). It comes with its own, Java-based interface, and supports the DIG-API.

- OntoBroker is a commercial Java based main-memory deductive database engine and query interface. It processes F-Logic ontologies and provides a number of additional features such as integration of relational databases and various built-ins. The new version of OntoBroker offers the KAON2 API.

- Pellet (Sirin et al., 2007) is a free open-source Java-based reasoner for SROIQ[5] with simple data types (i.e., for OWL 1.1). It implements a tableau-based decision procedure for general TBoxes (subsumption, satisfiability, classification) and ABoxes (retrieval, conjunctive query answering). It supports the OWL-API, the DIG-API, and Jena interface and comes with numerous other features.

- RacerPro is a commercial (free trials and research licenses are available) lisp-based reasoner for SHIQ with simple data types (i.e., for OWL-DL with qualified number restrictions, but without nominals). It implements a tableau-based decision procedure for general TBoxes (subsumption, satisfiability, classification) and ABoxes (retrieval, nRQL query answering). It supports the OWL-API and the DIG-API and comes with numerous other features.

- OWLIM is semantic repository and reasoner, packaged as a Storage and Inference Layer (SAIL) for the Sesame RDF database. OWLIM uses the TRREE engine to perform RDFS, and OWL DLP reasoning. It performs forward-chaining of entailment rules on top of RDF graphs and employs a reasoning strategy, which can be described as total materialization. OWLIM offers configurable reasoning support and performance. In the "standard" version of OWLIM (referred to as SwiftOWLIM) reasoning and query evaluation are performed in-memory, while a reliable persistence strategy assures data preservation, consistency and integrity.

In the following we additionally discuss two implementations of ontology repositories: Jena and Sesame are the two most popular implementations of RDF stores. They play a separate role, as their primary data model is that of RDF. However, they deserve discussion, as they offer some OWL functionalities and limited reasoning support.

- Sesame (http://openrdf.org, Broekstra et al., 2002) is an open source repository for storing and querying RDF and RDFS information. OWL ontologies are simply treated on the level of RDF graphs. Sesame

---

[5] That is another special description logic. For an overview see
http://www.cs.man.ac.uk/~ezolin/logic/complexity.html.

enables the connection to DBMS (currently MySQL, PostgreSQL and Oracle) through the SAIL (the Storage and Inference Layer) module, and also offers a very efficient direct to disk Sail called Native Sail. Sesame provides RDFS inferencing and allows querying through SeRQL, RQL, RDQL and SPARQL. Via the SAIL it is also possible to extend the inferencing capabilities of the system. (In fact, this is how the OWLIM reasoner is realized.) The main ways to communicate with the Sesame modules are through the Sesame API or through the Sesame Server, running within a Java Servlet Container.

- Jena is a Java framework for building Semantic Web applications (http://jena.sf.net). It offers the Jena/db module which is the implementation of the Jena model interface along with the use of a database for storing/retrieving RDF data. Jena uses existing relational databases for persistent storage of RDF data; Jena supports MySQL, Oracle and PostgreSQL. The query languages offered are RDQL and SPARQL. Just as in Sesame, the OWL support is realized by treating OWL ontologies as RDF graphs. However, in addition Jena also provides a separate OWL API and allows integration with external reasoners, such as Pellet.

2.2 Ontology development tools

A clear focus of current ontology management tools is to support the development of ontologies with a wide range of editing features. The following description of ontology tools is not meant to be complete. Instead we chose tools which represent different philosophies due to their history, their target users, etc.

Starting with Protégé as probably the most popular ontology development tool we describe an environment with a long history and a large number of features which go beyond pure editing of ontology-files. Other environments supporting a range of tasks in the broader context of ontology development include the commercial tools such as TopBraid Composer™. We then present tools that focus on certain aspects, such as providing a native OWL editor reflecting its characteristics as Semantic Web language (SWOOP), offering a rich graphical interface (Altova Semantic Works™) or rule-support and semantic integration (OntoStudio®).

While most of the tools focus on RDF(S) and/or OWL as ontology language, two of the presented environments support other languages. Protégé as a hybrid tool supports its own frame-based representation as well as OWL and RDF(S). The frame-based format, which from a historical point of view is the "original" native representation of Protégé, is related to formats used in expert system shells. OntoStudio® offers a couple of functionalities based on the F-Logic language, which mainly concerns the creation and management of rules. The latter functionalities differ from the rule-features some of the other tools offer, since those support SWRL rules as an extension to OWL ontologies.

The following sections focus on the characteristics of the tools from a user's perspective. The last sections provide a comparison of the core features and characterize the current state of ontology development tools.

2.2.1 Protégé

Protégé 3.2 (Gennari et al., 2002) is the latest version of the Protégé OWL editor (Knublauch et al., 2004), created by the Stanford Medical Informatics group at Stanford University. Protégé is a Java-based open source standalone application to be installed and run a local computer. It enables users to load and save OWL and RDF ontologies, edit and visualize classes, properties and SWRL rules (Horrocks et al., 2004), define logical class characteristics as OWL expressions and edit OWL individuals.

With respect to the supported languages Protégé is a hybrid tool. The internal storage format of Protégé is frame-based. Therefore Protégé has native frame-support. The support for OWL is provided by a special plugin that fits into the Protégé plugin architecture. Another example of plugin is the versioning support in Protégé (Noy et al., 2004).

The Protégé-OWL API is built on top of the frame-based persistence API using "frame-stores." The API provides classes and methods to load and save OWL files, to query and manipulate OWL data models, and to perform reasoning based on Description Logic engines. The API is designed to be used in two contexts: (1) development of components that are executed inside the Protégé UI, and (2) development of stand-alone applications (e.g. Swing applications, Servlets or Eclipse plugins).

The OWL APIs implementation rely both on the frame-based knowledge base for low level (file or DBMS based) triple storage, and both on the Jena[6] APIs for various services, such as OWL parsing and data type handling.

The Protégé-OWL API can be used to generate a Jena Model at any time in order to query the OWL model, for example by means of the SPARQL RDF query language (Prud'hommeaux et al., 2007). Reasoning can be

---

[6] Jena, developed by HP Labs, is one of the most widely used Java APIs for RDF and OWL (http://jena.sourceforge.net/).

performed by means of an API which employs an external DIG[7] compliant reasoner, such as RACER, FaCT++, Pellet or KAON2.

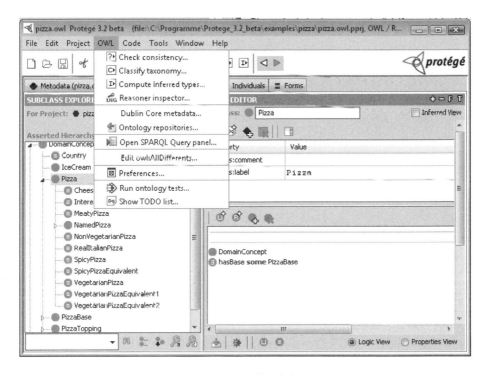

Figure 3-1. Protégé

Protégé offers a proprietary framework for plugins enabling users to extend the tool. The possible plugins include custom widgets as well as additional storage backends. In contrast to platforms like Eclipse there is a predefined set of possible extensions, which excludes "plugins of plugins."

Protégé has gained much popularity over the years and has a large user-base. Consequently a large number of plugins is available. The standard distribution contains plugins for graph-based visualization, import of different formats and many more. Additional plugins offer for example ontology merging functionalities. Apart from the community support through the Protégé website and mailing lists, there are Protégé regular user conferences.

---

[7] The DIG Interface (http://dig.sourceforge.net/) is a standardised XML interface to Description Logics systems developed by the DL Implementation Group (http://dl.kr.org/dig/).

For historical reasons Protégé has not been designed as a native OWL tool. As previously mentioned the OWL support is built on top of the frame-based storage API, but it also uses partly the Jena API for certain tasks. Protégé builds on a bridge between its internal triple store and the Jena API.

While Protégé offers a unique look and feel for both, frame-based ontologies and OWL ontologies, the implementation of an OWL API on top of a frame-based API has significant disadvantages over the design of a native OWL API. Consequently the next generation of Protégé OWL, which by the time of writing this text was only available as a prototype, is a standalone tool using a "pure" OWL API.

2.2.2 Altova SemanticWorks™

SemanticWorks™ is a commercial OWL editor offered by Altova[8]. The most outstanding feature of the tool is the graphical interface. SemanticWorks™ supports the visual editing of OWL and RDF(S) files using a rich, graph-based multi-document user interface. The latter supports various graphical elements including connections and compartments.

The visualization of ontologies utilizes very similar mechanisms from the other Altova products, which are XML-based. This means they are syntax-oriented. There is for example hardly any difference between the visualization of meta-objects of OWL like owl:Class and a user class. This makes it difficult to get an overview on the user content of an ontology.

Ontologies can be saved as .rdf, .rdfs, or .owl files and can be exported in their RDF/XML and N-Triples formats.

SemanticWorks™ does — in contrast to other tools presented in this section — not include direct interactions with reasoners for consistency checking, debugging, query processing etc. Thus the tool might be seen as a pure editor, rather than a development tool, especially when compared to tools like SWOOP. The latter also focuses on the creation and management of OWL-files, but includes for example debugging capabilities. The strength of SemanticWorks™ is the graphical interface with its navigation capabilities (e.g. dynamic expansion of elements with automatic layout).

2.2.3 TopBraid Composer™

TopBraid Composer™ is a modelling tool for the creation and maintenance of ontologies[9]. It is a complete editor for RDF(S) and OWL models. TopBraid Composer™ is built upon the Eclipse platform and uses Jena as its underlying API. The following list contains some of the

---

[8] At the time of this writing, SemanticWorks™ 2007 is the latest version available.

[9] At the time of this writing, the TopBraid Composer™ is available as version 2.2.

characteristics of the tool. It is implemented as an IDE-application using the Eclipse platform with all its advantages (such as the plugin concept). TopBraid Composer™ supports consistency checks and other reasoning tasks. The system has the open-source DL reasoner Pellet built-in as its default inference engine, but other classifiers can be accessed via the DIG interface.

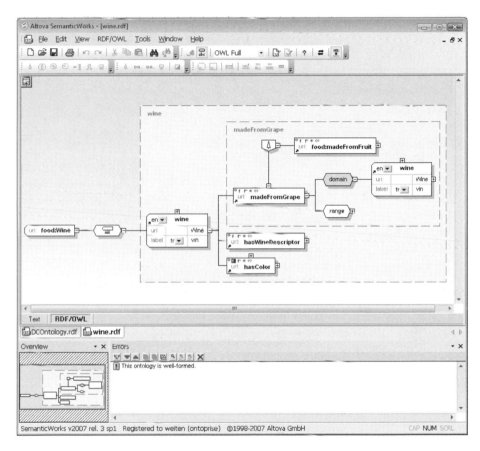

Figure 3-2. Altova SemanticWorks

Historically the development of TopBraid Composer™ has its roots in Protégé OWL[10]. Thus some of the concepts of TopBraid™ are similar to those of Protégé, such as the generation of schema-based forms for data acquisition. The most obvious difference from a technical perspective is the usage of the Eclise platform as a base and the lack of the frame-based part.

---

[10] As pointed out on the TopBraid website mid of 2006:
http://www.topbraidcomposer.com/tbc-protege.html

The latter allows TopBraid Composer™ to build on an OWL/RDF(S) based infrastructure, but excludes the support for frame-based technologies.

TopBraid Composer™ offers functionalities going beyond the creation and management of OWL/RDF(S) files. This includes the import of databases, XML-Schemas, UML and spreadsheets as well as a basic support for rules. The system supports rules in either the Jena Rules format or SWRL. Both types of rules are executed with the internal Jena Rules engine to infer additional relationships among resources. Rules can be edited with support of auto-completion and syntax checking.

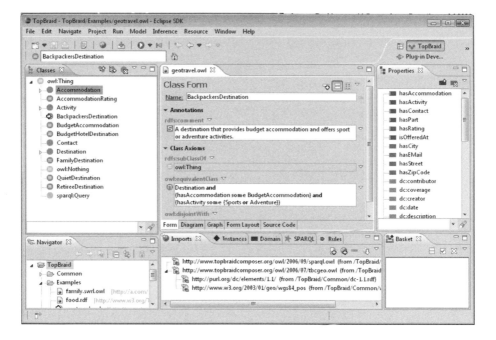

Figure 3-3. TopBraid Composer™

Other features of TopBraid Composer™ include the visualization of relationships in RDFS/OWL resources in a graphical format and the support for the concurrent editing of several ontologies. TopBraid Composer™ provides an explanation feature for OWL DL that is based on Pellet — similar to SWOOP.

TopBraid Composer™ represents a complex ontology development tool suitable for a number of tasks that go beyond the creation of OWL/RDF(S) files. As the other Eclipse-based implementations, TopBraid Composer™ is extensible by custom plugins. TopBraid Composer™ does — in contrast to the historically related Protégé — mainly (if not only) target professional users rather than a large community.

2.2.4   IODT

The Integrated Ontology Development Toolkit (IODT) was developed by IBM. This toolkit includes the Ontology Definition Metamodel (EODM), EODM workbench, and an OWL Ontology Repository (named Minerva). EODM is derived from the OMG's Ontology Definition Metamodel (ODM) and implemented in Eclipse Modelling Framework (EMF). In order to facilitate software development and execution, EODM includes RDFS/OWL parsing and serialization, reasoning, and transformation between RDFS/OWL and EMF-based formats. These functions can be invoked from the EODM Workbench or Minerva.

Minerva is an OWL ontology storage, inference, and query system based on RDBMS (Relational Database Management Systems). It supports DLP (Description Logic Program), a subset of OWL DL.

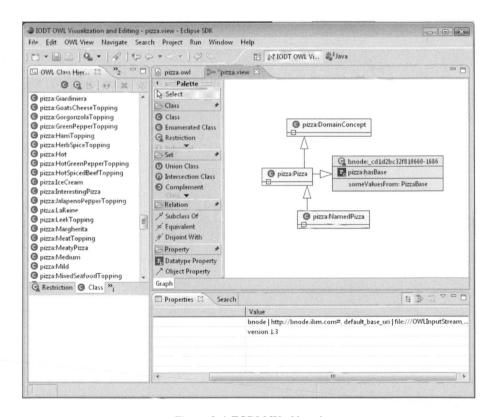

Figure 3-4. EODM Workbench

The EODM Workbench (see a screenshot in the following figure) is an Eclipse-based editor for users to create, view and generate OWL ontologies.

It has UML-like graphic notions to represent OWL class, restriction and property etc. EODM Workbench built by using EODM, EMF, Graphic Editing Framework (GEF), which provides the foundation for the graphic view of OWL. It also provides two hierarchical views for both OWL class/restriction and OWL object/datatype property.

As an Eclipse-based Tool the EODM workbench benefits from all advantages of the Eclipse platform (coupling with other plugins, etc.). In addition to traditional tree-based ontology visualization, EODM workbench provides UML-like graphic notion. Class, DatatypeProperty and ObjectProperty in OWL share the similar notion as Class, Attribute and Association in UML. Detailed properties of OWL constructs are shown in the Property view.

The EODM workbench supports multiple views for ontologies, enabling users to visually split large models. These views are independent from each other but synchronized automatically.

Being based on Eclipse, EODB is extensible, similar to products like TopBraid Composer™ and OntoStudio®. It does however not offer the direct interaction with an underlying reasoner in the form that the latter tools to and therefore lacks comfortable consistency checks or testing features.

EODM is deployed and installed as a set of Eclipse plugins. It therefore does not offer the easy-to-use installation routines of the other environments, which are deployed as standalone tools.

Offering an EMF-based implementation of an OWL and an RDF(S) metamodel, EODM offers interesting opportunities for developers, such as the combination with other EMF-based technologies or the extension of the metamodel itself.

2.2.5   SWOOP

SWOOP (Kalyanpur et al., 2005) is an open-source hypermedia-based OWL ontology editor. The user interface design of SWOOP follows a browser paradigm, including the typical navigation features like history buttons. Offering an environment with a look and feel known from Web browsers, the developers of swoop aimed at a concept that average users are expected to accept within short time. Thus users are enabled to view and edit OWL-ontologies in a "Web-like" manner, which concerns the navigation via hyperlinks but also annotation features. SWOOP therefore provides an alternative to Web-based ontology tools but offers additional features such as a plugin-mechanism.

SWOOP is designed as a native OWL-editor, which supports multiple OWL ontologies and consistency checking based on the capabilities of attached reasoners. Following the Web browser-approach, it reflects the characteristics of OWL being a language for the Semantic Web.

All ontology editing in SWOOP is done inline. Based on its HTML renderer, SWOOP uses different colour codes and font styles to emphasize ontology changes. Undo/redo options are provided with an ontology change log and a rollback option.

Some of the core features of SWOOP are the debugging features for OWL ontologies, exploiting features of OWL reasoners (in this case Pellet). This includes for example the automatic generation of explanations for a set of unsatisfiable axioms (e.g. for a particular class).

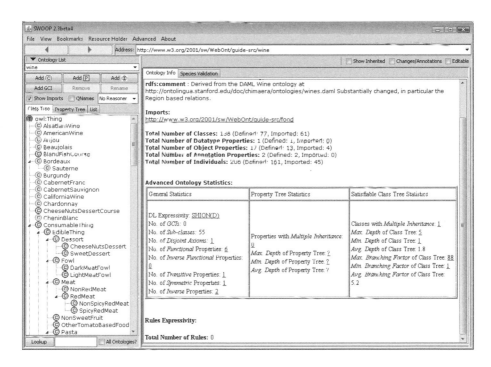

Figure 3-5. SWOOP

SWOOP can be characterized as a "pure" OWL tool, focusing on core features of the language rather then on general ontology development tasks. The tool has to offer additional features such as a basic version control, it does not include a couple of typical functionalities going beyond OWL editing, such as the integration or import of external (non-OWL/RDF-) sources.

2.2.6   OntoStudio®

OntoStudio® is a commercial product of ontoprise. It is a the front-end counterpart to OntoBroker®, a fast datalog based F-Logic inference machine. Consequently a focus of the OntoStudio® development has been on the support of various tasks around the application of rules. This includes the direct creation of rules (via a graphical rule editor) but also the application of rules for the dynamic integration of datasources (using a database schema import and a mapping tool).

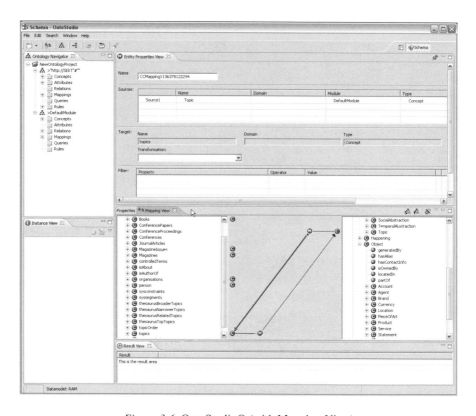

Figure 3-6. OntoStudio® (with Mapping-View)

OntoStudio® is available with a main memory- or database-based model, is therefore scaleable and is thus suitable for modelling even large ontologies. Based on Eclipse OntoStudio® provides an open framework for plugin developers. It already provides a number of plugins such as a query plugin, a visualizer and a reporting plugin supporting the Business Intelligence Reporting Tool (BIRT).

Just like TopBraid Composer™, OntoStudio® is implemented as IDE-application using the Eclipse platform with all the advantages such as the plugin concept.

OntoStudio® is tightly coupled to F-Logic (resp. its proprietary XML serialization OXML); the import and export from/to OWL/RDF is restricted mainly to concepts which can be expressed in F-Logic. Despite some minor syntactical details the Ontoprise F-Logic dialect conforms semantically to the F-Logic definition (Kifer, M. et al., 1995). Ontoprise is in close contact with the F-Logic forum to work on future versions of F-Logic and further standardization efforts.

OntoStudio® offers a graphical and a textual rule editor as well as debugging features as well as a form-based query-editor. It also includes a graphical editor for the creation and management of ontology mappings including conditional mappings, filters and transformations. Thus OntoStudio® takes advantage of the capabilities of F-Logic regarding rules (such as the support for function symbols).

2.3   Summary and remarks

In Table 3-1 we compare the described development tools by some important characteristics:

- Views: what type of representation is used to visualize the ontology elements;
- Basic infrastructure: what is the basic realisation infrastructure;
- Supported reasoner(s);
- Repository: which underlying repository is used?

Table 3-2 shows the important characteristics of the described reasoners:

- Interfaces: what are the client interfaces to access the reasoners
- Reasoning approach: what is the characteristic algorithm for the reasoning
- Supported Logic: which ontology language is supported.

The comparison shows that in many aspects the realisation of the reaoners is converging at least to only a few different approaches. For the interfaces the DIG interface is almost accepted as a service interface. For the Java client APIs the OWL API is very popular. For the reasoning approach the tableaux algorithm is very common. But several other realisations show that it is not sufficient especially for reasoning on large amount of instances. Most reasoners support OWL/DL or a subset of an equivalent description logic. However the support of rules either as DL safe rules or as F-Logic indicates that pure OWL functionality is not sufficient for semantic applications.

Table 3-1. Comparison Ontology development tools

	Protégé OWL	Semantic Works	TopBraid Composer™	IODT	SWOOP	OntoStudio®
Primary Ontology Language[11]	OWL	OWL	OWL	OWL	OWL	F-Logic
View	Form Text	Form Text Graph	Form Text (UML-like) Graph	(UML-like) Graph	Browser-like	Forms
Platform	Java	.NET	Eclipse	Eclipse	Browser + Java	Eclipse
Supported Reasoner	Via DIG	None	Pellet, (built-in) Via DIG	RACER, Pellet	Pellet	OntoBroker
Repository	Files, RDBMS	Files	Files, RDBMS	RDF on RDBMS	Files	Files, RDBMS

Table 3-2. Capabilities/Characteristics of Reasoners

	Cerebra	FACT++	KAON2	Pellet	Racer	Ontobroker	OWLIM
Interfaces	OWL API	DIG	KAON2 API	DIG OWL API, Jena API	DIG, OWL API	KAON2 API	Sesame API
Reasoning Approach	Tableaux	Tableaux	Resolution	Tableaux	Tableaux	Datalog	Forward Chaining
Supported Logic	OWL/DL	SHOIQ	SHIQ + DL safe rules	SROIQ + DL safe Rules	SHIQ	F-Logic	OWL DLP
Based on	C++	C++	Java	Java	Lisp	Java	Java

As mentioned in the introduction of this section, the tools focus on editing capabilities for OWL and RDF(S). They partially provide rich functionalities based on different editing paradigms, i.e. form-based editors or graph-based editors. In most cases those different editing features are not offered in parallel. The main exception is the TopBraid Composer®, which provides textual, graph-based and form-based editors and thus partially supports users with different levels of expertise or different profiles. In Protégé a number of wizards and two different class views ensure a certain degree of flexibility regarding the means of ontology creation and

---

[11] Most tools support additional languages via import/export.

management. However, the flexibility of the tools regarding the support for users with a different background is still limited.

As the popularity of semantic technologies increases and a wide range of ontology-based applications emerge the need for flexible and customizable environments will increase. A graph-based editor might not be the first choice for ontology experts but appropriate for domain experts with less in-depth knowledge. Tools building on extensible platforms like Eclipse (TopBraid Composer®, IODT, OntoStudio®) have clear advantages regarding their extension and customization as well as the reuse/integration of existing extensions.

The tools have a clear focus on ontology development in single-user environments. Only rarely more advanced features like the support of lifecycle aspects (e.g. in form of version management) or multi-user capabilities are available: e.g. Protégé offers a plugin for version management and TopBraid Composer® provides a multi-user mode. The latter is realized through an interface to the Sesame RDF repository. A tighter coupling of editor environments with backend technologies such as reasoners and repositories is a first step of going from single-user editors towards multi-user ontology engineering and management environments. The evolution of flexible environments will require modular approaches with efficient interfaces rather than monolithic editors. The tools currently available represent the first important steps in this direction.

With the exception of Protégé there is no really hybrid tool supporting different language paradigms — despite the fact that most tools support OWL and RDF(S) to a certain degree. With the exception of OntoStudio®, the rule support of the ontology engineering environments currently available is rather limited. OntoStudio® on the other hand does not (yet) offer sufficient OWL (DL) support.

However, a number of industrial applications and the activities around the standardization of rule languages show that the DL paradigm is comprehensive too but does not replace rule-based approaches. Large-scale rule-based applications on the other hand require full rule support, starting with a well-defined base in form of a rule-language. Other important features are rule-editing, visualization, debugging, profiling and explanation capabilities. At the same time there is need to support the current semantic Web standards including the core features of the languages.

3. REQUIREMENTS FOR ONTOLOGY MANAGEMENT INFRASTRUCTURES

The analysis shows that the current ontology management tools focus mainly on the development of single ontologies by single users. In order to use ontology management in commercial applications this approach has to be widened largely. Together with other important deficits found in our analysis we derive the following critical requirements.

3.1 Support for important ontology language paradigms

An important question for an ontology management tool is the kind of ontology language which is supported by the tool. The OWL ontology language is now well established as the standard ontology language for representing knowledge on the Web. At the same time, rule languages, such as F-Logic, have shown their practical applicability in industrial environments. Often, ontology-based applications require features from both paradigms — the description logics and the rule paradigm — but their combination remains difficult. This is not only due to the semantic impedance mismatch, but already because of the disjoint landscape in ontology engineering tools that typically support either the one or the other paradigm. An ideal ontology management environment will provide support for ontology languages satisfying a variety of needs. The role of OWL and Rules as ontology languages in the Semantic Web Stack is shown in Figure 3-7. It illustrates their parallel existence. A common subset like the DLP part of OWL is not powerful enough. The superset of a logic framework is still subject to research and cannot be efficiently handled. Therefore OWL and Rules have to be supported in parallel.

3.2 Support for networked ontologies

Next generation semantic applications will be characterized by a large number of networked ontologies, some of them constantly evolving, most of them being locally, but not globally consistent. In such scenarios it will become prohibitively expensive to adopt current ontology building models, where the expectation is to produce a single, globally consistent ontology which serves the application needs of developers and fully integrates a number of pre-existing ontologies.

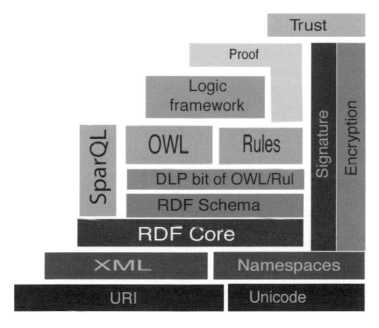

Figure 3-7 W3C Semantic Web Stack

To address distributed and networked ontology management, current ontology languages lack a number of features to explicitly express the relationships between ontologies and their elements. These features include in particular formalisms for expressing modular ontologies and mappings. Modular ontologies adopt the established notion of modules in order to separate ontologies into several parts, which can be developed and managed independently. Mappings (also called alignments) between ontologies allow defining relationships between concepts of different ontologies, without changing the ontologies themselves.

3.3 Lifecycle support

Lifecycle support is quite well established for traditional software artefacts like procedural programs or database schema. It means to govern the complete existence of a software artefact from its creation during software design and development via deployment, production, maintenance until deprecation and undeployment.

Whereas the initial development of single, static ontologies is well supported, ontology evolution has been, up to now, a rather poorly understood and supported aspect of the ontology lifecycle, especially in distributed environments involving large numbers of networked ontologies.

Therefore, we require means for supporting the application-driven evolution of ontologies and metadata while guaranteeing the "local consistency" of networked ontologies, when, for example, one of the involved ontologies undergoes a change.

While typically today's environments are 'closed,' and focus on a single or a few individual aspects/phases of the lifecycle, we require an environment that adequately supports the developer user loop over the *lifecycle* of *networked* ontologies.

Finally, we need to address not only the whole lifecycle of ontology developments but also the lifecycle of complex semantic applications. However it is important to emphasize that we are not concerned here with the "single ontology lifecycle," but the overall lifecycle of semantic models which may embed several networked sub-components, each of which may have its own evolutionary process. For a new generation of large-scale semantic applications, we will need to provide lifecycle support by developing appropriate tool support and a reference architecture, which will enable interoperability between distributed lifecycle support components. This requires ontology support in a general purpose registry, which keeps track of the state and other meta-information on all components of such semantic applications.

3.4   Collaboration support

Large ontologies are built by teams, often distributed across time and space. Ontology development environments will need to support collaborative development and, in parallel, provide mechanisms for detecting and reasoning about the provenance of ontological structures, in order to generate 'local,' consistent views for a single user or a particular (possibly multi-lingual) group or community.

Collaboration for networked ontologies consists of a set of methods, techniques, and tools to assist the users in distributed production of one particular type of formal content, namely *ontologies*. In addition to the initial production, the collaborative aspects that need a set of supportive methods and tools also emerge for the distributed management, maintenance and re-use of such ontologies.

Additionally, a collaborative framework also requires further infrastructure: the distributed repository of networked ontologies and a set of distributing components working as a middleware between the development environment itself and the distributed repository.

4. NEON REFERENCE ARCHITECTURE

In this section we present an overview on the NeOn architecture, which is targeted to become the reference architecture for ontology management in large-scale semantic applications. The NeOn reference architecture integrates functionalities common to today's ontology management tools and advances the state-of-the-art by addressing the discussed requirements that must be met in order to support the lifecycle of ontologies in networked, distributed, and collaborative environments.

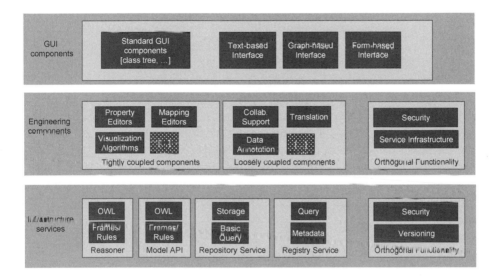

Figure 3-8 NeOn architecture

The general architecture of NeOn is structured into three layers (see Figure 3-8. The layering is done according to increasing abstraction together with the data- and process flow between the components. This results in the following layers:

- Infrastructure services: this layer contains the basic services required by most ontology applications.
- Engineering components: this middle layer contains the main ontology engineering functionality realized on the infrastructure services. They are differentiated between tightly coupled components and loosely coupled services. Additionally interfaces for core engineering components are defined, but it is also possible to realize engineering components with new specific ontology functionality.

- GUI components: user front-ends are possible for the engineering components but also directly for infrastructure services. There are also a predefined set of core GUI components.

4.1 Eclipse as an integration platform

The NeOn architecture relies on the architectural concepts of the Eclipse platform. The Eclipse IDE (integrated development environment) provides both GUI level components as well as a plugin framework for providing extensions to the base platform.

The Eclipse platform itself is highly modular. Very basic aspects are covered by the platform itself, such as the management of modularized applications (plugins), a workbench model and the base for graphical components. The real power in the Eclipse platform lies however in the very flexible plugin concept.

Plugins are not limited to certain aspects of the IDE but cover many different kinds of functionalities. For example the very popular Java-development support is not provided by the Eclipse platform but by a set of plugins. Even functionalities users would consider to be basic (such as the abstraction and management of resources like files or a help system) are realized through plugins. This stresses the modular character of Eclipse, which follows the philosophy that "everything is a plugin."

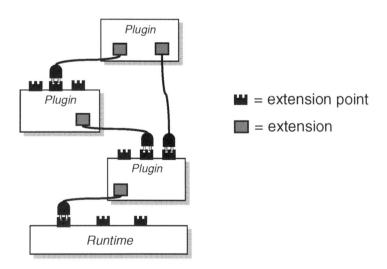

Figure 3-9 Plugin concept of Eclipse

A plugin itself can be extended by other plugins in an organized manner. As shown in Figure 3-9, plugins define extension points that specify the functionality which can be implemented to extend the plugin in a certain way. An extending plugin implements a predefined interface and registers itself via a simple XML file. In the XML file the kind of extension as well as additional properties (such as menu entries) are declared.

4.2 Infrastructure services

The infrastructure services cover support for the underlying ontology model via the Ontology Model API, as well as reasoning, repository and registry functionality.

4.2.1 Ontology model API

The NeOn ontology model API is the core ontology interface of the NeOn infrastructure. It is the main access point for the basic ontology-related operations such as reading, creating and manipulating models. The API is meant as a representation of the underlying languages encapsulating the details of interpretation, persistence, etc. The base of this API is the KAON2 API. The main feature of the API is its native support for both OWL and F-Logic as ontology languages.

The integration of OWL and F-Logic in the API is achieved via a common grounding in a First-Order-Logic (FOL) layer. The APIs for OWL and F-Logic are realized as extensions of the elements of the FOL API, for example the interface of OWLClass extends the interface of a FOL Predicate. While the API is a hybrid API supporting two languages it does not and is not meant to resolve the conceptual mismatch between different formal semantics of the languages. It is the base for hybrid applications and allows harmonizing infrastructure components (such as storage, reasoning components, etc.).

4.2.2 Reasoner

NeOn reasoners are a core component of the architecture on the infrastructure level. Accessing the reasoners is performed via a reasoner API that tightly integrates with the ontology model API described above. The API supports the management of ontologies as well as reasoning on ontologies. It thus supports engineering environments as well as runtime servers.

While in the reference architecture we foresee that both OWL and rule languages are supported for reasoning, actual implementations may also support either one of the ontology languages. In the first implementation of the NeOn reference architecture, we will provide reasoning support for OWL with the KAON2 reasoner and for F-Logic with the Ontobroker reasoner, both of which already support the NeOn ontology model and reasoning API.

4.2.3 Repository

The term repository subsumes often a wide variety of functionality. For the NeOn development architecture the functionality of a development repository for ontologies is essential. Another important aspect is the suitability of the repository for reasoning. This has been already discussed in the state of the art chapter for existing reasoners.

There are use cases where simple repository functionality is sufficient. However a realistic complete lifecycle support must handle large scale ontologies. Thus a more sophisticated repository functionality is needed. Reasoning on large ontologies additionally requires specific repository functionality for fast access to selected parts of many ontologies.

The repository manages ontologies identified by a unique name given as an URI in a persistent store. They are organized in a hierarchical, directory-like structure of collections. The functionality is based on the WebDAV protocol (Clemm et al., 2002).

The ontology repository manages directly all the artefacts needed for an ontology-based application including ontologies and other data like XML, text and binary data. For these artefacts the following basic operations are available: direct access via an URL, navigation on hierarchical collections and manipulation operations.

Another repository functionality is versioning. We provide basic versioning support for ontologies, which will be extended by more advanced collaboration facilities in specific engineering components. The basic versioning support is realized via WebDAV versioning, which is offered via the subversion protocol. The granularity is an ontology document. It includes check in and checkout facilities.

As ontologies are used to model all kind of data it is in many cases critical that the access to the ontologies can be controlled completely. This is especially true in open environments like the Semantic Web.

As the repository functionality is based on the WebDAV functionality the use of the powerful access control protocol (Clemm et al., 2004) is a consequent choice. It defines a powerful access protocol where the actors are user and groups. They can have privileges defined for all operations on any resource. These access control elements are grouped to access control list for each resource.

Multi-user capabilities are part of the versioning support. Transactions are not available at the interface level as the versioning support offers sufficient mechanisms for isolating the changes of concurrent users. The repository operations are atomic in the sense that their effect is either completely visible or not all. This is typically realised by transactions of DBMS. Nevertheless a simple file based realisation is also possible, which has not that guarantee.

4.2.4 Registry

With the increasing number of ontologies and their increased fragmentation into networked ontologies the need for an ontology registry is evident. This is not only true for the Semantic Web environment but also for large scale semantic applications in an enterprise environment.

The functionality of an ontology registry is based on an ontology meta model. For NeOn it will be based on the OMV ontology meta model (Palma et al., 2006). The ontology registry allows to register and query information about ontologies according to OMV. As this includes the location of an ontology in form of a directly accessible URL the ontology registry directly supports the management of networked ontologies.

Besides this functionality for certain scenarios other critical characteristics are needed.

- Integration with repository: For complete governance in enterprise environments the registry has to be integrated with the repository.
- Integration with general purpose registry: Opposite to specialized ontology registry it is necessary for many real world usages of ontologies that the same registry can handle also other artefacts of the complete applications. Therefore the integration of the ontology repository functionality into a general purpose registry is needed.
- Federation: Several registries can act as a federated registry. This means mechanisms to synchronize the content of the federated registries. Another functionality are federated registry queries. They will be distributed to all registries of the federation. The results are sent back to the registry initiating the federation.

4.3 Engineering components

The engineering components are the main source of functionalities that end-users typically make use of. An engineering component consists of one or more plugins. The basic engineering operations (managing elements of the ontology language) are supported through a core plugin.

Concerning the coupling of plugins to the toolkit we distinguish between two main categories: tightly and loosely coupled components.

The characteristics of tightly coupled components are

- Highly interactive behaviour
- Fine grained size
- Locally used components
- Repository access

Tightly coupled components are realized as conventional Eclipse plugins. Examples are Mapping editors or Ontology browsers, i.e. plugins with a rich graphical interface where frequent user actions invoke process on the infrastructure layer. A tightly coupled component directly interacts with the infrastructure layer without any transport layer in between.

The characteristics of loosely coupled components are

- Non interactive behaviour
- Large grain size
- Remotely used components
- own repositories

Thus the loose coupling allows using functionality, which was independently developed or cannot be easily deployed into the toolkit environment. Examples are specialized reasoning services or ontology annotation tools for text, which require a specialized infrastructure.

In the NeOn architecture the loosely coupled components are integrated as Web services. This requires the realisation of a usually thin Web service layer on top of the component. If not already available the Web service layer should be realized in the hosting environment of the component in order to avoid too many protocol indirections.

4.4   GUI components

The separation between GUI components and engineering components is — to a certain degree — arbitrary. A GUI component can be a separate Eclipse-plugin that is the counterpart to another plugin containing the engineering component or it can be one plugin together with its engineering component. The latter is suitable if only one GUI component is expected for the engineering component and both are strongly connected.

Basic GUI components will be part of a minimal configuration of the toolkit. This includes typical property editors for the management of language elements like classes and properties.

Additional GUI components include editors built on Eclipse frameworks such as the text-editor framework, the Eclipse Modeling Framework (EMF) and the Graphical Modeling Framework (GMF). The latter allows a declarative, model-driven approach for the creation of graph-based editors like UML tools. This requires a data model representing the supported language(s) or language subsets which is in line with the underlying ontology model API (see also section "infrastructure services").

GUI components require different modes of operation on the underlying data model. A form-based component e.g. for properties typically allows incremental updates using the event-management of its sub-components. A textual component can usually only be synchronized block-wise, depending on the part of the ontology that can be edited in the editor. In the extreme case it's the complete ontology.

5.   CONCLUSIONS

In this chapter we have explored infrastructures for ontology management. We have analyzed state-of-the-art systems for ontology management. From their deficits we derived critical requirements that must be met in order to support the lifecycle of ontologies in networked, distributed, and collaborative environments.

To support the development of next generation semantics-based applications, we have presented the NeOn architecture — a reference architecture for ontology management. The NeOn architecture is designed in an open and modular way and includes infrastructure services such as a registry and a repository and supports distributed components for ontology development, reasoning and collaboration in networked environments.

The NeOn toolkit as the reference implementation of the NeOn architecture is intended as the next generation ontology engineering environment and platform for semantic applications. In contrast to "traditional" ontology editors or engineering environments, the NeOn toolkit is based on a hybrid ontology model, as it natively supports the two major ontology modelling paradigms: OWL for DL-based ontologies and F-Logic for Rules and Frame based representations. It is based on the Eclipse infrastructure and heavily uses its mechanisms e.g. for extensibility and meta modelling.

It is currently under development and results on planned experiments with it usage will certainly refine also the reference architecture.

ADDITIONAL READING

To read about challenges that exist related to applying ontologies in real-world environments, we recommend (Maedche et al., 2003). The authors present an integrated enterprise-knowledge management architecture, focusing on how to support multiple ontologies and manage ontology evolution.

In (Gómez-Pérez et al., 2004) the authors have analyzed methodologies, tools and languages for building ontologies and argued that the future work in this field should be driven towards the creation of a common integrated workbench for ontology developers to facilitate ontology development, exchange, evaluation, evolution and management. The NeOn toolkit can be seen as a realization of this vision.

Another comparison and evaluation of ontology engineering environments can be found in (Mizoguchi, 2004).

REFERENCES

Broekstra, J., Kampman A., van Harmelen, F., 2002, Sesame: A Generic Architecture for Storing and Querying RDF and RDF Schema, International Semantic Web Conference, Sardinia, Italy.

Clemm et al., 2002, Web Distributed Authoring and Versioning (WebDAV) Versioning extensions, IETF Request for comments 3253, http://www.ietf.org/rfc/rfc3253.txt.

Gennari, J., Musen, M. A., Fergerson, R. W., Grosso, W. E., Crubezy , M., Eriksson, H., Noy N. F., Tu, S. W., 2002, The Evolution of Protégé: An Environment for Knowledge-Based Systems Development.

Ginsberg A., Hirtle D., McCabe F., Patranjan P., 2006, RIF use cases and requirements, Working Draft W3C http://www.w3.org/TR/rif-ucr/.

Gómez-Pérez, A, Corcho, O., Fernández-López, M., 2004, Ontological Engineering, Springer.

Grau, B. C., Motik B., Patel-Schneider P., 2006, OWL 1.1 Web Ontology Language, XML syntax, W3C Note, http://www.w3.org/Submission/owl11-xml_syntax/.

Horrocks, I. et al., 2004, SWRL: A Semantic Web Rule Language — Combining OWL and RuleML, W3C Member Submission, http://www.w3.org/Submission/SWRL/.

Kalyanpur, A., Parsia, B., Sirin, E., Cuenca, B., Grau, Hendler, J., 2005, SWOOP, A Web Ontology Editing Browser, *Elsevier's Journal Of Web Semantics (JWS), Vol. 4(2).*

Kifer, M., Lausen, G., Wu, J., 1995, Logical foundations of object-oriented and frame-based languages, Journal of the ACM, Volume 42 , Issue 4, ACM Press, New York.

Knublauch, H., Fergerson, R. W., Noy, N. F., Musen, M. A., 2004, The Protégé OWL Plugin: An Open Development Environment for Semantic Web Applications, 3rd International Semantic Web Conference, Hiroshima, Japan.

Maedche, A., Motik, B., Stojanovic, L., Studer, R., and Volz, R., 2003, Ontologies for Enterprise Knowledge Management. *IEEE Intelligent Systems* 18, 2, p. 26–33.

Motik, B., Sattler, U., 2006, A Comparison of Reasoning Techniques for Querying Large Description Logic ABoxes, Proc. of the 13th International Conference on Logic for Programming Artificial Intelligence and Reasoning, Phnom Penh, Cambodia.

Mizoguchi, R., 2004, Ontology Engineering Environments, in Studer, R., Staab, S. (eds), Handbook on Ontologies, Springer, p. 275–298.

Noy, N. F., Musen, M. A., 2004, Ontology Versioning in an Ontology Management Framework, *IEEE Intelligent Systems*, vol. 19, no. 4, p. 6–13.

Palma, R., Hartmann, J., Gomez-Perez, 2006, A., Towards an Ontology Metadata Standard, 3rd European Semantic Web Conference (ESWC), Budva.

Prud'hommeaux, E., Seaborne, A., 2007, SPARQL Query Language for RDF, W3C Working Draft, http://www.w3.org/TR/rdf-sparql-query/.

Sirin, E., Parsia, B., Grau, B. C., Kalyanpur, A., and Katz, Y., 2007, Pellet: A practical OWL-DL reasoner, *Journal of Web Semantics Vol 5(2)*.

Chapter 4

ONTOLOGY REASONING WITH LARGE DATA REPOSITORIES

Stijn Heymans[1], Li Ma[2], Darko Anicic[1], Zhilei Ma[3], Nathalie Steinmetz[1], Yue Pan[2], Jing Mei[2], Achille Fokoue[4], Aditya Kalyanpur[4], Aaron Kershenbaum[4], Edith Schonberg[4], Kavitha Srinivas[4], Cristina Feier[1], Graham Hench[1], Branimir Wetzstein[3], Uwe Keller[1]

[1]*Digital Enterprise Research Institute (DERI), University of Innsbruck, Technikerstrasse 21a, 6020 Innsbruck, {stijn.heymans|darko.anicic|nathalie.steinmetz|cristina.feier|graham.hench| uwe.keller}@deri.at;* [2]*IBM China Research Lab, Building 19 Zhongguancun Software Park, Beijing 100094, China, {malli| panyue|meijing}@cn.ibm.com;* [3]*Institute of Architecture of Application Systems (IAAS), University of Stuttgart, {zhilei ma| branimir.wetzstein}@iaas.uni-stuttgart.de;* [4]*IBM Watson Research Center, P.O.Box 704, Yorktown Heights, NY 10598, USA, {achille|adityakal|aaronk|ediths| ksrinivs}@us.ibm.com*

Abstract: Reasoning with large amounts of data together with ontological knowledge is becoming a pertinent issue. In this chapter, we will give an overviewof well-known ontology repositories, including native stores and database based stores, and highlight strengths and limitations of each store. We take Minerva as an example to analyze ontology storage in databases in depth, as well as to discuss efficient indexes for scaling up ontology repositories. We then discuss a scalable reasoning method for handling expressive ontologies, as well as summarize other similar approaches. We will subsequently delve into the details of one particular ontology language based on Description Logics called WSML-DL and show that reasoning with this language can be done by a transformation from WSML-DL to OWL DL and support all main DL-specific reasoning tasks. Finally, we illustrate reasoning and its relevance by showing a reasoning example in a practical business context by presenting the Semantic Business Process Repository (SBPR) for systemical management of semantic business process models. As part of this, we analyze the main requirements on a such a repository. We then compare different approaches for storage mechanisms for this purpose and show how a RDBMS in combination with the IRIS inference engine provides a suitable solution that deals well with the expressiveness of the query language and the required reasoning capabilities even for large amounts of instance data.

Keywords: business repository; IRIS; OWL DL; reasoning with large datasets; Semantic Business Process Management; WSML DL

1.   INTRODUCTION

Reasoning with large amounts of data together with ontological knowledge is becoming an increasingly pertinent issue. Especially in the case of Semantic Web applications, an important question is how to store respective ontologies and how to reason with them, without losing out of sight the need for scalability. In the end, the Semantic Web is envisaged to contain a huge amount of data, and reasoning with ontologies for maintaining semantical information requires scalable reasoners to extract the relevant information from these ontologies.

In order to give the reader an overview of existing solutions regarding the storage of ontologies, we will start this chapter by giving an overview of existing ontology stores. Furthermore, we will explore the use of relational databases extensively as an efficient means for storing ontologies.

After discussing how OWL — currently the most prominent ontology language on the Semantic Web — ontologies can be stored, we will investigate a particular language, WSML-DL and see how it can be translated to OWL-DL, thus giving the reader also insight in WSML-DL reasoning by relating it to the storing capabilities described for OWL in this chapter.

The first part of this chapter focuses on languages based on Description Logic, like OWL and WSML-DL. In the final part, we will discuss a Logic Programming approach, based on WSML-Flight, and see how reasoning with ontologies can be done in that context.

An important use case for scalable ontology repositories is given by the area of Business Process Management. The globalization of the economy and the ongoing change of the market situation challenge corporations to adapt their business processes in an agile manner to satisfy the emerging requirements on the market and stay. Business Process Management (BPM) is the approach to manage the execution of IT-supported business processes from a business expert's point of view rather than from a technical perspective (Smith et al. 2003). However, currently businesses have still very incomplete knowledge of and very incomplete and delayed control over their process spaces. Semantic Business Process Management (SBPM) extends the BPM approach by adopting Semantic Web and Semantic Web Service technologies to bridge the gap between business and IT worlds (Hepp et al., 2005).

In both BPM and SBPM, representations of business processes play a central role. As business processes manifest the business knowledge and logics of a corporation and normally more than one person or organization with different expertise and in different geographic locations are involved in management of business processes, it is advantageous to establish a business process repository (BPR) within a corporation for effective sharing of valuable business process knowledge. Furthermore, business users tend to reuse existing business process artifacts during process modeling, so that they are able to adapt the business processes in a more agile manner. However, as the number of business processes increases, it is difficult for them to manage the process models by themselves and to find the required business process information effectively. A BPR helps business users by providing a systematic way to manage and obtain information on business processes.

In SBPM, business process models are based on process ontologies and make use of other ontologies, such as organizational ontologies or a Semantic Web Service ontology (Hepp et al. 2007). The BPR has to be able to cope with these ontological descriptions when storing and retrieving process models, and in particular support efficient querying and reasoning capabilities based on the ontology formalism used. In order to distinguish from traditional BPR technology, we call this kind of repository a Semantic Business Process Repository (SBPR).

We first analyze the functional requirements on the SBPR. We describe what kind of functionality the SBPR should offer to its clients, which is primarily a process modeling tool. We then compare different approaches for data storage and querying based on the ontological descriptions. The comparison is based on the expressiveness of the query language, the scalability of the query processing and the effort for the integration of the query processing with the underlying data storage. We then finally describe the overall architecture of the SBPR.

2. ONTOLOGY STORAGE AND REASONING: AN OVERVIEW

2.1 Ontology repositories

In the past decade, we have seen the development of numerous ontology repositories for use in Semantic Web applications. In this section, we classify some well-known repositories based on their storage schemes, summarize methods to store ontologies in relational databases, and introduce reasoning methods used by these repositories briefly.

From the representational perspective, an ontology is in essence a directed, labeled graph, which makes ontology storage highly challenging. Figure 4-1 shows a classification scheme for ontology repositories based on

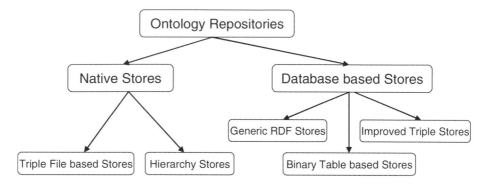

Figure 4-1. A taxonomy to classify ontology repositories

their storage models. In general, ontology repositories can be divided into two major categories, which are **native stores** and **database-based stores**. Native stores are directly built on top of the file system, whereas database-based repositories use relational or object-relational databases as the underlying backend store; that is, they can build on top of the storage and retrieval mechanisms and optimizations of those databases. Popular native stores include OWLIM (Kiryakov at al., 2005), HStar (Chen et al., 2006), and AllegroGraph (AllegroGraph, 2006). OWLIM and AllegroGraph adopt simple triple (N-triple) files to store all data, which results in the extremely fast speed for load and update. It is reported that AllegroGraph can load RDF data at the speed of more than 10,000 triples per second. OWLIM uses B+ trees to index triples and AllegroGraph just sorts triples in the order of (S, P, O), (P, O, S), and (O, S, P), respectively, for indexing purposes. The triple reasoning and rule entailment engine (TRREE) is utilized by OWLIM, which performs forward chaining reasoning in main memory, and inferred results are materialized for query answering. AllegroGraph can expose RDF data to Racer, a highly optimized DL reasoner (Haarslev & Moller, 2001), for inference. HStar is a hierarchy store and organizes *typeOf* triples (namely concept assertions in description logics terminology) using a class hierarchy and other non-typeOf triples (namely role assertions) using a property hierarchy. Because of its hierarchical tree models, it can leverage XML techniques to support a scalable store. Range labeling, which assigns labels to all nodes of an XML tree such that the labels encode all ancestor-descendant relationships between the nodes (Wu et al., 2004), can also largely improve query performance. Also, HStar uses B+ trees to index triples. A set of rules derived from OWL-lite is categorized into two groups, which are executed at load time using forward chaining and are evaluated at query time using backward chaining, respectively. In particular, reasoning on *SubClassOf* or *SubPropertyOf* could be easily implemented via its hierarchical trees.

Compared with database-based stores, native stores, in general, greatly reduce the load and update time. However, database systems provide many query optimization features, thereby contributing positively to query response time. It is reported in (Ma et al., 2006) that a simple exchange of the order of triples in a query may increase the query response time of native stores by 10 times or even more. Furthermore, native stores need to re-implement the functionality of a relational database such as transaction processing, query optimization, access control, logging and recovery. One potential advantage of database-based stores is that they allow users and applications to access both (1) ontologies and (2) other enterprise data in a more seamless way at the lower level, namely the level of the database. For instance, the Oracle RDF store translates an RDF query into a SQL query which can be embedded into another SQL query retrieving non-RDF data. In this way, query performance can be improved by efficiently joining RDF data and other data using well-optimized database query engines. Currently, lots of research efforts are made on database-based stores. We thus focus on ontology storage and reasoning in databases in the following, while comparing it with native stores.

A generic RDF store mainly uses a relational table of three columns (Subject, Property, Object) to store all triples, in addition to symbol tables for encoding URIs and literals with internal, unique IDs. Both Jena and the Oracle RDF store are generic RDF stores. In Jena2 (Wilkinson et al., 2003), most of URIs and literal values are stored as strings directly in the triple table. Only the URIs and literals longer than a configurable threshold are stored in separated tables and referenced by IDs in the triple table. Such a design trades storage space for time. The property table is also proposed to store patterns of RDF statements in Jena2. An n-column property table stores $n–1$ statements (one column per property). This is efficient in terms of storage and access, but less flexible for ontology changes. Jena2 provides by default several rule sets with different inference capability. These rule sets could be implemented in memory by forward chaining, backward chaining or a hybrid of forward and backward chaining. The Oracle RDF store (Murray et al., 2005) is the first commercial system for RDF data management on top of RDBMS. Particularly, it supports so-called *rulebases* and *rule indexes*. A rulebase is an object that contains rules which can be applied to draw inferences from RDF data. Two built-in rulebases are provided, namely RDFS and RDF (a subset of RDFS). A rule index is an object containing pre-calculated triples that can be inferred from applying a specified set of rulebases to RDF data. Materializing inferred results would definitely speed up retrieval. Different from the generic RDF store, improved triple stores, such as Minerva (Zhou et al., 2006) and Sesame on top of the MySQL database (Broekstra et al., 2002), manage different types of triples using different tables. As we can see from the storage schema of Minerva shown in Figure 4-3, class and property information is separated from instances, and *typeOf* triples are isolated from other triples. The improved triple store is efficient since some self-joins on a big triple table are changed to some joins among small-sized tables. Both the generic RDF store and the improved triple store make use of a fixed database schema. That is, the schema is independent of the ontologies in use. The schema of binary table based stores, however, changes with ontologies. These kinds of stores, such as DLDB-OWL (Pan & Heflin, 2003) and Sesame on PostgreSQL (Broekstra et al., 2002), create a table for each class (resp. each property) in an ontology. A class table stores all instances belonging to the same class and a property table stores all triples which have the same property. Such tables are called binary tables. For the subsumption of classes and properties, DLDB-OWL exploits database views to capture them, whereas Sesame leverages the sub-tables from object relational databases so as to handle them naturally. One of advantages of the binary table based store is to decrease the traversal space and improve data access for queries. That is, instances of unrelated classes or properties to a query will not be accessed. An obvious drawback is the alteration of the schema (e.g., deleting or creating tables) when ontologies change. Also, this binary table based approach is not suitable for very huge ontologies having tens of thousands of classes, such as SnoMed ontology (SnoMed, 2006). Too many tables will increase serious overhead to the underlying databases.

   The above gives an overall introduction to some well-known ontology repositories, including native stores and database based stores, and highlights strengths and limitations of each store. It is reported in (Ma et al., 2006) that Minerva achieves good performance in benchmarking tests. Next, we will take Minerva as an example to analyze ontology storage in databases in depth, as well as to discuss efficient indexes for scaling up ontology repositories. We will then discuss a scalable reasoning method for handling expressive ontologies, as well as summarize other similar approaches.

2.2   Practical Methods for ontology storage and index in relational databases

   This section discusses methods to store and index ontologies in relational databases by investigating an improved triple store, namely Minerva (Zhou et al., 2006). Figure 4-2 shows the component diagram of Minerva, which is consists of four modules: Import Module, Inference Module, Storage Module (viz. an RDBMS schema), and Query Module.

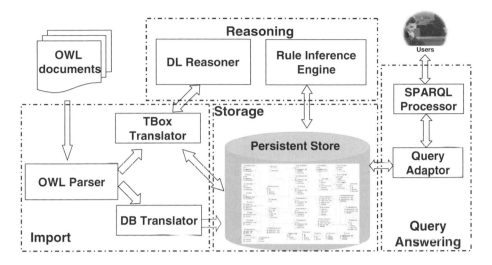

Figure 4-2. The component diagram of Minerva

The import module consists of an OWL parser and two translators. The parser parses OWL documents into an in-memory EODM model (EMF ontology definition metamodel) (IODT, 2005), and then the DB translator populates all ABox assertions into the backend database. The function of the TBox translator is two-fold: One task is to populate all asserted TBox axioms into a DL reasoner, and the other is to obtain inferred results from the DL reasoner and to insert them into the database. A DL reasoner and a rule inference engine comprise the inference module. Firstly, the DL reasoner infers complete subsumption relationships between classes and properties. Then, the rule engine conducts ABox inference based on the description logic programs (DLP) rules (Grosof et al., 2003). Currently, the inference rules are implemented using SQL statements. Minerva can use well-known Pellet (Sirin & Parsia, 2004) or a structural subsumption algorithm for TBox inference (IODT, 2005). The storage module is intended to store both original and inferred assertions by the DL reasoner and the rule inference engine. However, there is a way to distinguish original assertions from inferred assertions by a specific flag. Since inference and storage are considered as an inseparable component in a complete storage and query system for ontologies, a specific RDBMS schema is designed to effectively support ontology reasoning. Currently, Minerva can take IBM DB2, Derby, MySQL and Oracle as the back-end database. The query language supported by Minerva is SPARQL (Prud'hommeaux & Seaborne, 2006). SPARQL queries are answered by directly retrieving inferred results from the database using SQL statements. There is no inference during the query answering stage because the inference has already been done at the loading stage. Such processing is expected to improve the query response time.

In summary, Minerva combines a DL reasoner and a rule engine for ontology inference, followed by materializing all inferred results into a database. The database schema is well designed to effectively support inference and SPARQL queries are answered by direct retrieval from the database. Jena and Sesame have provided support for ontology persistence in relational databases. They persist OWL ontologies as a set of RDF triples and do not consider specific processing for complex class descriptions generated by class constructors (boolean combinators, various kinds of restrictions, etc). The highlight of Minerva's database schema is that all predicates in the DLP rules have corresponding tables in the database. Therefore, these rules can be easily translated into sequences of relational algebra operations. For example, Rule *Type(x,C) :- Rel(x,R, y).Type(y,D).SomeValuesFrom(C,R,D)* has four terms in the head and body, resulting in three tables: *RelationshipInd*, *TypeOf* and *SomeValuesFrom*. It is straightforward to use SQL statements to execute this rule. We just need to use simple SQL *select* and *join* operations among these three tables. Leveraging well-optimized database engines for rule inference is expected to significantly improve the efficiency. Figure 4-3 shows the relational storage model of Minerva.

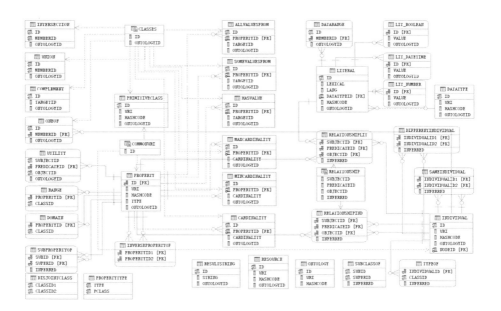

Figure 4-3. Database schema of Minerva

We categorize tables of the database schema of Minerva into four types: atomic tables, TBox axiom tables, ABox fact tables and class constructor tables. The atomic tables include: Ontology, PrimitiveClass, Property,

Datatype, Individual, Literal and Resource. These tables encode the URI with an integer (the ID column), which reduces the overhead caused by the long URI to a minimum. The hashcode column is used to speed up search on URIs and the ontologyID column denotes which ontology the URI comes from. The Property table stores characteristics (symmetric, transitive, etc.) of properties as well. To leverage built-in value comparison operations of databases, boolean, date time and numeric literals are separately represented using the corresponding data types provided by databases. There are three important kinds of ABox assertions involved in reasoning: TypeOf triples, object property triples and datatype property triples. They are stored in three different tables, namely tables TypeOf, RelationshipInd and RelationshipLit. A view named *Relationship* is constructed as an entry point to object property triples and datatype property triples. Triples irrelevant to reasoning, such as those with rdfs:comment as the property, are stored in the table Utility. The tables SubClassOf, SubPropertyOf, Domain, Range, DisjointClass, InversePropertyOf are used to keep TBox axioms. The class constructor tables are used to store class expressions. Minerva decomposes the complex class descriptions into instantiations of OWL class constructors, assigns a new ID to each instantiation and stores it in the corresponding class constructor table. Taking the axiom Mother = Woman $\sqcap$ $\exists$ hasChild.Person as an example, we first define S1 for $\exists$ hasChild.Person in Table SomeValuesFrom. Then I1, standing for the intersection of Woman and S1, will be defined in Table IntersectionClass. Finally, {Mother $\sqsubseteq$ I1, I1 $\sqsubseteq$ Mother} will be added to the SubClassOf table. Such a design is motivated by making the semantics of complex class description explicit. In this way, all class nodes in the OWL subsumption tree are materialized in database tables, and rule inference can thus be easier to implement and faster to execute via SQL statements. Also, a view named *Classes* is defined to provide an overall view of both named and anonymous classes in OWL ontologies.

The triple table of three columns (Subject, Property, Object) is also called a vertical table in data management. In (Agrawal et al., 2001), Agrawal et al. discussed the advantages of vertical tables over binary tables in terms of manageability and flexibility. Improved triple stores, including Minerva, generally adopt vertical tables to store ABox facts. The vertical table is efficient in space, but its retrieval often requires a 3-way join. This becomes a bottleneck in the case of complex queries or a large number of records involved, although using some indexes. Wang et al. (Wang et al., 2002) gives an insight into why the vertical table sometimes results in long query response time. Most relational databases transform a user query into a physical query plan which represents the operations, the method of performing the operations, and the order of processing the different operations (Garcia-Molina et al., 2000). A query optimizer of the database considers multiple physical plans and estimates their costs, and then selects a plan with the least estimated cost and passes it to the execution engine. So, the accuracy of the cost estimation seriously affects the efficiency of a query execution. Usually statistics collected from the base data are used to estimate the cost of a query plan. The query optimizer builds a histogram for each column. The histogram contains information about the distribution of the corresponding column and is stored in a database catalog (Wang et al., 2002, Poosala et al., 1996, Matias et al., 1998). Apparently, if the statistical information represented by the histogram is inaccurate, the query optimizer may make a wrong selection among different physical query plans. Since values of different properties are stored in the same column of the vertical table, the corresponding histogram can not accurately reflect the value distribution of each property. This may affect the query plan selection and execution of a query which needs to access information in the vertical table. Wang et al. proposed to build external histograms for values of different attributes and rewrite the physical query plan based on these external histograms. That is, with the external histograms, the DBMS query engine could generate an optimal query plan. Therefore, we can adopt this optimization method for the performance of triple stores. Sometimes, it is impossible to apply this method since one needs to access the core engine of the database. So, it is desirable to leverage indexes as much as possible to improve ontology repositories.

Currently, most commercial database systems provide primary clustering indexes. In this design, an index containing one or more keyparts could be identified as the basis for data clustering. All records are organized on the basis of their attribute values for these index keyparts by which the data is ordered on the disk. More precisely, two records are placed physically close to each other if the attributes defining the clustering index keyparts have similar values or are in the same range. Clustering indexes could be faster than normal indexes since they usually store the actual records within the index structure and the access on the ordered data needs less I/O costs. In practice, it is not suitable to create an index on a column with few distinct values because the index does not narrow the search too much. But, a clustering index on such a column is a good choice because similar values are grouped together on the data pages. Considering that real ontologies have a limited number of properties, the property column of triple tables, such as the RelationshipInd table of Minerva, could be a good candidate for clustering. So, it is valuable to use clustering indexes on triple tables for performance purpose.

Similar to normal unclustered indexes, the clustering index typically contains one entry for each record as well. More recently, Multi-

Dimensional Clustering (MDC) (Bhatt et al., 2003) is developed to support block indexes which is more efficient than normal clustering indexes. Unlike the primary clustering index, an MDC index (also called MDC table) can include multiple clustering dimensions. Moreover, the MDC supports a new physical layout which mimics a multi-dimensional cube by using a physical region for each unique combination of dimension attribute values. A physical block contains only records which have the same unique values for dimension attributes and could be addressed by block indexes, a higher granularity indexing scheme. Block indexes identify multiple records using one entry and are thus quite compact and efficient. Queries using block indexes could benefit from faster block index scan, optimized prefetching of blocks, as well as lower path length overheads while processing the records. Evaluation results from (Brunner et al., 2007) showed that the MDC indexes could dramatically improve query performance (20 times faster and even more) and the set of indexes P*, (P,O), (S,P,O) on the triple table gives the best result for most queries on Minerva using DB2, where P* means an MDC index, other two represent composites unclustered indexes. Additionally, the MDC index could be built on the table defining *typeOf* information, grouping the records by classes.

Currently, the MDC index is a unique feature of DB2. But other popular databases provide advanced index functionalities as well. Oracle supports range partitioning which is a single dimension clustering of the data into partitions. It allows tables, indexes, and index-organized tables to be subdivided into smaller pieces, enabling these objects to be managed and accessed at a finer level of granularity. SQL Server and Teradata Non StopSQL support B+ tree tables. In this scheme, one can define the entire table as a B+ tree itself clustered on one or more columns. These features are helpful for the performance of triple stores.

2.3 A scalable ontology reasoning method by summarization and refinement

Reasoning algorithms that could be scaled to realistic databases are a key enabling technology for the use of ontologies in practice. Unfortunately, OWL-DL ontology reasoning using the tableau algorithm is intractable in the worst case. As we discussed previously, rule inference is adopted for OWL reasoning by some ontology repositories, and sometimes, inferred results are materialized for retrieval. But, rule inference cannot realize complete and sound reasoning of OWL-DL ontologies and maintaining the update of materialized results is also a non-trivial problem. Here, we introduce a novel method that allows for efficient querying of SHIN ontologies with large ABoxes stored in databases. Currently, this method focuses on instance retrieval that queries all individuals of a given class in the ABox. This summarization and refinement based method can also be treated as an optimization that any tableau reasoner can employ to achieve scalable ABox reasoning.

It is well known that all queries over DL ontologies can be reduced to a consistency check (Horrocks & Tessaris, 2002), which is usually checked by a tableau algorithm. As an example, an instance retrieval algorithm can be realized by testing if the addition of an assertion $a : \neg C$ for a given individual a results in an inconsistency. If the resulting ABox is inconsistent, then a is an instance of C. But, it is impractical to apply such a simple approach to every individual. In most real ontologies, we can observe that 1) individuals of the same class tend to have the same assertions with other individuals and 2) most assertions are in fact irrelevant for purposes of consistency check. Motivated by these observations, Fokoue et al. (Fokoue et al., 2006) proposed to group individuals which are instances of the same class into a single individual to generate a summary ABox of a small size. Then, consistency check can be done on the dramatically simplified summary ABox, instead of the original ABox. By testing an individual in the summary ABox, all real individuals mapped to it are effectively tested at the same time.

The SHER reasoner (Dolby et al., 2007) implemented this reasoning approach on top of Minerva's storage component (Zhou et al., 2006) and proved its effectiveness and efficiency on the UOBM benchmark ontology. It is reported that SHER can process ABox queries with up to 7.4 million assertions efficiently, whereas the state of the art reasoners could not scale to this size.

2.4   Other approaches to scaling reasoning over large knowledge bases

The issue of scaling reasoning over large ABoxes has recently received a lot of attention from the Semantic Web and Description Logics communities. Two main approaches have been proposed to tackle it. The first approach consists in building new algorithms, heuristics and systems that exhibit acceptable performance on realistic large and expressive knowledge bases. Proponents of the second approach, on the other hand, advocate reducing the expressiveness of TBoxes describing large ABoxes so that the worst-case data complexity[1] of reasoning becomes tractable. The summarization and refinement technique to scale reasoning over large and expressive ABoxes

---

[1] Data complexity refers to the complexity of reasoning over the ABox only assuming that the TBox is fixed. It measures the complexity of reasoning as a function of the ABox size only.

presented in the previous section is an illustration of research work guided by the first approach. In this section, we present other important recent work on reasoning over large and expressive knowledge bases as well as Description Logics that have been defined with a tractable worst-case data complexity.

Since state-of-the-art in-memory reasoners, such as Pellet (Sirin & Parsia, 2004) and Racer (Haarslev & Moller, 2001), offer good performance on realistic expressive but small knowledge bases, Guo et al. have recently proposed to decompose large and expressive ABoxes into possibly overlapping small components that could be separately fed to state-of-the-art in-memory reasoners. The decomposition is such that the answer to a conjunctive query over the original ABox is the union of the answers of the same conjunctive query over each component of the decomposition. Conservative analyses of the inference rules of the considered DL provide the understanding of interdependency between ABox assertions. Two ABox assertions depend on each other if they might be used together to infer new assertions. The decomposition is such that two assertions that depend on each other always appear together in a component. Results of initial experimental evaluation presented in (Guo & Heflin, 2006) are very promising. Another approach (Hustadt et al., 2004) to efficiently answer conjunctive queries over large and expressive knowledge bases consists in transforming any SHIN(D)[2] knowledge base into a disjunctive Datalog program. The advantages of this approach are twofold. First, it leverages decades of research on optimizations of disjunctive datalog programs (e.g. magic set transformation). Second, it naturally supports DL-safe rules (Motik et al., 2004), which can straightforwardly be translated into datalog rules.

Other researchers have advocated reducing the expressive power in order to obtain tractable reasoning over large ABoxes. Calvanese et al. have introduced a family of inexpressive Description Logics, the DL-Lite family, with data complexity varying from LogSpace to co-NP-hard (Calvanese et al., 2006). DL-Lite$_{core}$, the least expressive language in the DL-Lite family, consists of existential restriction and a restricted form of negation (Calvanese et al., 2005). The language for DL-Lite$_{core}$ concepts and roles is defined as follows:

$$C_l \rightarrow A \mid \exists R; \qquad C_r \rightarrow A \mid \exists R \mid \neg A \mid \neg \exists R$$
$$R \rightarrow P \mid P^-$$

where C_l (resp. C_r) denotes a concept that may appear in the left (resp. right) hand side of a concept inclusion axiom in the TBox. Two simple extensions

---

[2] SHIN(D) is the subset of OWL DL without nominal.

of DL-Lite$_{core}$, DL-Lite$_{F,6}$ and DL-Lite$_{R,6}$, have been defined and shown to be FOL-reducible: i.e. answering a conjunctive query in DL-Lite$_{core}$ or in one of these extensions can be reduced to evaluating a SQL query over the database corresponding to the ABox. The advantages of these FOL-reducible languages are straightforward for applications with very limited expressiveness needs. DL-Lite$_{F,6}$ extends DL-Lite$_{core}$ by allowing intersections on the left hand side of concept inclusion axioms and functional roles; while DL-Lite$_{R,6}$ extends DL-Lite$_{core}$ by allowing inclusion axioms between roles, intersections on the left hand side of concept inclusion axioms, and qualified existential restrictions on the right hand side of concept inclusion axioms. All the other extensions[3] to DL-Lite$_{core}$ are not FOL-reducible, but, for the most part, they remain tractable. Other Description Logics with polynomial data complexity include Horn-SHIQ (Hustadt et al., 2005, Krotzsch et al., 2006), a fragment of SHIQ analogous to the Horn fragment of first-order logic, and description logic programs (Grosof et al., 2003).

2.5   Bridging discrepancies between OWL ontologies and databases

Recently, Semantic Web and ontologies are receiving extensive attention from data management research. One source of this interest is that ontologies can be used as semantic models which are able to represent more semantics of the underlying data. OWL provides numerous constructs to define complex and expressive models. However, it is gradually recognized that there are remarkable discrepancies between description logics (the logical foundation of OWL) and databases. As is well-known, DL is based on an open world assumption (OWA), permitting incomplete information in an ABox, while DB adopts a closed world assumption (CWA) requiring information always understood as complete. The unique name assumption (UNA) is often emphasized in DB but not in DL. OWL Flight (Bruijn et al., 2005), furthermore, clarifies restrictions in DL and constraints in DB, of which the former is to infer and the latter to check. With negation, DBs prefer to "non-monotonic negation," while DLs rely on "monotonic negation." The following simple example gives us an intuitive understanding of such discrepancies. In a relational database, if "each employee must be known to be either male or female" is specified as an integrity constraint, the database system would check whether the gender of a person is given and set to be male or female during database updates. If the gender is not specified as male or female, the update would fail. In an ontology, the same

---

[3] We are not considering extension allowing n-ary predicate with n>2.

requirement would naturally be represented by an axiom that Employee is subsumed by the union of Male and Female. Adding an employee without expressing he/she is an instance of Male or Female to the ontology would not result in any errors, and just imply that the employee could be either Male or Female.

Some research work on extending DLs with integrity constraints are mainly based on autoepistemic extensions of DLs, such as the description logics of minimal knowledge and negation-as-failure (MKNF) (Donini et al., 2002) and some nonmonotonic rule extensions of DLs (Motik et al., 2007). This may be inspired by Reiter's observation that integrity constraints describe the state of the database and have an epistemic nature (Reiter, 1992). Motivated by representing integrity constraints in MKNF, Mei et al. imposed epistemic operators on union and existential restrictions and explained them using integrity constraints in an ontology (Mei et al., 2006). Given the ABox of an SHI ontology is satisfiable with regard to its epistemic TBox, reasoning on such an ontology could be done by a datalog program.

More recently, (Motik et al., 2006) proposes an extension of OWL that attempts to mimic the intuition behind integrity constraints in relational databases. Integrity constraints, introduced in (Mei et al., 2006), are used for conveying semantic aspects of OWL that are not covered by deductive databases, while (Motik et al., 2006) extends standard TBox axioms with constraint TBox axioms, s.t., for TBox reasoning, constraints behave like normal TBox axioms; for ABox reasoning, however, they are interpreted in the spirit of relational databases. Acting as checks, constraints are thrown away, if satisfied, without losing relevant consequences. Algorithms for checking constraint satisfaction are also discussed in (Motik et al., 2006), and the complexity of constraint checking is primarily determined by the complexity of the standard TBox. As a result, answering queries under constraints may be computationally easier due to a smaller input of the standard TBox concerning. Currently, (Motik et al., 2006) plans to implement such an approach in the OWL reasoner KAON2 and tests its usefulness on practical problems.

Technically, (Motik et al., 2006) defines constraints in the same way as subsumptions, having the form of $C \sqsubseteq D$ where C and D are DL concepts. Keeping the semantics of DLs unchanged, constraints rely on Herbrand models for checking satisfiability. Query answering is another reasoning service, provided the constraints are satisfied, and again uses the standard semantics of DLs after throwing those constraints away. That is, authors define TBox axioms, of which some are for inferring (namely, standard TBox axioms) and some for checking (namely, constraint TBox axioms). The extended DL system will provide support for DL reasoning as usual, in addition to checking constraint satisfiability using the well-known methods of logic programming.

By definition, an extended DL knowledge base is a triple $K=(S, C, A)$ such that S is a finite set of standard TBox axioms, C is a finite set of constraint TBox axioms, and A is a finite set of ABox assertions, $D(a)$, $\neg D(a)$, $R(a,b)$, $a \approx b$, $a \neq b$, for D an atomic concept, R a role, and a, b individuals. Checking C in the minimal models of $A \cup S$, the algorithm is sketched as follows (Motik et al., 2006).

1. The standard TBox S is translated into a first-order formula $\pi(S)$ according to the standard DL semantics, and the results are further translated into a (possibly disjunctive) logic program $LP(S) = LP(\pi(S))$ which can be exponentially larger than S. For each rule in $LP(S)$ in which a variable x occurs in the head but not in the body, the atom $HU(x)$ is added to the rule body. Additionally, for each individual a occurring in $A \cup S$, an assertion $HU(a)$ is introduced.
2. The constraint TBox C is translated into a first-order formula $\pi(C)$, and $CN(C) = CN(\pi(C))$ is constructed as a stratified datalog program. For each formula φ, a unique predicate E_φ is associated, also $\mu(\varphi)$ and $sub(\varphi)$ are defined, where $\mu(\varphi)$ is a translation rule for φ and $sub(\varphi)$ is the set of sub-formulae of φ, s.t. the following logic program is computed: $CN(\varphi) = \mu(\varphi) \cup \bigcup_{\phi \in sub(\varphi)} CN(\phi)$.

As a consequence, $K=(S, C, A)$ satisfies the constraint TBox C if and only if $A \cup LP(S) \cup CN(C) \models_c E_C$, where $\models_c$ denotes the well-known entailment in stratified (possibly disjunctive) logic programs, and $E_C = E_{\pi(C)}$.

Intuitively, $CN(C)$ simply evaluates C and ensures that E_C holds in a model if and only if C is true in the model. Thus, E_C is derived if and only if C is satisfied in all minimal models. Finally, suppose $K=(S, C, A)$ be an extended DL knowledge base that satisfies C. For any union of conjunctive queries $\gamma(v)$ over $K=(S, C, A)$ and any tuple of constants u, it holds that $A \cup S \cup C \models \gamma(u)$ if and only if $A \cup S \models \gamma(u)$.

Not surprising, in query answering, constraints are thrown away, if they are satisfied. All other reasoning problems look like before, and the existing DL algorithms can be applied to solve them.

3. REASONING WITH WSML-DL

In this section, we take the approach of looking at another practical language for ontology reasoning. We focus on reasoning with the Description Logic-based Ontology language WSML-DL. We use WSML-

DL as a more intuitive surface syntax for an expressive Description Logic (DL) in the WSML family of knowledge representation languages. Its syntax is inspired by First-order Logic modelling style. The WSML family of ontology languages is strongly related to the work on the Web Service Modeling Ontology WSMO and thus potentially very relevant in Semantic Web Services environments.

WSML-DL is less expressive than OWL DL, given that WSML-DL does not support nominals. This reduces the complexity of WSML-DL, which is important for reasoning. In fact, until recently many state-of-the-art DL reasoners did not support reasoning with nominals, since no good optimization techniques were known.

To enable the use of existing DL reasoning engines for WSML, we transform WSML-DL to OWL DL. This is because OWL DL is the appropriate syntax for DL reasoners as e.g. Pellet or KAON2. Then we integrate the reasoners into a flexible WSML reasoner framework.

In the following, we first point out the particularities of DL reasoning. Next we describe the WSML-DL syntax and its correspondence to DLs. We show the translation from WSML-DL to OWL DL abstract syntax and explain the architecture and implementation of the WSML2Reasoner framework.

3.1 Reasoning with description logics

Description Logics can be seen as particularly restricted subset of Predicate Logic and constitute a family of logic-based knowledge representation formalisms. They have become a cornerstone of the Semantic Web for its use in the design of ontologies.

DL knowledge bases are separated into two components: TBoxes, containing the terminological knowledge of a knowledge base (e.g. concept definitions), and ABoxes, containing the assertional knowledge (knowledge about the individuals of a domain).

In DLs, there are different basic reasoning tasks for reasoning with TBoxes or ABoxes. As described in Baader et al. (2003), the main inference procedures with TBoxes are concept subsumption and concept satisfiability. With ABoxes, the main reasoning tasks are ABox consistency and instance checking.

The OWL community focuses on entailment and query answering as the key inference services. Entailment can be reduced to satisfiability, while query answering amounts to compute the result of a query for instances with specific properties over a database, or an ABox respectively.

http://tools.deri.org/wsml2reasoner/DIPFactSheet.html -
ReasWSMLDLDescriptions of the main standard DL reasoning tasks, as

well as of some main non-standard inference tasks can be found in Baader et al. (2003).

3.2   WSML-DL

The Web Service Modeling Language WSML (de Bruijn et al., 2005) is a family of formal Web languages based on the conceptual model of WSMO (Roman et al., 2004). Conforming to different influences, as e.g. Description Logics (Baader et al., 2003), Logic Programming (Lloyd, 1987) and First-order Logic (Fitting, 1996), there exist five variants of WSML: WSML-Core, WSML-DL, WSML-Flight, WSML-Rule and WSML-Full.

The WSML-DL variant captures the expressive Description Logic SHIQ(D). The following sections will introduce the WSML-DL syntax and its correspondence to Description Logics.

3.2.1   WSML-DL syntax

WSML makes a clear distinction between the modelling of conceptual elements (Ontologies, Web Services, Goals and Mediators) and the specification of logical definitions. Therefore the WSML syntax is split in two parts: the conceptual syntax and the logical expression syntax. The following sections will provide an overview of the WSML-DL conceptual and the logical expression syntax. A more detailed description can be found in de Bruijn et al. (2005).

3.2.1.1   WSML-DL conceptual syntax

A WSML ontology specification may contain concepts, relations, instances, relation instances and axioms. Concepts form the basic terminology of the domain of discourse and may have instances and associated attributes. A concept can be defined as subconcept of another concept, and in this case, a concept inherits all attribute definitions of its superconcept.

A concept may have an arbitrary number of instances associated to it. The instance definition can be followed by the attribute values associated with the instance. Instead of being explicitly defined in the ontology, instances can exist outside the ontology in an external database.

There are two sorts of attribute definitions that a concept may contain: inferring definitions with the keyword *impliesType* and constraining definitions with the keyword *ofType*. The constraining definitions may only be used for datatype ranges. Inferring attribute definitions are similar to range restrictions on properties in RDFS (Brickley and Guha, 2004) and OWL (Bechhofer et al., 2004).

In WSML-DL only binary relations are allowed. They correspond to the definition of attributes. The usage of inferring and constraining definitions in relations corresponds to their usage in attribute definitions. A relation can be defined as a subrelation of another relation.

A relation may contain relation instances with parameter values associated to it.

Axioms can be used to refine the definitions already given in the conceptual syntax, e.g. the subconcept and attribute definitions of concepts. By defining respective axioms one can define cardinality restrictions and global transitivity, symmetricity and inversity of attributes, just like in DLs or OWL. The logical expression syntax is explained in the following section.

3.2.1.2   WSML-DL logical expression syntax

The form of WSML-DL logical expressions and their expressiveness is based on the Description Logic SHIQ(D). The WSML-DL logical expression syntax has constants, variables, predicates and logical connectives, which all are based on First-order Logic modelling style.

An atom in WSML-DL is a predicate symbol with one or two terms as arguments. WSML has a special kind of atoms, called molecules. There are two types of molecules that are used to capture information about concepts, instances, attributes and attribute values: "isa molecules," that are used to express concept membership or subconcept definitions, and "object molecules," that are used to define attribute and attribute value expressions.

These molecules build the set of atomic formulae in WSML-DL. Using First-order connectives, one can combine the atomic formulae to descriptions and formulae. How exactly the molecules can be combined to build descriptions and formulae can be seen in detail in de Bruijn et al. (2005).

3.2.2   WSML-DL vs. SHIQ(D)

Table 4-1 illustrates the relationship between the WSML-DL semantics, the Description Logics syntax and the OWL DL syntax. The table follows de Bruijn et al (2005), Volz (2004) and Borgida (1996).

In the table, "id" can be any identifier, "dt" is a datatype identifier, "X" can be either a variable or an identifier and "Y" is a variable.

3.3   Translation of WSML-DL to OWL DL

The following sections show the translation from WSML-DL to OWL DL abstract syntax (Steinmetz, 2006). The mapping is based on a mapping from WSML-Core to OWL DL, which can be found in de Bruijn et al. (2005), and can be applied to WSML ontologies and logical expressions.

Table 4-1. WSML-DL logical expressions — DL syntax

WSML-DL	DL Syntax	OWL DL
τ(lexpr **impliedBy** rexpr)	$rexpr \subseteq lexpr$	subClassOf
τ(lexpr **or** rexpr)	$lexpr \cup rexpr$	unionOf
τ(lexpr **and** rexpr)	$lexpr \cap rexpr$	intersectionOf
τ(**neg** expr)	$\neg\ expr$	complementOf
τ(**forall** Y expr)	$\forall R.\ expr$	allValuesFrom
τ(**exists** Y expr)	$\exists R.\ expr$	someValuesFrom
τ(X **memberOf** id)	$X : id$	Type
τ(id1 **subConceptOf** id2)	$id1 \subseteq id2$	subClassOf
τ(X1[id **hasValue** X2])	$< X1, X2 > : id$	Property
τ(id1[id2 **impliesType** id3])	$id1 \subseteq \forall id2.id3$	subPropertyOf
τ(id1[id2 **ofType** dt])	$id1 \subseteq \forall id2.dt$	subPropertyOf
τ(p(X_1,…,X_n))	$< X_1,…X_n > : p$	Type
τ(X1 :=: X2)	$X1 \equiv X2$	equivalentClass

3.3.1   Transformation steps

The transformation of a WSML-DL ontology to an OWL DL ontology is done in a line of single transformation steps that are executed subsequently.

- Relations, subrelations and relation instances are replaced by attributes and axioms, according to the preprocessing steps described in Steinmetz (2006).
- All conceptual elements are converted into appropriate axioms specified by logical expressions. The resulting set of logical expressions is semantically equivalent to the original WSML ontology.
- Equivalences and right implications in logical expressions are replaced by left implications.
- Conjunctions on the left side and disjunctions on the right side of inverse implications are replaced by left implications.
- Complex molecules inside of logical expressions are replaced by conjunctions of simple ones.

As last step, the resulting axioms and logical expressions are transformed one by one into OWL descriptions according to the mapping presented in the following section.

3.3.2   Mapping tables

Tables 4-2 and 4-3 contain the mapping between the WSML-DL syntax and the OWL DL abstract syntax. The mapping is described through the mapping function τ. In Table 4-3 we will introduce the functions α and ε, which are needed for the correct translation of WSML-DL descriptions.

Boldfaced words in the tables refer to keywords in the WSML language. "X" and "Y" are meta-variables and are replaced with actual identifiers and variables during the translation, while "DES" stands for WSML-DL descriptions. IRIs[4] are abbreviated by qualified names. The prefix 'wsml' stands for 'http://wsmo. org/wsml/wsml-syntax#' and 'owl' stands for 'http://www.w3.org/2002/07/owl#.'

Table 4-3 shows the mapping of WSML-DL descriptions that are used inside of axioms, as can be seen in Table 4-2. The descriptions are translated to concept expressions and to axioms. Concept expressions are again used within other expressions, while the axioms are added as such to the OWL ontology. The mapping τ is translated into a tuple of concept expressions and axioms as follows: τ (DES) = (ε (DES), α (DES)).

The table also indicates a mapping for Qualified Cardinality Restrictions (QCRs). In WSML-DL the QCRs are represented by a combination of WSML-DL descriptions. The mapping to OWL DL is done according a workaround with OWL subproperties, described in Rector (2003).

3.3.3 Restrictions to the transformation

The transformation is not complete, i.e. WSML-DL supports features that cannot be expressed in OWL DL and that can thus not be translated. Concretely, OWL DL does not support datatype predicates. They are lost during the transformation.

3.3.4 Translation example

Table 4-4 shows two simple translation examples of both WSML-DL conceptual syntax and logical expression syntax. More examples can be found in Steinmetz (2006).

3.3.5 Architecture and implementation

In the following we will discuss the architecture and the implementation of a reasoner prototype that allows us to perform reasoning with WSML-DL ontologies using state-of-the-art reasoning engines by means of a wrapper component.

---

[4] http://www.ietf.org/rfc/rfc3987.txt

Table 4-2. Mapping WSML-DL ontologies and axioms to OWL DL

WSML-DL	OWL-DL	Remarks
Mapping for ontologies		

τ(**ontology** id
    header$_1$
    ...
    header$_n$
    ontology_element$_1$
    ...
    ontology_element$_n$
)
	Ontology(id
	    τ(header$_1$)
	    ...
	    τ(header$_n$)
	    τ(ontology_element$_1$)
	    ...
	    τ(ontology_element$_n$)
	)
		A header can contain
		nonFunctionalProperties,
		usesMediator and
		importsOntology statements. An
		ontology_element can be a
		concept, a *relation*, an *instance*,
		a *relation instance* or an *axiom*.

τ(**nonFunctionalProperties**
    id$_1$ **hasValue** value$_1$
    ...
    id$_n$ **hasValue** value$_n$
endNonFunctionalProperties)
	Annotation(id$_1$ τ(value$_1$))
	    ...
	Annotation(id$_n$ τ(value$_n$))
		For non functional properties on
		the ontology level "Annotation"
		instead of "annotation" has to
		be written.

τ(**importsOntology** id)	Annotation(owl#import id)	"id" stands for the identifier of a WSML file.
τ(**usesMediator** id)	Annotation(wsml#usesMediator id)	As OWL doesn't have the concept of a mediator, a wsml#usesMediator annotation is used.
τ(datatype_id(x$_1$,...,x$_n$))	datatype_id(x$_1$,...,x$_n$)^^ τ$_{datatypes}$(datatype_id)	τ$_{datatypes}$ maps WSML datatypes to XML Schema datatypes, according to de Bruijn et al. (2005).
τ(id)	id	In WSML an IRI is enclosed by _" and ", which are omitted in OWL abstract syntax.
Mapping for axioms		
τ(**axiom** id log_expr **nfp**)	τ(log_expr)	A log_expr can be a logical expression like the following. The axiom does not keep its non functional properties.

τ(id[att_id **impliesType**
    range_id])
	Class(id
	    restriction (att_id
	    allValuesFrom range_id))
	ObjectProperty (att_id)	

τ(id[att_id **ofType** range_id])	Class(id
	    restriction (att_id
	    allValuesFrom range_id))
	DatatypeProperty (att_id)	

τ(id1 **subConceptOf** id2)	Class(id1 partial id2)	
τ(id[att_id **hasValue** value])	Individual (id value (att_id τ(value)))	

Continued

WSML-DL	OWL-DL	Remarks
τ(id1 **memberOf** id2)	Individual(id1 type(id2))	
τ(?x[att_id2 **hasValue** ?y] **impliedBy** ?x[att_id **hasValue** ?y])	SubProperty(att_id att_id2)	A left implication with attribute values as left-hand and right-hand sides is mapped to an OWL subProperty.
τ(?x[att_id **hasValue** ?y] **impliedBy** ?x[att_id **hasValue** ?z] and ?y[att_id **hasValue** ?z])	ObjectProperty(att_id Transitive)	Transitive Property
τ(?x[att_id **hasValue** ?y] **impliedBy** ?y[att_id **hasValue** ?x])	ObjectProperty(att_id Symmetric)	Symmetric Property
τ(?x[att_id **hasValue** ?y] **impliedBy** ?y[att_id2 **hasValue** ?x])	ObjectProperty(att_id inverseOf(att_id2))	Inverse Property
τ(?x **memberOf** concept_id2 **impliedBy** ?x **memberOf** concept_id)	Class(concept_id partial concept_id2)	Equivalence of concepts can be expressed as follows, with A and B being membership molecules: "A equivalent B" :=: "A impliedBy B and B impliedBy A".
τ(?x **memberOf** concept_id **impliedBy** ?x[att_id **hasValue** ?y])	ObjectProperty(att_id domain(concept_id))	
τ(?y **memberOf** concept_id **impliedBy** ?x[att_id **hasValue** ?y])	ObjectProperty(att_id range(concept_id))	
τ(DES1 **impliedBy** DES2)	α(DES1) α(DES2) subClassOf(ε(DES2) ε(DES1))	"A impliedBy B" can be written as "subClassOf(B,A)".
τ()		If τ is applied for a non-occurring production no translation has to be made

Table 4-3. Mapping WSML-DL descriptions to OWL DL

WSML-DL	OWL-DL — concept expression ε	OWL-DL — axiom α	Remarks
Mapping for descriptions (DES)			
τ(?x **memberOf** id)	id	Class(id)	Membership molecule.
τ(?x[att_id **hasValue** ?y])	restriction(att_id allValuesFrom(owl:Thing))	ObjectProperty(att_id)	Attribute value molecule with ?y being an unbound variable within the logical expression.

continued

WSML-DL	OWL-DL — concept expression ε	OWL-DL — axiom α	Remarks
τ(?x[att_id **hasValue** ?y] **and** ?y **memberOf** id)	restriction (att_id someValuesFrom(id))	Class(id) ObjectProperty(att_id)	Attribute value molecule with ?y being a bound variable.
τ(DES$_1$ **and** … **and** DES$_n$)	intersectionOf(ε(DES$_1$),…,ε(DES$_n$))	α(DES$_1$) … α(DES$_n$)	Conjunction.
τ(DES$_1$ **or** … **or** DES$_n$)	unionOf(ε(DES$_1$),…,ε(DES$_n$))	α(DES$_1$) … α(DES$_n$)	Disjunction.
τ(**neg** DES)	complementOf(ε(DES))	α(DES)	Negation.
τ(**exists** ?x (?y[att_id **hasValue** ?x] **and** DES))	restriction(att_id someValuesFrom(ε(DES)))	α(DES) ObjectProperty(att_id)	Existential quantification.
τ(**exists** ?x (?x[att_id **hasValue** ?y] **and** DES))	restriction(inverseOf(att_id) someValuesFrom(ε(DES)))	α(DES) ObjectProperty(att_id)	Existential quantification with inverse role.
τ(**forall** ?x (DES **impliedBy** ?y[att_id **hasValue** ?x]))	restriction(att_id allValuesFrom(ε(DES)))	α(DES) ObjectProperty(att_id)	Universal quantification.
τ(**forall** ?x (DES **impliedBy** ?x[att_id **hasValue** ?y]))	restriction(inverseOf(att_id) allValuesFrom(ε(DES)))	α(DES) ObjectProperty(att_id)	Universal quantification with inverse role.
τ(**exists** ?y1,…,?yn (?x [att_id **hasValue** ?y1] **and** … **and** ?x[att_id **hasValue** ?yn] **and** DES **and neg**(?y1 :=: ?y2) **and** … **and neg**(?yn−1 :=: ?yn)))	restriction(att_id' minCardinality(n))	α(DES) ObjectProperty(att_id) ObjectProperty(att_id' range(ε(DES))) SubPropertyOf(att_id' att_id)	(Qualified) minCardinality restriction.
τ(**forall** ?y1,…,?yn+1 (?y1 :=: ?y2 **or** … **or** ?yn :=: ?yn+1 **impliedBy** ?x[att_id **hasValue** ?y1] **and** … **and** ?x[att_id **hasValue** ?yn+1] **and** DES)	restriction(att_id' maxCardinality(n))	α(DES) ObjectProperty(att_id) ObjectProperty(att_id' range(ε(DES))) SubPropertyOf(att_id' att_id)	(Qualified) maxCardinality restriction.

Table 4-4. Translation Example

WSML-DL	OWL DL

concept Human
   hasChild **impliesType** Human
   hasBirthday **ofType** date
	ObjectProperty(hasChild
	   domain(Human) range(Human))
	DatatypeProperty(hasBirthday
	   domain(Human) range(xsd:date))
	Class(Human partial)

axiom definedBy
  ?x **memberOf** Man **implies neg**(?x
  memberOf Woman).
	Class(Man partial)
	Class(Woman partial)
	SubClassOf(Man complementOf(Woman))

The WSML2Reasoner framework[5] is a flexible and highly modular architecture for easy integration of external reasoning components. It has been implemented in Java and is based on the WSMO4J[6] project, which provides an API for the programmatic access to WSML documents. Instead of implementing new reasoners, existing reasoner implementations can be used for WSML through a wrapper that translates WSML expressions into the appropriate syntax for the reasoner.

As already said above, the appropriate syntax for many DL Reasoners is OWL DL. We have implemented the transformation from WSML-DL to OWL DL using the Wonderweb OWL API (Bechhofer et al., 2003). The OWL API allows a programmatic access to OWL ontologies. It offers a high-level abstraction from the Description Logics underlying OWL DL, what increases the usage of DL knowledge bases in the Semantic Web area.

The WSML2Reasoner framework infrastructure offers an interface that represents a façade to various DL reasoning engines. The façade provides a set of usual DL reasoning task methods and mediates between the OWL DL ontologies produced by the transformation and the reasoner-specific internal representations. For each new DL reasoning engine that is integrated into the framework, a specific adapter façade has to be implemented.

The framework currently comes with façades for two OWL DL reasoners: Pellet[7] and KAON2[8]:

- **Pellet** — Pellet is an open-source Java based OWL DL reasoner. It can be used directly in conjunction with the OWL API.
- **KAON2** — KAON2 is an infrastructure to manage, amongst others, OWL DL ontologies. It provides a hybrid reasoner that allows datalog-style rules to interact with structural Description Logics knowledge bases.

---

[5] http://tools.deri.org/wsml2reasoner/
[6] http://wsmo4j.sourceforge.net/
[7] http://pellet.owldl.com/
[8] http://kaon2.semanticweb.org/

4.   SEMANTIC BUSINESS PROCESS REPOSITORY

In the final section of this chapter, we take a look at a practical use of ontological reasoning with large instance data. In particular, we describe the requirements on an ontology repository for Semantic Business Process Management (SBPM) and discuss how the various approaches described in the previous sections can be combined in order to meet those requirements.

4.1   Requirements analysis

In general, a repository is a shared database of information about engineered artifacts produced or used by an enterprise (Bernstein et al. 1994). In SBPM, these artifacts are semantic business process models or process models for short.

Process models are often modeled by business users with help of a process modeling tool. To support process modeling, the SBPR has to provide standard functionality of a database management system, such as storage of new process models, update, retrieval or deletion of existing process models, transaction support for manipulation of process models and query capability. The query capability enables business users or client applications to search process models in the SBPR based on the criteria specified. We classify the queries into two categories. The first category of queries can be answered based on the artifacts explicitly stored in the SBPR. This kind of queries is of the same kind as the queries that traditional database systems can process. The second category of queries are "semantic queries", which can only be processed when the ontological knowledge of the process models is taken into account.

The modeling of process models can be a time-consuming task. It may take days or even months for business users to finish modeling a given business process. Therefore, treating the entire modeling activity related to a process model as a single transaction is impractical. The SBPR has to provide check-in and check-out operations, that support long running interactions, enable disconnected mode of interaction with the SBPR, and are executed as separate short transactions. In this case the modeling tool could work in a disconnected mode regarding the SBPR. The process model in the SBPR can be locked when the modeling tool obtains it (check-out), so that no other users can modify the process model in the SBPR in the meantime. After the modeling work has been done the process model is updated in the SBPR and any locks that have been held for the process model are released (check-in). Note that the locking mechanism refers only to the locking of the process models in the SBPR. The process ontologies, that are stored separately in an ontology store and have been referenced by the process models, are not locked simultaneously. Furthermore, in a distributed modeling environment several business users may work on the same process model simultaneously. A fine-grained locking of elements in a process model enables different business users to lock only the part of the process model they are working on, thus avoiding producing inconsistent process models.

Process models may undergo a series of modifications undertaken by business users. The series of modification is called change history of the process model. The SBPR represents the change history as versions. A version is a snapshot of a process model at a certain point in its change history (Bernstein et al. 1994). In certain industry sectors corporations must record all the change histories of their process models for government auditing or for some legal requirements. From the modeling perspective it is meaningful to keep process models in different versions, so that business users can simply go back to an old version and develop the process model from the old version further. Due to these reasons the SBPR has to provide also versioning functionality, so that the change history of process models can be documented.

4.2   Comparison of storage mechanisms

As storing and querying process models stored are the main requirements for the SBPR, we evaluate in this section several options for storage mechanism and their query capabilities.

A process model is an instance of a process ontology. Process ontologies which are developed in the SUPER project (SUPER, Hepp et al. 2007) include the Business Process Modeling Ontology (BPMO); the semantic Business Process Modeling Notation ontology (sBPMN), which is an ontological version of Business Process Modeling Notation (BPMN); the semantic Event Process Chain ontology (sEPC), which is an ontological version of Event Process Chain (EPC) (Keller 1992); the semantic Business Process Execution Language ontology (sBPEL), which is a ontological version of Business Process Execution Language (BPEL) (Andrews 2003). These ontologies are described using the ontology formalism Web Service Modeling Language (WSML) (de Bruijn et al. 2005). As said, there are five variants of WSML available, namely WSML-Core, WSML-DL, WSML-Flight, WSML-Rule, and WSML-Full, differing in logical expressiveness and underlying language paradigm. The ontologies considered in this chapter are formalized using WSML-Flight, which is a compromise between the allowed expressiveness and the reasoning capability of the ontology language. In the following, we assume thus that a process model is an instance of a process ontology, which is specified in WSML-Flight.

For each option we take into account the expressiveness of the query language, the scalability of the query processing and the effort for the integration of the query processing with the underlying data storage. Scalability is a rather fuzzy term. In general, one would understand that in the context of reasoning. Reasoning is used to infer conclusions that are not explicitly stated but are required by or consistent with a known set of data (cf. (Passin, 2004)). A system or a framework is scalable if enlarging the data-set, which is in our context the set of actual process models that described using ontologies, leads to a performance loss that is tolerable. More formal, one could say that reasoning is scalable if augmenting the input size of the problem, which in this case refers to the ontologies plus the instance data of the ontologies, leads at most to a polynomial increase of the time in which reasoning can be performed. With regards to the reasoning capability, we consider two options, namely the storage mechanism with or without reasoning capability.

4.2.1　Option 1: Without reasoning capability

For storage mechanisms without reasoning capability we considered Relational Database Management System (RDBMS) and RDF store, which have been widely adopted at the time of writing.

Queries against RDBMS are normally formalized using the Structured Query Language (SQL). SQL is quite powerful and bases on both the relational algebra and the tuple relational calculus (Siberschatz 2006). However, it has still some limitations. For example, take a simple query such as "Find all supervisors of the employee John Smith," where *supervisor* is a binary relation indicating which employees are supervisors of other employees. This query requires computation of transitive closures on the personnel hierarchies. It is known that transitive closure can not be expressed using relational algebra (Libkin 2001, Abiteboul 1995). In SQL one can express transitive closures using *WITH RECURSIVE* to create recursive views, which could be very expensive. Furthermore the "supervisor" relationship must be stored explicitly in the database system. Because SQL can express queries that aim at the explicitly stored data, it has no capability to take into account of the implicit data, which can be derived from the instances of the ontologies based on the axioms specified there. This is not sufficient for the requirements on query processing of the SBPR.

De Bruijn (2006) defined a RDF representation of WSML, which allows storing WSML data in a RDF store. RDF (RDF 2004) store is a framework providing support for the RDF Schema (RDFS 2004) inference and querying, which uses a relational database system as the underlying storage for the RDF data. In this section we only consider RDF stores without third-party inference engine or reasoner integrated. The inference here refers to the RDFS entailments supported by the RDFS semantics. There are already several reference implementations of RDF stores like Sesame[9]. The inference in such RDF stores is normally based on the RDF schema, which provides only restricted number of constructs to describe the relationships between the resources, as well as these between the properties, such as rdfs:subClassOf, rdfs:subPropertyOf. The query processing of RDF stores is based on special query languages for RDF data like Simple Protocol and RDF Query Language (SPARQL) or Sesame RDF Query Language (SeRQL). Using these query languages, one cannot express transitivity or transitive closure. Furthermore, these query languages take only into account explicitly stored data. The implicit data can be derived by the inference capability. However, the inference capability is very limited in RDF stores.

4.2.2   Option 2: With reasoning capability

Quite naturally, ontology stores (cf. Section 2.1) are a candidate technology for a Semantic Business Process repository. Jena 2, for example, is a RDF store, which supports not only native entailment of RDFS semantics but also third-party inference engines or reasoners. The primary use of plug-in such inference engine or reasoner is to support the use of languages such as RDFS and OWL which allow additional facts to be inferred from instance data and class descriptions, while the default OWL reasoner in Jena can only perform reasoning on a subset of OWL semantics. To provide complete support of OWL DL reasoning, one can use external OWL DL reasoners such as Pellet[10], Racer[11] or FaCT[12]. Jena can handle OWL DL, but there is only a partial bi-directional mapping defined between WSML-Core and OWL DL, which is not sufficient to fulfill the requirements of SBPR.

Besides Jena, OWLIM (OWLIM, 2006) is a candidate implementation. OWLIM enables RDF storage with reasoning capability. OWLIM is a high performance Storage and Inference Layer (SAIL) for the Sesame repository. It provides OWL Description Logic Programs (DLP) (Grosof, 2003) reasoning, based on forward-chaining of entailment rules (Kiryakov, 2005). As argued in (Kiryakov 2005), OWLIM can query the Knowledge Base (KB) of 10 million statements with an upload and storage speed of about 3000 statements per second. In order to achieve this, OWLIM materializing the KB. This means that for every update to the KB, the inference closure of

---

[9] http://www.openrdf.org/index.jsp

[10] http://pellet.owldl.com/

[11] http://www.racer-systems.com/

[12] http://www.cs.man.ac.uk/~horrocks/FaCT/

the program is computed. In an SBPM scenario this means that all conclusions that can be recursively obtained by applying process ontology rules, given certain instance data (process models), are computed. This approach has the advantage that querying or other reasoning tasks are performed fast because the reasoning was done beforehand. Moreover, one could store the inference closure in the persistent storage, effectively using optimization methods for storage. The approach taken in OWLIM shows that taking into account ontologies does not need to lead to a significant performance loss per se. Nonetheless, the approach has some disadvantages.

First, OWLIM provides support for a fraction of OWL only. The supported fragment is close to OWL DLP and OWL-Horst (ter Horst 2005), which can be mapped to WSML and vice versa. However, the expressiveness of OWL DLP corresponds to WSML-Core. OWL-Horst is more powerful than WSML-Core, but it is still not as powerful as WSML-Flight.

Second, as we already discussed, the reasoning in OWLIM takes the forward-chaining approach. Forward-chaining means that the reasoner starts from the facts that are already known and infers new knowledge in an inductive fashion. The result of forward-chaining can be stored for reuse. This enables efficient query answering, because all facts needed for the query processing are already available in the data storage. But in the meanwhile this introduces also the expensive time and space consuming operations of data manipulation such as update or delete. Newly added or updated data leads to computing the inference closure in the SBPR again. Removal of process models is even more problematic, as facts from the inference closure that were introduced by this removed process models have also to be removed from the SBPR, which could lead to additional removal operations. In the worst case, this could require the recalculation of a large part of the inference closure. In practice, however, the removal of process models from the SBPR seems to be an action that is less common. The OWLIM approach also relies heavily on the fact that the semantics of OWL DLP and extensions towards OWL Lite are monotonic. The monotonic semantics allows for incremental additions to the process library, i.e., one can extend the current inference closure with new inferences. In the presence of non-monotonism, e.g., negation as failure as for example in WSML-Flight (de Bruijn 2006), such an incremental approach no longer works, as adding knowledge may prohibit previously made deductions.

These limitations excluded the direct use of OWLIM as a repository for process models in the described scenario.

IRIS (Integrated Rule Inference System)[13] is an inference engine, which together with the WSML2Reasoner framework[14], supports query answering

---

[13] http://sourceforge.net/projects/iris-reasoner/

for WSML-Core and WSML-Flight. In essence, it is a datalog engine extended with stratified negation[15]. The system implements different deductive database algorithms and evaluation techniques. IRIS allows different data types to be used in semantic descriptions according the XML Schema specification and offers a number of built-in predicates. Functionality for constructing complex data types using primitive ones is also provided. The translation from a WSML ontology description to datalog is conducted using the WSML2Reasoner component. This framework combines various validation, normalization and transformation functionalities which are essential to the translation of WSML ontology descriptions to set of predicates and rules. Further on, rules are translated to expressions of relational algebra and computed using the set of operations of relational algebra (i.e., union, set difference, selection, Cartesian product, projection etc.). The motivation for this translation lies in the fact that the relational model is the underlying mathematical model of data for datalog and there are a number of database optimization techniques applicable for the relational model. Finally optimized relational expressions serve as an input for computing the meaning of recursive datalog programs.

The core of the IRIS architecture, as shown in Figure 4-4, is defined as a layered approach consisting of three components:

- Knowledge Base API,
- Invocation API, and
- Storage API.

The knowledge base API is a top API layer encapsulating central abstractions of the underlying system (e.g., rule, query, atom, tuple, fact, program, knowledge base, context etc.). The purpose of this layer is to define the basic concepts of the data model used in IRIS as well as to define the functionality for the knowledge base and program manipulation.

The invocation API characterizes a particular evaluation strategy (e.g., bottom-up, top-down or a blend of these two strategies) and evaluation methods for a given strategy which are used with respect to a particular logic program. IRIS implements the following evaluation methods[16]:

- Naive evaluation,
- Semi-naive evaluation, and
- Query-subquery (QSQ) evaluation.

---

[14] WSML2Reasoner framework: http://tools.deri.org/wsml2reasoner/

[15] IRIS is continuously being developed and the support for non-stratified negation and unsafe rules is envisioned in coming releases.

[16] More evaluation techniques are under development.

The storage layer defines the basic API for accessing data and relation indexing. A central abstraction in this layer is a relation which contains a set of tuples and serves as an argument in each operation of relation algebra. The implementation of IRIS relation is based on Collection and SortedSet Java interfaces where red-black binary search trees are utilized for indexing.

Current inference systems exploit reasoner methods developed rather for small knowledge bases. Such systems either process data in the main memory or use a Relational Database Management System (RDBMS) to efficiently access and do relational operations on disk persistent relations. Main memory reasoners cannot handle datasets larger than their memory. On the other side, systems based on RDBMSs may feature great performance improvement comparing with main memory systems, but efficient database techniques (e.g., cost-based query planning, caching, buffering) they utilize are suited only for EDB relations and not fully deployable on derived relations.

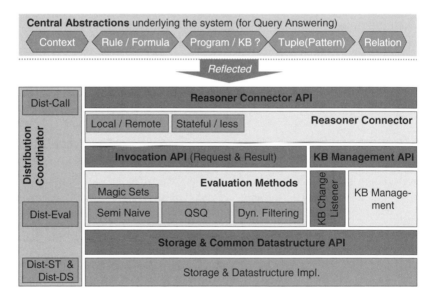

Figure 4-4. IRIS architecture

IRIS is designed to meet the requirements of large-scale reasoning. Apart from the state-of-the-art deductive methods, the system utilizes database techniques and extends them for implicit knowledge in order to effectively process large datasets. We are building an integrated query optimizer. The estimation of the size and evaluation cost of the intentional predicates will be based on the adaptive sampling method (Liption 1990, Ruckhaus 2006), while the extensional data will be estimated using a graph-based synopses of data sets similarly as in Spiegel (2006). Further on, for large scale reasoning (i.e., during the derivation of large relations which exceeds main memory), run time memory overflow may occur. Therefore in IRIS we are developing novel techniques for a selective pushing of currently processed tuples to disk. Such techniques aim at temporarily lessening the burden of main memory, and hence to make the entire system capable of handling large relations.

Based on this comparison, a RDBMS integrated with the IRIS inference engine was regarded as the most suitable solution to fulfill the requirements of the SBPR in our use case.

4.3   Proposed solution

In this section, we present the overall architecture of the SBPR based on the integration of RDBMS technology and the IRIS inference engine. We utilize a layered architecture consisting of the three layers (1) Semantic Business Process Repository API, (2) Service Layer, and (3) Persistence Layer, as illustrated in Figure 4-5.

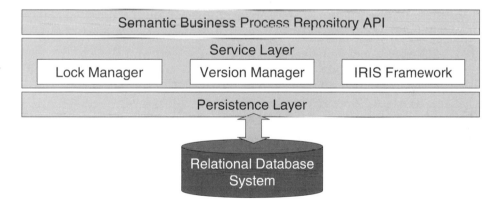

Figure 4-5. SBPR architecture

Semantic Business Process Repository API

The Semantic Business Process Repository API provides the programmatic access to the SBPR. It includes the API designed after the CRUD pattern, which represents the four basic functions of persistent storage, namely create, retrieve, update and delete. Besides the CRUD API, the SBPR API also provides check-in and check-out functions for long-running process modeling. The query API rounds off the SBPR API by providing programmatic access to the IRIS Framework for query answering.

Service Layer

The Service Layer implements the SBPR API and processing logic of the SBPR. The Service Layer contains three modules: Lock Manger, Version Manager, and the IRIS Framework. The Lock Manager takes charge of requests on locking and unlocking for the process models in the SBPR. A locking request can only be granted when the process model is not yet locked. The Version Manager takes care of the management of the versions of process models. To record the modeling history, every new process model or changed process model is stored as a new version in the SBPR. The IRIS Framework takes the responsibility for the query processing in SBPR.

Persistence Layer

The Persistence Layer manages the data access to the underlying relational database system and provides an abstraction for data access operations. It provides persistent solutions for persistent objects by adopting Object Relational Mapping (ORM) middleware such as Hibernate and Data Access Object (DAO) pattern.

The proposed solution is currently used and evaluated in the SUPER project[17], in which a reference architecture and practical usc cases of Semantic Business Process Management is being developed.

5. CONCLUSIONS AND DIRECTIONS FOR FUTURE RESEARCH

In this chapter, we have tried to summarize the theoretical challenges and practical problems of storing ontologies and associated data in a scalable way while considering the implicit facts of the ontology for query answering and other tasks.

We gave an overall introduction to some well-known ontology repositories, including native stores and database based stores, and highlighted strengths and limitations of each store. It is reported in (Ma et al., 2006) that Minerva achieves good performance in benchmarking tests. We took Minerva as an example to analyze ontology storage in databases in

---

[17] http://www.ip-super.org

depth, as well as discussed efficient indexes for scaling up ontology repositories. We then discussed a scalable reasoning method for handling expressive ontologies, as well as summarized other similar approaches.

We have presented a framework for reasoning with Description Logic based on WSML as a formalism of particular relevance in the field of Semantic Web services. Our framework builds on top of a transformation from WSML-DL to OWL-DL and supports all main DL-specific reasoning tasks. We thus linked the work for storing OWL ontologies, to the work on WSML-DL, providing the reader with an insight in storing and reasoning with both OWL-DL and WSML-DL ontologies.

As a practical use case of storing ontologies and reasoning with them, we presented our work on developing aSemantic Business Process Repository (SBPR) for the semantically supported management of business process models. We first analyzed the main requirements on SBPR. Then, we compared different approaches for storage mechanisms and showed how combining a RDBMS with the IRIS inference engine was a suitable solution, due to the expressiveness of the query language and the required reasoning capability. The IRIS inference engine is currently a WSML-Flight reasoner. The system is extensively being developed to support reasoning with WSML-Rule (i.e., support for function symbols, unsafe rules and non-stratified negation). Further on, IRIS will tightly integrate a permanent storage system designed for distributed scalable reasoning. One of our major objectives is the implementation of Rule Interchange Format (RIF)[18] in IRIS. Implementing RIF, IRIS will be capable of handling rules from diverse rule systems and will make WSML rule sets interchangeable with rule sets written in other languages that are also supported by RIF. Finally, IRIS will implement novel techniques for reasoning with integrating frameworks based on classical first-order logic and nonmonotonic logic programming as well as techniques for Description Logics reasoning.

ADDITIONAL READING

For more information on reasoning with ontologies and knowledge representation in general we suggest the two books by Baader et al (2003) and Baral (2003). The former provides an excellent introduction to Description Logic reasoning, while the second will get the reader up-to-date in the area of declarative knowledge representation with logic programming.

---

[18] Rule Interchange Format-W3C Working Group: http://www.w3.org/2005/rules/

REFERENCES

AllegroGraph, http://www.franz.com/products/allegrograph/index.lhtml, 2006

SnoMed Ontology, http://www.snomed.org/snomedct/index.html, 2006

IODT, IBM's Integrate Ontology Development Toolkit, http://www.alphaworks.ibm.com/tech/semanticstk, 2005

Abiteboul, Serge; Hull, Richard; Vianu, Victor: Foundations of Databases. Addison-Wesley, 1995

Agrawal, R., Somani, A., and Xu, Y., 2001, Storage and Querying of E-Commerce Data. In Proceedings of the 27th International Conference on Very Large DataBases, pages 149–158, Morgan Kaufmann.

Andrews, Tony; Curbera, Francisco; Dholakia, Hitesh; et al.: Business Process Execution Language for Web Services Version 1.1. 5 May 2003

Baader, F., Calvanese, D., McGuinness, D. L., Nardi, D. and Patel-Schneider, P. F., 2003, *The Description Logic Handbook*. Cambridge University Press.

Baral, C.Knowledge Representation, Reasoning and Problem Solving. Cambridge University Press, 2003.

Bechhofer, S., van Harmelen, F., Hendler, J., Horrocks, I., McGuinness, D. L., Patel-Schneider, P. F., and Stein, L. A., 2004, Owl web ontology language reference. Technical report. Available from: http://www.w3.org/TR/owl-ref/.

Bechhofer, S., Volz R. and Lord P.W., 2003, Cooking the Semantic Web with the OWL API, in: *International Semantic Web Conference*, pp. 659–675.

Bernstein, Philip A.; Dayal, Umeshwar: An Overview of Repository Technology. In VLDB 1994.

Bhattacharjee, B., Padmanabhan, S., and Malkemus, T., 2003, Efficient Query Processing for Multi-Dimensionally Clustered Tables in DB2, In Proceedings of the 29th Conference on Very Large Data Bases, pages 963–974, Morgan Kaufmann.

Borgida, A., 1996, On the relative expressiveness of description logics and predicate logics. *Artificial Intelligence* 82(1–2):353–367. Available from: http://citeseer.ist.psu.edu/borgida96relative.html.

BPMN, Business Process Modeling Notation Specification. OMG Final Adopted Specification, February 6, 2006

Brickley, D. and Guha, R. V., 2004, Rdf vocabulary description language 1.0: Rdf schema. Technical report. Available from: http://www.w3.org/TR/rdf-schema/.

Broekstra, J., Kampman, A., and Harmelen, van F., 2002, Sesame: A generic architecture for storing and querying RDF and RDF schema. In Proceedings of the 1st International Semantic Web Conference, volume 2342 of Lecture Notes in Computer Science, pages 54–68, Springer.

de Bruijn, J.; Kopecký, Jacek; Krummenacher, Reto: RDF Representation of WSML. 20 December 2006

de Bruijn, J., Lausen, H., Krummenacher, R., Polleres, A., Predoiu, L., Kifer, M., and Fensel, D., 2005, The web service modeling language WSML. WSML Final Draft D16.1v0.21, WSML. Available from: http://www.wsmo.org/TR/d16/d16.1/v0.21/.

de Bruijn, J., Polleres, A., Lara, R., and Fensel, D., 2005, OWL DL vs. OWL Flight: Conceptual Modeling and Reasoning on the Semantic Web. In Proceedings of the 14th International Conference on the World Wide Web.

Brunner, J., Ma, L., Wang, C., Zhang, L., Wolfson, D. C., Pan, Y., and Srinivas, K., 2007, Explorations in the Use of Semantic Web Technologies for Product Information Management. In Proceedings of the 16th International Conference on the World Wide Web. To appear.

Calvanese, D., De Giacomo, G., Lembo, D., Lenzerini, M., and Rosati, R., 2005, DL-Lite: Tractable Description Logics for Ontologies. In Proceedings of the 12th National Conference on Artificial Intelligence, pages 602–607.

Calvanese, D., De Giacomo, G., Lembo, D., Lenzerini, M., and Rosati, R., 2006, Data Complexity of Query Answering in Description Logics. In Proceedings of the 10th International Conference on the Principles of Knowledge Representation and Reasoning, pages 260–270, AAAI Press.

Chen, Y., Ou, J., Jiang, Y., and Meng, X., 2006, HStar-a Semantic Repository for Large Scale OWL Documents. In Proceedings of the 1st Asian Semantic Web Conference, volume 4185 of Lecture Notes in Computer Science, pages 415–428, Springer.

Das, S., Chong, E.I., Eadon, G., and Srinivasan, J., 2004, Supporting Ontology-Based Semantic matching in RDBMS. In Proceedings of the 30th International Conference on Very Large Data Bases, pages 1054–1065.

Dolby, J., Fokoue, A., Kalyanpur, A., Kershenbaum, A., Ma, L., Schonberg, E., and Srinivas, K., 2007, Scalable semantic retrieval through summarization and refinement. IBM Technical report, 2007.

Donini, M. F., Nardi, D., and Rosati, R., 2002, Description Logics of Minimal Knowledge and Negation as Failure. ACM Transactions on Computational Logic, 3(2):177–225.

Fitting, M., 1996, *First-Order Logic and Automated Theorem Proving*. 2nd ed., Springer-Verlag, New York.

Fokoue, A., Kershenbaum, A., Ma, L., Schonberg, E., and Srinivas, K., 2006b, The summary abox. Cutting ontologies down to size. In Proceedings of the 5th International Semantic Web Conference, volume 4273 of Lecture Notes in Computer Science, pages 343–356, Springer.

Garcia-Molina, H., Ullman, J., and Widom, J., 2000, Database System Implementation. Prentice-Hall.

Grosof, B., Horrocks, I., Volz, R., and Decker, S., 2003, Description logic programs: combining logic programs with description logic. In Proceddings of the 12th International Conference on the World Wide Web, pages 48–57.

Guo, Y., and Heflin, J., 2006, A Scalable Approach for Partitioning OWL Knowledge Bases. In Proceedings of the 2nd International Workshop on Scalable Semantic Web Knowledge Base Systems.

Haarslev, V., and Moller, R., 2001, RACER System Description. In Proceedings of Automated Reasoning, the 1st International Joint Conference.

Hepp, Martin; Leymann, Frank; Domingue, John; Wahler, Alexander; Fensel, Dieter: Semantic Business Process Management: A Vision Towards Using Semantic Web Services for Business Process Management. Proceedings of the IEEE ICEBE 2005, October 18–20, Beijing, China, pp. 535–540.

Hepp, Martin; Roman, Dumitru: An Ontology Framework for Semantic Business Process Management, Proceedings of Wirtschaftsinformatik 2007, February 28–March 2, 2007, Karlsruhe.

Horrocks I., Patel-Schneider P.F., van Harmelen F., 2003, From SHIQ and RDF to OWL: The making of a Web Ontology Language, *J. of Web Semantics*, 1570–8268, pp. 7–26, Available from: http://www.cs.man.ac.uk/~horrocks/Publications/download/2003/HoPH03a.pdf

Horrocks, I., and Tessaris, S., 2002, Querying the semantic web: a formal approach. In Proceedings of the 1st International Semantic Web Conference, volume 2342 of Lecture Notes in Computer Science, pages 177–191, Springer.

Hustadt, U., Motik, B., and Sattler, U., 2004, Reducing SHIQ Descrption Logic to Disjunctive Datalog Programs. In Proceedings of the 9th International Conference on Knowledge Representation and Reasoning, pages 152–162.

Hustadt, U., Motik, B., and Sattler, U., 2005, Data Complexity of Reasoning in Very Expressive Description Logics. In Proceedings of the 19th International Joint Conference on Artificial Intelligence, pages 466–471.

JENA, http://jena.sourceforge.net/index.html

Keller, G.; Nüttgens, M.; Scheer, A.-W.: Semantische Prozeßmodellierung auf der Grundlage "Ereignisgesteuerter Prozeßketten (EPK)", in: Scheer, A.-W. (Hrsg.): Veröffentlichungen des Instituts für Wirtschaftsinformatik, Heft 89, Saarbrücken 1992.

Kiryakov, A., Ognyanov, D., and Manov, D, 2005, OWLIM — a pragmatic semantic repository for OWL. In Proceedings of the 2005 International Workshop on Scalable Semantic Web Knowledge Base Systems.

Kiryakov, Atanas; Ognyanov, Damyan; Manov, Dimitar: OWLIM — a Pragmatic Semantic Repository for OWL. In Proc. of Int. Workshop on Scalable Semantic Web Knowledge Base Systems (SSWS 2005), WISE 2005, 20 Nov, New York City, USA.

Krotzsch, M.., Rudolph, S., and Hitzler, P., 2006, On the complexity of Horn description logics. In Proceedings of the 2nd Workshop OWL Experiences and Directions.

Libkin, Leonid: Expressive Power of SQL. The 8th International Conference on Database Theory. London, United Kingdom, 2001

Lipton, Richard and Naughton, Jeffrey. Query size estimation by adaptive sampling (extended abstract). In PODS '90: Proceedings of the ninth ACM SIGACTSIGMOD-SIGART symposium on Principles of database systems, pages 40–46, New York, NY, USA, 1990. ACM Press.

Lloyd, J. W., 1987, *Foundations of Logic Programming*. 2nd ed., Springer-Verlag, New York.

Ma, L., Yang, Y., Qiu, Z., Xie, G., Pan, Y., and Liu. S., 2006, Towards a complete owl ontology benchmark. In Proceedings of the 3rd Europe Semantic Web Conference, volume 4011 of Lecture Notes in Computer Science, pages 125–139, Springer.

Matias, Y., Vitter, J. S., and Wang, M., 1998, Wavelet-based histograms for selectivity estimation. In Proceedings of the ACM SIGMOD International Conference on Management of Data.

Mei, J., Ma, L., and Pan, Y., 2006, Ontology Query Answering on Databases. In Proceedings of the 5th International Semantic Web Conference, volume 4273 of Lecture Notes in Computer Science, pages 445–458, Springer.

Motik, B., Sattler, U., and Studer, R., 2004, Query Answering for OWL-DL with Rules. In Proceedings of the 3th International Semantic Web Conference, volume 3298 of Lecture Notes in Computer Science, pages 549–563, Springer.

Motik, B., Horrocks, I., and Sattler, U., 2006, Integrating Description Logics and Relational Databases. Technical Report, University of Manchester, UK.

Motik, B., and Rosati, R., 2007, A Faithful Integration of Description Logics with Logic Programming. In Proceedings of the 20th International Joint Conference on Artificial Intelligence.

Murray C., Alexander N., Das S., Eadon G., Ravada S., 2005, Oracle Spatial Resource Description Framework (RDF), 10g Release 2 (10.2).

OWLIM — OWL semantics repository. 2006. http://www.ontotext.com/owlim/

Pan, Z., and Heflin, J., 2003, DLDB: Extending relational databases to support semantic web queries. In Procedding of Workshop on Practical and Scaleable Semantic Web Systems.

Passin, Thomas B.: Explorer's Guide to the Semantic Web. Manning, 2004.

Prud'hommeaux, E., Seaborne, A., eds., 2005, SPARQL Query Language for RDF.W3C Working Draft.

Poosala, V., Ioannidis, Y. E., Haas, P. J., and Shekita, E., 1996, Improved histograms for selectivity estimation of range predicates. In Proceedings of the ACM SIGMOD International Conference on Management of Data.

RDF Primer, W3C Recommendation 10 February 2004. http://www.w3.org/TR/rdf-primer

RDF Vocabulary Description Language 1.0: RDF Schema. W3C Recommendation 10 February 2004

Rector, A., 2003, Message to public-webont-comments@w3.org: "case for reinstatement of qualified cardinality restrictions." Available from: http://lists.w3.org/Archives/Public/public-webontcomments/2003Apr/0040.html.

Reiter, R., 1992, What Should a Database Know? Journal of Logic Programming, 14(1–2):127–153.

Roman, D., Lausen, H., and Keller, U., 2004, Web service modeling ontology (WSMO). WSMO final draft d2v1.2. Available from: http://www.wsmo.org/TR/d2/v1.2/.

Rosati, R., 2006, DL + log: A Tight Integration of Description Logics and Disjunctive Datalog. In Proceedings of the 10th International Conference on the Principles of Knowledge Representation and Reasoning, pages 68–78, AAAI Press.

Ruckhaus, Edna and Ruiz, Eduardo. Query evaluation and optimization in the semantic web. In Proceedings of the ICLP'06 Workshop on Applications of Logic Programming in the Semantic Web and Semantic Web Services (ALPSWS2006), Washington, USA, August 16 2006.

Siberschatz, Abraham; Korth, Henry F.; Sudarshan, S.: Database System Concepts. Fifth Edition, McGraw-Hill, 2006.

Sirin, E., and Parsia, B., 2004, Pellet: An OWL DL Reasoner. In Proceedings of Workshop on Description Logic.

Smith, Howard; Fingar, Peter: Business Process Management. The Third Wave. Meghan-Kiffer,US 2003.

Spiegel, J. and Polyzotis, N. Graph-based synopses for relational selectivity estimation. In SIGMOD '06: Proceedings of the 2006 ACM SIGMOD international conference on Management of data, pages 205–216, New York, NY, USA, 2006. ACM Press.

Steinmetz, N., 2006, WSML-DL Reasoner. Bachelor thesis, Leopold-Franzens University Innsbruck. Available from: http://www.deri.at/fileadmin/documents/thesis/dlreasoner.pdf

SUPER, The European Integrated Project — Semantics Utilised for Process Management within and between Enterprises. http://www.ip-super.org/

ter Horst, Herman J.: Combining RDF and Part of OWL with Rules: Semantics, Decidability, Complexity. In Proc. of ISWC 2005, Galway, Ireland, November 6–10, 2005. LNCS 3729, pp. 668–684.

Volz, R., 2004, Web Ontology Reasoning with Logic Databases. PhD thesis, Fridericiana University Karlsruhe.

Wang, M., Chang, Y., and Padmanabhan, S., 2002, Supporting Efficient Parametric Search of E-Commerce Data: A Loosely-Coupled Solution. In Proceedings of the 8th International Conference on Extending Database Technology, pages 409–426.

Wilkinson, K., Sayers, C., Kuno, H. A., and Reynolds, D., 2003, Efficient RDF storage and retrieval in Jena2. In Proceedings of VLDB Workshop on Semantic Web and Databases, pages 131–150.

Wu, XD, Lee, ML, Hsu, W., 2004, A prime number labeling scheme for dynamic ordered XML trees. In Proceedings of the 20th Int'l Conf. on Database Engineering (ICDE). pages 66–78, IEEE Computer Society.

Zhou, J., Ma, L., Liu, Q., Zhang, L., Yu, Y., and Pan, Y., 2006, Minerva: A Scalable OWL
    Ontology Storage and Inference System. In Proceedings of the 1st Asian Semantic Web
    Conference, volume 4185 of Lecture Notes in Computer Science, pages 429–443,
    Springer.

III. EVOLUTION, ALIGNMENT, AND THE BUSINESS PERSPECTIVE

Chapter 5

ONTOLOGY EVOLUTION
State of the Art and Future Directions

Pieter De Leenheer[1] and Tom Mens[2]

(1) Semantics Technology & Applications Research Lab, Vrije Universiteit Brussel, Pleinlaan 2, B-1050 BRUSSELS 5, Belgium, pdeleenh@vub.ac.be; (2) Software Engineering Lab, Université de Mons-Hainaut, 6 Avenue du champ de Mars, B-7000 MONS, Belgium, tom.mens@umh.ac.be; (2) LIFL (UMR 8022), Université Lille 1 - Projet INRIA ADAM Cité Scientifique, 59655 Villeneuve d'Ascq Cedex, France

Abstract: The research area of ontology engineering seems to have reached a certain level of maturity, considering the vast amount of contemporary methods and tools for formalising and applying knowledge representation models. However, there is still little understanding of, and support for, the evolutionary aspects of ontologies. This is particularly crucial in distributed and collaborative settings such as the Semantic Web, where ontologies naturally co-evolve with their communities of use. For managing the evolution of single ontologies, established techniques from data schema evolution have been successfully adopted, and consensus on a general ontology evolution process model seems to emerge. Much less explored, however, is the problem of evolution of interorganisational ontologies. In this "complex" and dynamic setting, a collaborative change process model requires more powerful engineering, argumentation and negotiation methodologies, complemented by support for context dependency management.. It turns out that much can be learned from other domains where formal artefacts are being collaboratively engineered. In particular, the field of system engineering offers a wealth of techniques and tools for versioning, merging and evolving software artefacts, and many of these techniques can be reused in an ontology engineering setting. Based on this insight, this chapter gives a unified overview of the wide variety of models and mechanisms that can be used to support all of the above aspects of ontology evolution. The key remaining challenge is to construct a single framework, based on these mechanisms, which can be tailored for the needs of a particular environment.

Keywords: collaborative ontology engineering; context dependency management; ontology evolution; ontology versioning

1.   INTRODUCTION

The considerable amount of methods and tools for formalising (Sowa, 1984; Gruber, 1993; Guarino, 1998; Meersman, 1999) and applying knowledge representation (KR) models that is available today, suggests that the area of knowledge engineering has come to a state of stable maturity. However, there is still little understanding of, and support for, the evolutionary aspects of knowledge — in its most concrete manifestation called an ontology. This is particularly crucial in distributed and collaborative settings such as the Semantic Web, where ontologies naturally co-evolve with their communities of use (de Moor et al., 2006).

For managing the evolution of single ontologies, established techniques from data schema evolution have been successfully adopted, and consensus on a generally agreed ontology evolution process model seems to emerge (Maedche et al., 2003). Much less explored, however, is the evolution of interorganisational ontologies, which are usually engineered in distributed and collaborative settings. In such settings, different organisations collaboratively build a common ground of the domain. Ontologies are instrumental in this process by providing formal specifications of shared semantics. Such semantics are a solid basis to define and share (business) goals and interests, and ultimately develop useful collaborative services and systems.

However, scalable ontology engineering is hard to do in interorganisational settings where there are many pre-existing organisational ontologies and ill-defined, rapidly evolving collaborative requirements. A complex socio-technical process of ontology alignment and meaning negotiation is therefore required (de Moor et al., 2006). Furthermore, sometimes it is not necessary (or even possible) to reach for context-independent ontological knowledge, as most ontologies used in practice assume a certain context and perspective of some community (Schoop et al., 2006). Much valuable work has been done in the Semantic Web community on the formal aspects of ontology *elicitation* and *application*. However, the socio-technical aspects of the ontology engineering process in complex and dynamic realistic settings are still little understood, and introduce new problems in ontology evolution that where so far not unified.

One of the most important problems in collaborative ontology engineering is the detection and resolution of meaning ambiguities and conflicts during the elicitation and application of ontologies (De Leenheer and de Moor, 2005). The problem is principally caused by three facts: (i) no matter how expressive ontologies might be, they are all in fact lexical representations of concepts, relationships, and semantic constraints; (ii) linguistically, there is no bijective mapping between a concept and its lexical representation; and (iii) terms can have different meaning in different contexts of use. Consider for example phenomena such as synonyms and homonyms. Furthermore, ontologies are particularly elicited from tacit knowledge which is subjective and difficult to articulate. Resulting misunderstandings and ambiguities can have adverse consequences for the cost-effectiveness and viability of ontologies as a solution to a given problem.

Therefore, more powerful support for versioning and merging is required in order for domain experts to collaboratively and incrementally, build and manage increasingly complex versions of ontological elements and their diverging and converging relationships. Instead of being frustrated by out-of-control change processes, proper ontology versioning support will allow human experts to focus on the much more interesting meaning elicitation, interpretation, and negotiation process. It turns out that much can be learned from other domains where formal artefacts are being collaboratively engineered. In particular, the field of system engineering offers a wealth of techniques and tools for versioning, merging and evolving software artefacts (Mens, 2002), and many of these techniques can be reused in an ontology engineering setting.

Regardless of the complexity of the ontology engineering setting, what is currently lacking is a unified overview of the wide variety of models and mechanisms that can be used to support all of the above aspects of ontology evolution. Such an overview should not be restricted to data and knowledge engineering literature above as apparently much can be learned from other domains where formal artefacts are being engineered and evolved (De Leenheer et al., 2007). The key remaining challenge is to construct a single change management framework, based on these mechanisms, which can be tailored for the needs of a particular community of use.

This chapter is organised as follows. In **Section 2** we consider the dynamic aspects of ontology engineering. Next, in **Section 3**, we introduce a context-independent evolution process model for ontologies that are developed and evolved by a single user. We describe the essential activities of this process and substantiate these with a survey of existing approaches, including work that has been done in other system engineering domains such as software engineering and database engineering. **Section 4** considers the collaborative and distributed aspects of ontology engineering. From these observations we come up with a community-goal-driven change process model. We characterise the alternative methodological approaches and socio-technical aspects to be considered when multiple knowledge workers collaborate to the ontology. We address typical problems in this setting such as meaning negotiation and argumentation methods, and context dependency management. We provide a survey of existing approaches from different system engineering domains, and discuss future challenges (**Section 5**). Finally, we complete with an overview of state-of-the-art ontology evolution tools (**Section 6**), a digest for additional reading (**Section 7**).

2.   THE DYNAMIC ASPECTS OF ONTOLOGY ENGINEERING

Communication is the primary basis for coordinated action (and hence achieving *goals*) between different and diverse communities. When a communication *breakdown* occurs, it is important to capture and agree on the semantics of the concepts being communicated. Consider for example the business goal for delivering goods between the producer of the goods, and its delivery service. Implementing such a new delivery line requires agreement about a new workflow model, and the types of products that are to be delivered. This implies a number of change requests, which are formulated by the knowledge engineer in terms of ontology engineering processes.

2.1   Ontology engineering processes

In (De Leenheer et al., 2007), we identified some important types of context-driven ontology engineering processes that address these issues. These are macro-level processes in that they (in a particular methodological combination) provide the goals of the ontology engineering *process*. These include *lexical grounding (*and *word sense disambiguation), attribution* (of concepts), *specialisation, axiomatisation*, and *operationalisation*. In their operational implementation, which we respectively call OE *micro-processes*, methodologies differ widely.

Figure 5-1 illustrates a middle-out approach to ontology engineering: central are the processes, where each process is dependent on the result of the previous process (bottom-up semantic freedom). Each of these processes have optional constraints imposed by depending artefacts or running (Semantic Web) services (top-down-framing). Finally, the axiomatised artefact is operationalised and fed into the actual knowledge structures.

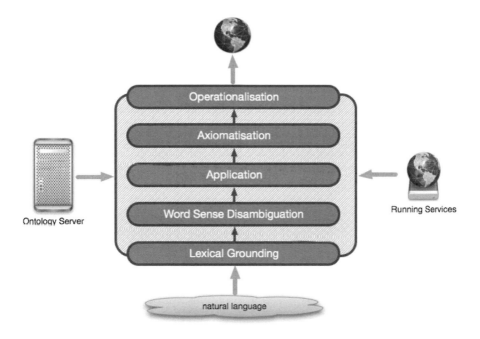

Figure 5-1. A middle-out approach to ontology engineering: central are the processes, where each process is dependent on the result of the previous process (bottom-up semantic freedom). Each of these processes have optional constraints imposed by depending artefacts or running (Semantic Web) services (top-down-framing).

2.1.1   Natural language grounding and lexical disambiguation

All meaning (semantics) is for communication purposes about a universe of discourse. It is represented independent of language but necessarily must be entirely rooted and described in (natural) language. Linguistic "grounding" of meaning is achieved through elicitation contexts, which can be mappings from identifiers to source documents such as generalised glosses, often in natural language (Jarrar, 2006; De Leenheer *et al.*, 2007). Natural language labels for concepts and relationships bring along their inherent ambiguity and variability in interpretation (Bouaud *et al.*, 1995), therefore this process is inseparable from lexical disambiguation.

Data models, such as data or XML schemas, typically specify the structure and integrity of data sets. Hence, building data schemas for an enterprise usually depends on the specific needs and tasks that have to be performed within this enterprise. Data engineering languages such as SQL aim to maintain the integrity of data sets and only use a typical set of language constructs to that aim (Spyns *et al.*, 2002), e.g., foreign keys.

The schema vocabulary is basically to be understood intuitively (via the terms used) by the human database designer(s). The semantics of data schemas often constitute an informal agreement between the developers and an intended group of users of the data schema (Meersman, 1999), and finds its way only in application programs that use the data schema instead of manifesting itself as an agreement that is shared amongst the community. When new functional requirements pop up, the schema is updated on the fly. This schema update process is usually controlled by one designated individual.

In (collaborative) ontology engineering, however, absolute meaning is essential for all practical purposes, hence all elements in an ontology must ultimately be the result of agreements among human agents such as designers, domain experts, and users. In practice, correct and unambiguous *reference* to concepts or entities in the schema vocabulary is a real problem; often harder than agreeing about their properties, and obviously not solved by assigning system-owned identifiers. At the start of the *elicitation* of an ontology, its basic knowledge elements (such as concepts and relationships) are extracted from various resources such as a text corpus or an existing schema, or rashly formulated by human domain experts through, e.g., tagging. Many ontology approaches focus on the conceptual modelling task, hence the distinction between lexical level (term for a concept) and conceptual level (the concept itself) is often weak or ignored. In order to represent concepts and relationships lexically, they usually are given a uniquely identifying term (or label). However, the context of the resource the ontology element was extracted from is not unimportant, as the meaning of a concept behind a lexical term is influenced by this *elicitation context*. When eliciting and unifying information from multiple sources, this can easily give rise to misunderstandings and ambiguities. An analysis of multiple contexts is therefore generally needed to disambiguate successfully (Bachimont et al., 2002; De Leenheer and de Moor, 2005).

2.1.2   Application

For the *application* of an ontology, the interpretation of the knowledge artefacts (which are referred to by terms) of the ontology is ambiguous if the context of application, such as the purpose of the user, is not considered. Different domain experts might want to "contextualise" elements of an ontology individually for the purpose of their organisation, for example by selection, specialisation or refinement, leading to multiple diverging ontologies that are context-dependent on (read: contextualisations of) the same (part of an) ontology.

Divergence is the point where domain experts disagree or have a conflict about the meaning of some knowledge element in such a way that consequently their ontologies evolve in widely varying directions. Although they share common goals for doing business, divergent knowledge positions appear as a natural consequence when people collaborate in order to come to a unique common understanding. Divergence arises because of differences among individuals. Individuals' experiences, personalities, and commitments become the potential for conflicts. According to Putnam and Poole (1987), a *conflict* is:

> *"the interaction of interdependent people who perceive opposition of goals, aims, and values, and who see the other party as potentially interfering with the realisation of these goals."*

This definition mainly underlines three characteristics of conflict: interaction, interdependence, and incompatible goals. In our context, goals should be understood as meaning. Incompatible meaning refers to the divergent ontological elements caused by alternative perspectives. Diaz (2005) refers to this as *cognitive conflict*.

Rather than considering this to be a problem, conflicts should be seen as an opportunity to negotiate about the subtle differences in interpretation, which will ultimately converge to a shared understanding disposed of any subjectivity. However, meaning conflicts and ambiguities should only be resolved when relevant. It is possible that people have alternative conceptualisations in mind for business or knowledge they do not wish to share. Therefore, in building the shared ontology, the individual ontologies of the various partners only need to be aligned insofar necessary, in order to avoid wasting valuable modelling time and effort. Furthermore, even if considered relevant from the community point of view, the changes that are caused by convergence or divergence are not always desired to be propagated to dependent artefacts in a push-based way: some applications might desire to decide on their own pace when to commit to the new version (Maedche *et al.*, 2003).

2.1.3   Axiomatisation

Domain constraints (e.g., database constraints), rules and procedures are essential to achieve an understanding about a domain's semantics but agreement about them is very difficult and nearly always specific to a context of application. An optimal ontological commitment constrains the possible interpretations of an ontology so that they can be understandable and usable (Gruber, 1993; Guarino, 1998). Furthermore, from an ontology application's point of view, constraints describe permitted updates of data stores that exist entirely within that application's realm.

This suggests an approach were an ontology is composed of separate inter-dependent layers, with on the lowest level the *conceptualisation* (i.e., lexical representation of concepts and their interrelationships), and continued with a number of increasingly restricting *axiomatisation* (i.e., semantic constraints) layers articulating different levels of ontological commitment. The goal of this separation, referred to as the *double articulation* principle (Spyns *et al.*, 2002), is to enhance the potential for re-use and design scalability. Reuse is only engendered by letting the application determine its own level of commitment to the ontology, i.e., by only committing to that layer that best approximates its intended meaning. The latter ought to be an optimal trade-off between a general-purpose and application-specific axiomatisation.

2.1.4   Operationalisation

Once (a version of) an ontology has been verified and validated (see further Sect. 3.2.4), it can be translated into an operational language that is in accordance with the application pool. For example, the most widely used recommendations on the Semantic Web are XML, RDF(S) and OWL. However, as community goals tend to shift depending on the changing shared business interests, an operationalised ontology version will soon become obsolete. An ontology should capture these changes continuously in order to co-evolve driven by the ontology engineering activities described so far.

2.2   Context dependencies

Context dependencies between artefacts play an important role for the elicitation, application, and analysis of ontologies (e.g., Maedche *et al.*, 2003; Haase *et al.*, 2004), but also for their correct interpretation (De Leenheer and de Moor, 2005). The question is how to apply and integrate them to increase the quality of such ontology engineering processes. For example, in Fig. 5-2: the interpretation of the terms *A, B, C*, and *F* on the right-hand side is dependent on their lexical grounding and disambiguation on the left-hand side. The dependency is further formalised by a sequence of operations defining relationships between the terms.

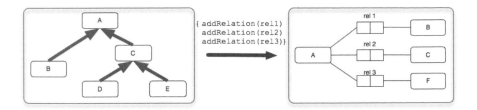

Figure 5-2. An illustration of a context dependency: the interpretation of the terms *A, B, C,* and *F* on the right-hand side is dependent on their lexical grounding and disambiguation on the left-hand side. The dependency is further formalised by a sequence of operations defining relationships between the terms.

Another particular example in the sense of conceptual graph theory (Sowa, 1984) would be a specialisation dependency for which the dependency constraint is equivalent to the conditions for contextual graph specialisation (Sowa, 1984: pp. 97). A specialisation dependency corresponds to a monotone specialisation. For instance, an organisational definition of a particular task (the entity) can have a specialisation dependency with a task template (its context). The constraint in this case is that each organisational definition must be a specialisation of the template (de Moor *et al.*, 2006). Furthermore, ontologies naturally co-evolve with their communities of use: whenever the template evolves, all context-dependent specialisations should evolve along.

In (De Leenheer *et al.*, 2007), we give a non-exhaustive analysis of context dependency types and meaning conflicts between diverging meanings as a natural consequence of interorganisational ontology engineering. We illustrate these dependencies by formally describing and decomposing the OE macro-processes in terms of a non-exhaustive set of primitives such as change operators for selecting, linking, and changing knowledge elements.

Tracing context dependencies by means of micro-process primitives, provides a better understanding of the whereabouts of knowledge elements in ontologies, and consequently makes negotiation and application less vulnerable to meaning ambiguities and conflicts, hence more practical. Instead of being frustrated by out-of-control change processes, proper context dependency management support will allow human experts to focus on the much more interesting meaning interpretation and negotiation processes.

Particularly in collaborative applications where humans play an important role in the interpretation and negotiation of meaning (de Moor, 2005), such frustrating misunderstanding and ambiguity can have adverse consequences for the cost-effectiveness and viability of ontologies as a solution to bring the Semantic Web to its full potential.

3.   SINGLE ONTOLOGY EVOLUTION

The key challenge of this chapter was to provide a unified framework and process model for ontology evolution that describes and supports all high-level activities related to evolving ontologies in a collaborative and distributed setting. Before undertaking this challenge, however, let us first focus on the more humble task of coming up with an evolution process for ontologies developed and evolved by a single user. This single user ontology evolution view seems to become generally accepted, since it has been proposed in various forms by different authors. For example, Maedche et al. (2003) have proposed a basic process model for evolving ontologies. We first take a look at the work that has been done in data schema evolution.

3.1   Data schema evolution

Although the issues in schema evolution are not entirely the same as in ontology evolution, the philosophy and results from schema evolution in general[1] have been fruitfully reconsidered for the treatment of the ontology evolution problem. The resemblances and differences between ontologies and data models are widely discussed in literature such as Meersman (2001), Spyns *et al.* (2002), and Noy and Klein (2004). The basic argumentation behind comparing ontologies and data schemas is that (i) formally, all such kinds of formal artefacts are lexically represented by sets of predicates (data models); and (ii) they describe some domain by means of conceptual entities and relationships in a (not necessarily) shared formal language[2] (Meersman, 2001).

Furthermore, the following rigorously cited definitions for schema evolution and versioning by Roddick (1995), indicate the similar situation we are confronted with in ontology evolution.

- *Schema evolution* is the ability to change a schema of a populated database without loss of data, the latter which means providing access to both old and new data through the new schema.

---

[1] object-oriented (OO) database schemas, relational schemas, entity-relationship (ER) schemas, fact-oriented schemas (NIAM (Verheijen and Van Bekkum, 1982), ORM (Halpin, 2001), *etc.*) in particular

[2] e.g., (De Troyer, 1993) presents a language that is able to represent ER, BRM, or relational schemas

- *Schema versioning* is the ability to access all the data (both old and new) through user-definable version interfaces. A version is a reference that labels a quiet point in the definition of a schema.

Similarly, in our survey we will consider versioning as a supportive activity along the different phases of the evolution process.

Looking at ontology evolution merely from this "formal" point of view, we can adopt methods and techniques from data schema evolution. Significant examples include transformation rules (in terms of pre- and post-conditions) to effect change operators on data schemas and change propagation to the data (Banerjee *et al.*, 1987), frameworks for managing multiple versions of data schemas coherently (Kim and Chou, 1988; Roddick, 1995) and models for different levels of granularity in change operators, viz. compound change operators[3] (Lerner, 2000). Furthermore, changes in one part of a schema might trigger a cascade of changes in other parts (Katz, 1990).

Main results in ontology evolution have been reported by Oliver *et al.* (1999), Heflin (2001), Klein *et al.* (2002), Stojanovic *et al.* (2002), Maedche et al. (2003), and Plessers (2006). They base their work predominantly in the previous mentioned schema evolution techniques, next to addressing particular needs for evolution of ontologies. Next, we will elaborate on this work by positioning it in the appropriate activities within a generic process model for single ontology evolution.

3.2 Single user change process model

All ontology engineering processes define a change process that involves several activities. In this section, we propose a more sophisticated single user change process model, based on the experience borrowed from the domain of software and systems engineering, where the use of process models is commonly accepted. Over the years, various process models have been proposed, and dedicated tools to support these process models are in active use today.

When it comes to evolution, there are various so-called "evolutionary process models," that explicitly consider software evolution as a crucial activity.[4] There are even dedicated models that detail the different subactivities of the evolution process itself, and explain how they are related. One such process model, that we will refer to as the *change process model* is

---

[3] e.g., moving an attribute x from a class A to a class B, means (more than) successively deleting x in A and adding x in B

[4] Examples of such models are the so-called *spiral model* of software development (Boehm, 1988) and the staged model for software evolution (Bennett and Rajlich, 2000)

depicted in Fig. 5-3. It is based on Bennett and Rajlich (2000) and essentially distinguishes four activities over three phases (*initiation*, *execution*, and *evaluation*) in the process of making a change: *requesting* a change, *planning* the change, *implementing* the change, and *verifying and validating* the change. It is an iterative process that needs to be applied for each requested change. The process requires decisions on whether the requested change is relevant, whether it is feasible to implement this change, and whether the change has been implemented properly.

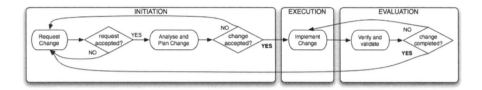

Figure 5-3. A context-independent change process model.

Interestingly, the activities of the proposed change model of Fig. 6-1 are generic, in the sense that they are not typical to software systems, but can be applied to any type of artefact that is subject to changes. As such, this change process can be interpreted and reused in the context of ontology evolution without any difficulty whatsoever. In the remainder of this section, we will explore the different activities of the change process model in more detail, seen from the *single user* ontology evolution point of view.

3.2.1   Requesting the change

Requesting the change has to do with initiating the change process. Some stakeholder wants to make a change to the ontology under consideration for some reason, and will post a so-called *change request*.

Change representation: Usually a change request is formalised by a finite sequence of elementary *change operators*. The set of applicable *change operators* to conduct these change operators is determined by the applied KR model. In principle, this set should subsume every possible type of ontology access and manipulation (*completeness* issue), and in particular, the manipulation operators should only generate valid ontologies (*soundness* issue) (Banerjee *et al.*, 1987; Peters and Özsu, 1997). In practice, however, ontology evolution frameworks only consider a non-exhaustive set of operators, tuned to the particular needs of the domain.

In the data schema and ontology evolution literature, much work focuses on devising taxonomies of elementary change operators that are sound and complete. Banerjee *et al.* (1987) chose the ORION object-oriented data model, devised a complete and sound taxonomy of possible change operators, and finally defined *transformation rules* (in terms of pre- and post-conditions) in order to effect change operators on data schemas and change propagation to the data. Lerner (2000) introduces models for different levels of granularity in change operators, viz. *non-elementary* or *compound* change operators.

Also in ontology evolution literature, it has become common practice to derive a taxonomy of change operators in terms of a particularly chosen KR model. E.g., Heflin (2001) takes the definition of Guarino (1998) as basis for his model, while Klein *et al.* (2002) refer to the definition of Gruber (1993). Heflin's model is formal, but his definition of an ontology (being a logical theory) is very much akin to the formal definition of a data schema as in De Troyer (1993). On the other hand, Klein *et al.* are more pragmatical in a way that they take Gruber's definition quite literally, and infer that there are three parts of the ontology (i.e., the model) to consider: the specification, the shared conceptualisation and the domain, and infer different types of change respectively. Klein and Fensel (2001) exemplify this.

Inspired by Lerner (2000), Stojanovic argues that change representation in terms of elementary operators is not always appropriate, and hence she defines a taxonomy of *composite* and *complex* change operators that are on a more coarse level than atomic change operators. Composite change operators are restricted to modify one level of neighbourhood of entities in the ontology. Examples are, given a concept taxonomy: "pull concept up," "split concept," etc. Complex change operators are combinations of at least two elementary and one composite change operator.

Prioritisation: Multiple change requests may be pending, in which case one of the requests needs to be selected. This requires setting up a prioritisation scheme for mapping the change requests, in order to decide which change should be implemented first. Prioritisation of requests can be based on the role of the change requester; however this remains undefined when assuming only one single administrator.

Change request types: Plessers (2006) distinguishes between changes *on request* and changes *in response*. He mainly concentrates on the changes on response that concern the process of changing an artefact as a consequence of changes to a sub-ontology it is depending on. A change on request is further divided by Stojanovic (2004) in *top-down* and *bottom-up* change requests.

Top-down change requests are explicit and are centrally driven by an entitled knowledge engineer who wants to adapt the ontology to the new requirements spawned by explicit user feedbacks. Bottom-up requests, on the other hand are implicit, reflected in the behaviour of the system, and can only be discovered through analysing this behaviour.

These types of change requests correspond to the two typical methods for knowledge acquisition[5]. *Top-down (deductive) changes* are the result of *knowledge elicitation* techniques that are used to acquire knowledge directly from human domain experts. *Bottom-up (inductive) changes* correspond to *machine learning*[6] techniques, which use different methods to infer patterns from sets of examples.

Change discovery: Stojanovic (2004) states that based on heuristics knowledge and/or data mining algorithms, suggestions for changes that refine the ontology structure may be induced by the analysis of the following data sources: (i) the ontology structure itself, (ii) the ontology instances or (iii) the information describing patterns of ontology usage. This results in three change discovery strategies. First, structure-driven changes are discovered from the ontology structure itself. Second, data-driven changes are induced from updates in the underlying instance sets and documents that are annotated with the ontology. Different definitions can be found in Stojanovic (2004) and Klein and Noy (2003). Finally, user-driven changes are discovered from certain usage patterns emerged over a period of time. Examples of such patterns include querying and browsing behaviour (Klein and Noy, 2003).

3.2.2   Planning the change

Planning the change has to do with understanding *why* the change needs to be made, *where* the change needs to be made (i.e., which parts of the artefact under consideration need to be modified), and *whether* the change should be made (i.e., do the benefits outweigh the risk, effort and cost induced by making the change).

Impact analysis: A crucial activity in planning the change has to do with *change impact analysis*, which is "the process of identifying the potential consequences (side effects) of a change, and estimating what needs to be

---

[5] Knowledge acquisition is a subfield of Artificial Intelligence (AI) concerned with eliciting and representing knowledge of human experts so that it can later be used in some application

[6] Machine learning provides techniques for extracting knowledge (e.g., concepts and rules) from data

modified to accomplish a change" (Bohner and Arnold, 1996). This impact analysis is very helpful to estimate the cost and effort required to implement the requested change.

A result of this activity may be to decide to implement the change, to defer the change request to a later time, or to ignore the change request altogether (for example, because its estimated impact and effort may be too high to afford).

Ontologies often reuse and extend (parts of) other ontologies. Many different types of dependencies exist within and between ontological artefacts of various levels of granularity, ranging from individual concepts of definitions to full ontologies. Other dependent artefacts include instances, as well as application programs committing to the ontology. Hence, a change on request in one artefact might imply a cascade of changes in response to all its dependent artefacts (Plessers, 2006). A viable tool should generate and present the administrator with a complete list of all implications to the ontology and its dependent artefacts.

Cost of evolution: Plessers (2006) determines the *cost of evolution* as a key element in the decision whether to propagate change to a dependent artefact or not. He does this by checking to which *intermediate* version[7] the ontology can update without any cost, i.e., without any need for change propagation to the depending artefact. Simperl et al. (2007) propose a *parametric cost estimation* model for ontologies by identifying relevant cost drivers having a direct impact on the effort invested in ontology building. Finally, Hepp (2007) gives an excellent overview about how realistic factors constrain ontology benefits.

Also in the software engineering community, a lot of research has been carried out in estimating the cost of software evolution (Sneed, 1995) (Ramil, 2003). Whether and how these results can be adapted to ontology engineering remains an open question.

3.2.3   Implementing the change

The activity of *implementing the change* seems to be self-explanatory, although it is more complicated than it looks. The application of a change request should have transactional properties, i.e., atomicity, consistency, isolation, and durability (Gray, 1981). Our process model realises these

---

[7] Plessers (2006: pp. 53) uses the term 'intermediate version' to refer to: "*one of the versions in the version log that together have lead to a publicly available version, but that never has been published as a public version on its own. An intermediate version is rather a version in-between towards a public version*".

requirements by strictly separating the change request specification and subsequent implementation, as suggested by Stojanovic (2004).

Implementing a change is a difficult process that necessitates many different sub-activities: change propagation, restructuring and inconsistency management.

Change propagation: During the change planning phase, the impact of the change has been analysed, and it may turn out that a seemingly local change will *propagate* to many different types of dependent artefacts. Based on the cost and impact analysis, the administering knowledge engineer might consider to cancel the change or not. Techniques for dealing with this *change propagation,* such as the one proposed by Rajlich (1997), need to be put in place.

In data schema evolution, the principal dependent artefacts are the instances representing the database population. In order to keep the instances meaningful, either the relevant instances must be coerced into the new definition of the schema or a new version of the schema must be created leaving the old version intact. In literature four main approaches have been identified (Peters and Özsu, 1997), which can be reconsidered for updating ontology instances as well: *immediate conversion* (or *coercion*) (Penney and Stein, 1987; Skarra and Zdonik, 1986; Nguyen and Rieu, 1989; Lerner and Habermann, 1990) and *deferred conversion* (lazy, *screening*) (Andany *et al.*, 1991; Ra and Rundensteiner, 1997) propagate changes to the instances only at different times. Third, *explicit deletion* allows for (i) the explicit deletion of all instances of all dependent component classes when the referencing class is dropped; and (ii) explicit deletion of all instances when their class is dropped (Banerjee *et al.*, 1987). Four, *filtering* (Andany *et al.*, 1991; Ra and Rundensteiner, 1997) is a solution for versioning that attempts to maintain the semantic differences between versions of schema. Other hybrid approaches take a combination of the above four methods.

For propagating changes to dependent artefacts, Maedche *et al.* (2003) propose two strategies: *push-based* and *pull-based* synchronisation. Push-based synchronisation is a variant of immediate conversion. With pull-based synchronisation, the changes are propagated at explicit request, which implies a deferred approach.

Change logging: All information about the performed change operations are usually tracked and recorded in a change log. This facilitates change detection, merging and conflict management, as we will see further.

Restructuring: In some cases the requested change may turn out to be too difficult to implement, given the current structure of the ontology. In that case, the ontology needs to be *restructured* first, before the actual desired change can be implemented. According to Chikofsky and Cross (1990), *restructuring* is "the transformation from one representation form to another at the same relative abstraction level, while preserving the subject system's external behaviour (functionality and semantics)."

In conceptual schema modelling, a schema change can be formalised by a transformation that either enriches, reduces or preserves the *information capacity* (Miller, 1993). Information capacity is not a kind of quantitive measure crediting the quality of a schema. It is explicated as a "semantic" ordering between schemas. Hence, different notions of *semantics* and *semantic equivalence* were defined, such as mathematical and conceptual equivalence (Proper and Halpin, 1998). Proper and Halpin (1998) distinguish roughly three reasons to apply transformation: (i) to select an alternative conceptual schema which is regarded as a better representation of the domain, (ii) to enrich the schema with derivable parts creating diverse alternative views on the same conceptual schema as a part of the original schema, (iii) to optimise a finished conceptual schema before mapping it to a logical design. Schema equivalence in the relational model concerns normalisation using *lossless decomposition* transformations (Codd, 1972).

Inconsistency management: Yet another problem is that the change may introduce *inconsistencies* in the ontology. Nuseibeh *et al.* (2000) state succinctly:

"An inconsistency is any situation in which a set of descriptions does not obey some relationship that should hold between them. The relationship between descriptions can be expressed as a consistency rule against which the descriptions can be checked."

According to Spanoudakis and Zisman (2001), an inconsistency corresponds to

"a state in which two or more overlapping elements of different software models make assertions about aspects of the system they describe which are not jointly satisfiable."

Obviously, this definition can be used for ontology models as well.

In research literature, we can discern two schools of thought. Proponents of "consistency maintenance" try to keep the system under consideration consistent at all costs. This is typically a conservative approach, where certain changes are disallowed, as they would lead the system into an inconsistent state. The second school of thought, that we will refer to as "inconsistency management" is more liberal, since it relies on the hypothesis that inconsistencies are inevitable, and that we need to live with them. Either way, we need to define and use formalisms and techniques for detecting and resolving inconsistencies in ontologies, as well as mechanisms and processes to manage and control these inconsistencies.

In data schema evolution, most work is situated in consistency maintenance, where it is usually denoted as *semantics of change*. In ORION (Banerjee et al., 1987), the semantics for each schema change is determined. They first identify a set of invariant properties intrinsic to the object-oriented model, ensuring semantic integrity. The invariants strictly depend on the underlying model. Then for each schema change where there are theoretically multiple alternative ways to preserve the invariant properties, they define a set of transformation rules guiding the change process through the most meaningful way that preserves the semantic integrity of the schema. Similar approaches are found in Gemstone (Penney and Stein, 1987), Farandole2 (Andany *et al.*, 1991), and OTGen (Lerner and Habermann, 1990). In ontology evolution this work was adopted by Stojanovic (2004) and De Leenheer *et al.* (2007).

A semantic approach was taken by Franconi *et al.* (2000). They adopt a description logic framework for a simplified object-oriented model (ignoring class behaviour), and extend it with versions. Each elementary schema change between two versions specifies how the axiomatisation of the new version will be in terms of the previous version, and refers to the evolution of the objects through the change. The only elementary change operator that can refer to a new object is "add class." That is the reason that changing the domain type of an attribute with a new domain type that is compatible with the old one, leads to an inconsistent version. A legal instance of a schema should satisfy the constraints imposed by the class definitions in the initial schema version and by the schema changes between schema versions. Franconi *et al.* also propose a reasoning mechanism for investigating evolution consistency. Franconi's approach is very similar to the declarative approach taken by Stojanovic (2004). Finally, Jarrar *et al.* (2006) describe algorithms for detecting unsatisfiability of ORM schemas. There, conflict patterns for detecting conflict between semantic constraints on the same pair of paths in the semantic network.

A sound and complete axiomatic model for dynamic schema evolution in object-based systems is described in (Peters and Özsu, 1997). This is the first effort in developing a formal basis for the schema evolution research which provides a general approach to capture the behaviour of several different systems, and hence is useful for their comparison in a unified framework.

In software engineering, there is a plethora of research on inconsistency management. Spanoudakis and Zisman (2001) provide an excellent survey of this research field. In the domain of ontology engineering, on the other hand, research on inconsistencies is still in its infancy. Haase and Stojanovic

(2005) present an approach to localise inconsistencies based on the notion of a minimal inconsistent sub-ontology. Plessers and De Troyer (2006) use a variant of description logics to detect and resolve certain kinds of inconsistencies in OWL ontologies.

Evolution strategies: As already mentioned above, Banerjee *et al.* (1987) provide for each change multiple alternative ways to preserve the invariant properties. This idea was further adopted by Stojanovic *et al.* (2002). They introduce resolution points where the evolution process or the user has to determine one of a set of possible evolution strategies to follow. In order to relieve the engineer of choosing evolution strategies individually, four advanced evolution strategies are introduced. The choice of how a change should be resolved can depend on characteristics of the resulting ontology state (*structure-driven*); on characteristics of the change process itself, such as complexity (*process-driven*); on the last recently applied evolution strategy (*frequency-driven*); or on an explicitly given state of the instances to be achieved (*instance-driven*). Mens *et al.* (2006) also provide alternative strategies to resolve model inconsistencies. Furthermore, they exploit the mechanism of critical pair analysis to analyse dependencies and conflicts between inconsistencies and resolutions, to detect resolution cycles and to analyse the completeness of resolutions.

3.2.4   Verification and validation

The last, but certainly not the least important, activity in the change process has to do with *verification* and *validation*. Verification addresses the question "did we build the system right?", whereas validation addresses the question "did we build the right system?" A wide scale of different techniques has been proposed to address these questions, including: testing, formal verification, debugging and quality assurance.

Formal verification relies on formalisms such as state machines and temporal logics to derive useful properties of the system under study. Well-known techniques for formal verification are model checking and theorem proving (Clarke *et al.*, 2000). While formal verification can be very useful, it is a technique requiring considerable expertise, and it does not always scale very well in practice. Therefore, other more pragmatic approaches are needed as well.

Testing is one of these approaches. For a well-chosen representative subset of the system under consideration, tests are written to verify whether the system behaves as expected. Whenever one of the tests fails, further actions are required.

Debugging is the task of localising and repairing errors (that may have been found during formal verification or testing). Some work on ontology debugging is starting to emerge, see Parsia *et al.* (2005) and Wang *et al.* (2005).

A final activity has to do with *quality assurance*. The goal is to ensure that the developed system satisfies all desired qualities. This typically concerns non-functional qualities, since the behaviour of the system has already been verified during formal verification or testing. Examples of useful quality characteristics may be: reusability, adaptability, interoperability, and so on. Currently, efforts are being made for editing and publishing a concise list of ontology quality guidelines in the context of the Ontology Outreach Advisory[8].

3.3   Versioning

In the case of ontology management, some of the activities in the process model above suggest additional versioning support. *Versioning* is a mechanism that allows users to keep track of all changes in a given system, and to *undo* changes by *rolling back* to any previous version. Furthermore, it can be used to keep track of the history of all changes made to the system.

The most common variant of versioning is known as *state-based versioning*. At any given moment in time, the system under consideration is in a certain *state*, and any change made to the system will cause the system to go to a new state. Typically (but not always), this state is associated with a unique version number. A more sophisticated variant of versioning is known as *change-based versioning*. It treats changes as first-class entities, i.e., it stores information about the precise changes that were performed. A particular flavour of change-based versioning is *operation-based versioning*. It models changes as explicit operations (or transformations). These evolution operations can be arbitrarily complex, and typically correspond to the commands issued in the environment used to perform the changes.

Explicit information about changes can be used to facilitate comparing and merging parallel versions. Compared to state-based versioning, change-based versioning is more flexible. For example, it makes it easier to compute the difference between versions, or to implement a multiple *undo/redo mechanism*. For *undo*, it suffices to perform the last applied operations in the opposite direction, and for *redo*, we simply reapply the operations.

In the context of database systems, Katz (1990) and Roddick (1993,1995) provide an excellent survey on schema versioning issues for CAD objects and data schemas respectively. Schema versioning allows to view all data

---

[8] http://www. ontology-advisory.org

both *retrospectively* and *prospectively*, through user-definable version interfaces. A *version* is a reference that labels a quiet point in the definition of the schema, forced by the user:

1. **prospective use** is the use of a data source conforming to a previous version of the schema, via a newer version of the schema — the new schema must be backwards compatible;
2. **retrospective use** is the use of a data source conforming to a newer version of the schema, via a previous version of the schema — the new schema must be forwards compatible;

where *use* can be either viewing or manipulating. Schema evolution, however, actually does not require this ability: essentially, change can be propagated by means of coercion, screening or filtering (see Sect. 3.2.3).

Conradi and Westfechtel (1998) provided a similar, yet considerably more extensive survey on the use of versioning in software engineering. This also included so-called change-based version models, which were not treated by Roddick (1995).

Klein *et al.* (2002) propose a system offering support for ontology versioning. It is a state-based approach to versioning. In contrast, Maedche *et al.* (2003) propose to use a change-based approach, which tracks and records all information about the performed changes, thus facilitating change detection, integration, and conflict management (see further).

3.3.1   Version differences

Noy and Musen (2002) propose PROMPTDiff, an algorithm to find differences between two versions of a particular ontology. The algorithm distinguishes between three kinds of mismatches of two versions of a frame: (i) unchanged (nothing has changed in the definition), (ii) isomorphic (the frames have slots, and facet values are images of each other but not identical), and (iii) changed (the frames have slots or facet values that are not images of each other). The algorithm is inspired by classical difference algorithms, such as *diff*, that are used to discover changes or differences between versions of a document (Hunt and McIllroy, 1976).

PROMPTDiff only detects differences between two versions based on their structural difference. Therefore, Klein (2004) proposed several complementary alternatives (change logs, conceptual relations and transformation sets) that provide a richer semantic description of the changes that the original ontology has undergone. Research on *semantic differencing* in software engineering may also be relevant in this context (Jackson and Ladd, 1994).

3.3.2   Compatibility

Backward compatibility was first mentioned by Heflin (2001). Its goal is to provide data accessibility between different versions of an ontology by means of binary mappings between ontological elements of the respective versions (Klein et al., 2002). We refer to Chapter 5, for an in-depth elaboration on such mapping languages.

According to Plessers (2006), an ontology version is backward compatible with a previous version for a given depending artifact if the depending artifact remains consistent and a set of *compatibility requirements* hold. Compatibility requirements allow maintainers of depending artifacts to express which facts that could be inferred from the old version of an ontology must still be inferable from the new version. All compatibility requirements must be met for an ontology to be considered backward compatible for that specific depending artifact. The compatibility requirements are specified in terms of a Change Definition Language.

4.   COLLABORATIVE ONTOLOGY ENGINEERING

The process model we presented above addresses the principal ontology management activities from a single administrator point of view. We have shown that for each of these activities a considerable amount of methods and techniques are available. The key challenge of this chapter, however, was to come up with a unified framework and process model for ontology evolution and change management that scales up ontology engineering to a collaborative and distributed setting.

As an illustrative example of the additional complexity introduced by the distributed and collaborative nature of interorganisational ontology engineering, consider the scenario depicted in Figure 5-4. It describes the situation of two different organisations, each having their own particular organisational ontology (OO_1 and OO_2, respectively). Assume that these organisations have the same domain of interest, and they wish to share their common knowledge by agreeing upon a shared interorganisational ontology IOO. Evolution problems start to arise since these three ontologies OO_1, OO_2 and IOO have to be maintained and kept synchronised while they can all be subject to changes. For example, Figure 5-4 shows what happens if version 1 of OO_1 is revised into a new version. This requires integrating, if necessary, these changes into a new version of IOO as well. As a result of updating the IOO, the changes will need to be propagated to OO_2 in order to keep it synchronised. The situation becomes even more complex if OO_1 and OO_2 are subject to parallel independent changes (indicated by the parallel revisions of OO_1 and OO_2 to version 3 in Figure 5-4). As before, these parallel changes need to be integrated into the IOO, but since these changes come from different sources, it is likely that conflicts arise, and that a negotiation process is required to decide how to merge all changes into a new version of the IOO.

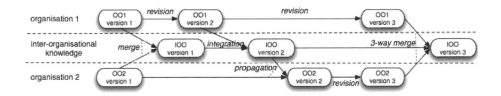

Figure 5-4. An example of interorganisational ontologies.

In this section, we will explore the above problem in detail, and discuss which additional mechanisms and activities are required to provide a solution.

4.1 Collaborative change process model

Collaboration aims at the accomplishment of shared objectives and an extensive coordination of activities (Sanderson, 1994). Successful virtual communities and communities of stakeholders are usually self-organising. The knowledge creation and sharing process is driven by implicit community *goals* such as mutual concerns and interests (Nonaka and Takeuchi, 1995). Hence, in order to better capture *relevant* knowledge in a *community-goal-driven* way, these community goals must be externalised appropriately. They may then be linked to relevant *strategies* underlying the collaborative ontology engineering process and its support.

In a collaborative setting, we replace the single knowledge engineer by multiple knowledge *workers*, the latter being community members that have expertise about the domain in particular, rather than in knowledge engineering in general. Furthermore, we leverage the single user change process model to a community-goal-driven change process model, by embedding it in its real and "complex" environment or context (Figure 5-5), characterised as a system consisting of following two parts:

1. A *formal* system part, being the Ontology Server storing actual shared networked structures of inter-dependent knowledge artefacts. In the single user change process model, we only considered this part and further assumed a context-independent environment.

2. A *social* system part, encompassing the community or organisation
   governing the shared knowledge. Ultimately, this requires us to model
   communities completely (i.e., establish their formal semantics) in terms
   of their intrinsic aspects such as *goals, actors, roles, strategies,
   workflows, norms*, and *behaviour*, and to so integrate the concept of
   community as first-class citizen in the knowledge structures of the
   evolving system.

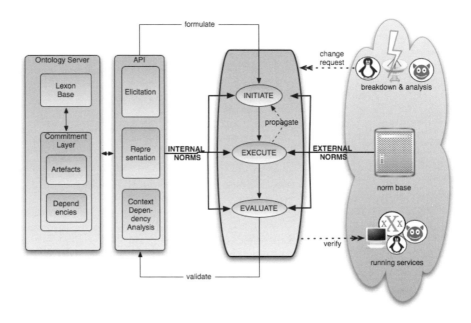

Figure 5-5. A community-goal-driven change process model, embedded in its real
environment.

This *holistic* approach is breaking with current practice, where evolution
processes are usually reduced to only the non-human parts, with the possible
exception of the field of *organisational semiotics* and the *language/action
perspective* (e.g., RENESYS (de Moor and Weigand, 2007)) that already
involved a few socio-technical aspects of communities such as norms and
behaviour (e.g., MEASUR (Stamper, 1992)) in legitimate user-driven
information system specification.

These rapidly evolving community aspects, and the many dependencies
they have with the actual knowledge *artefacts* in the knowledge structures,
lead to knowledge structures that can be extremely volatile. Hence, research
into a special-purpose, disciplined and comprehensive framework and
methodology will be needed to address the manageable evolution of
knowledge structures, taking into account crucial issues such as conflict and

dependency management, and ontology integration, while respecting the autonomous yet self-organising drives inherent in the community.

Next, we give an overview of socio-technical aspects that currently bootstrap practice in context-driven ontology engineering.

4.2   Socio-technical requirements

When formulating a change request in a collaborative context, at least the following questions need to be considered:

1. **What** *ontology engineering processes are required in order to achieve the goal or resolve the communication breakdown?* We already touched upon this in Section 2. As multiple knowledge workers will collaborate, we will need additional methods for integrating their divergent conceptualisations, including negotiation and argumentation.
2. **How** *to conduct the activities?* This relates to the *epistemological dimension* of knowledge: it examines to which extent subjective tacit knowledge from multiple knowledge workers can be made explicit, and universally acceptable (read: objective) for the community. This ultimately requires alternative epistemological approaches to ontology elicitation.
3. **Who** *will be coordinating these activities?* As already mentioned, shared objectives can only be achieved through extended coordination. E.g., through implicit and explicit norms, the authority for the control of the process is *legitimately distributed* among many different participants, independent of their geographical location. This requires specification methods for legitimate action.

4.2.1   Epistemological approaches

Knowledge Explication: During the ontology engineering process, the subjective knowledge held by the individual domain experts is amplified, internalised, and externalised as part of a shared ontology (Nonaka and Takeuchi, 1995). Knowledge moves in an *upward spiral* starting at the individual level, moving up to the organisational level, and finally up to the interorganisational level. This requires an alternative approach to ontology engineering.

The radical constructivist approach: *Constructivism* rejects the existence of a unique objective reality, hence its reflecting "transcendent" conceptualisation. Analogously, in a collaborative setting, however, organisation members, including middle managers, users, and domain experts play an important role in the interpretation and analysis of meaning during the different knowledge elicitation and application activities. Furthermore, it might be the case that multiple members turn out to be relevant to participate in one contextualised change process when it is related to a topic for which they all share the necessary expertise. Hence, given the diversity and the dynamics of knowledge domains that need to be accommodated, a viable ontology engineering methodology should not be based on a single, monolithic domain ontology that presumes a unique *objective* reality that is maintained by a single knowledge engineer. It should instead take a *constructivist* approach where it supports multiple domain experts in the gradual and continuous externalisation of their *subjective* realities contingent on relevant formal community aspects (De Leenheer *et al.*, 2007).

No free lunch: divergence meets convergence: The constructivist approach engenders meaning divergence in the respective organisational contexts. This requires a complex socio-technical meaning *argumentation* and *negotiation* process, where the meaning is aligned, or converged. Figure 5-6 shows the effect of the constructivist approach on ontology engineering processes: an explosion of increasingly mature versions of *contextualised* ontological artefacts (conceptualising their divergent subject realities), and of their *inter-dependencies.*

This confronts us with a seemingly unscalable alignment task. However, sometimes it is not necessary (or even possible) to achieve context-independent ontological knowledge, as most ontologies used in practice assume a certain professional, social, and cultural perspective of some community (Diaz, 2005). The key is to reach the *appropriate* amount of consensus on *relevant* conceptual definitions through *effective* meaning negotiation in an *efficient* manner. This requires powerful strategies for selected integration, supported by argumentation and negotiation methodologies, while allowing for management of context dependencies.

4.2.2   Modelling communities: coordination and negotiation

By grounding evolution processes in terms of community aspects such as composition norms and conversation modes for specification, the knowledge-intensive system can be precisely tailored to the actual needs of the community (de Moor, 2002).

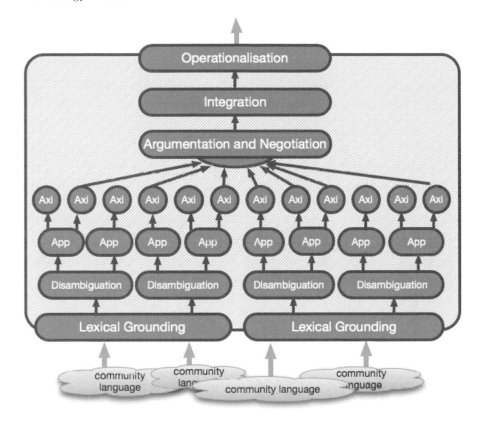

Figure 5-6. The middle-out approach applied when multiple knowledge workers are engaged in the change request. This requires additional support for integration, including argumantation and negotiation.

Conversation: The RENISYS method conceptualises community information system specification processes as *conversations for specification* by relevant community members. It therefore uses formal *composition norms* to select the relevant community members who are to be involved in a particular conversation for specification. Next, it adopts a formal model of conversations for specification to determine the acceptable conversational moves that the selected members can make, as well as the status of their responsibilities and accomplishments at each point in time.

Composition norms: Among other community aspects that will orchestrate the collaborative ontology engineering processes, in this paper we only distinguish between two kinds of composition norms: (i) *external* norms that *authorise* relevant actors in the community for an action within a particular ontological context, and (ii) *internal* norms that, independently from the involved actors, constrain or propagate the evolution steps, enforced by the dependencies the involved ontological context has with other contexts in the knowledge structures.

Inspired by Stamper and de Moor, an external norm is defined as follows:

if precondition **then** actor **is** *{permitted/required/obliged}* **to** *{initiate/execute/evaluate}* action **in** ontological context

The *precondition* can be a boolean, based on a green light given by an entitled decision organ, or triggered by some pattern that detects a trend or inconsistency in the actual ontological structures. The *deontic status* states whether an *actor* is permitted, obliged, or required to perform a particular *role* (initiation, execution, validation) within the scope of a certain *action* (e.g., a micro-level OE process or macro-level OE activity).

An internal norm is defined as follows:

{initiate/execute/evaluate} action **in** ontological_context **is constrained to** $\cup_i$ primitive$_i(e^1_i,\ldots,e^n_i)$ **where** $\forall_i$ $\{e^j_i,\ldots,e^k_i\} \in$ ontological_context$_i$ ($1 \le j \le k \le n$)

Performing a particular action role in some ontological context is (in order to perform that action) constrained to use a restricted toolbox of primitives ($\cup_i$ primitive$_i$), of which some parameters are bound to ontological elements $e^j_i,\ldots,e^k_i$, that were already grounded in some ontological contexts.

4.3   Context dependency management

We now present a generic model for understanding the inter-organisational ontology engineering process, which collects the epistemological and legitimate assumptions we made above. It is an extension of the one inspired by de Moor *et al.* (2006) and Templich *et al.* (2005). The main focus lies on how to capture *relevant* commonalities and differences in meaning by supporting domain experts in an *efficient* way by assigning them *scalable* knowledge elicitation tasks driven by *incentives* such as templates that represent the current insights. Differences are aligned insofar necessary through meaning argumentation and negotiation.

In the model, we make the following assumptions:

1. An interorganisational ontology needs to be modelled not by external knowledge engineers, but constructively by domain experts themselves. Only they have the tacit knowledge about the domain and can sufficiently assess the real impact of the conceptualisations and derived collaborative services on their organisation.

2. An interorganisational ontology cannot be produced in one session, but needs to evolve over time. Due to its continuously changing needs, expectations, and opportunities, different versions are needed.
3. The common interest only partially overlaps with the individual organisational interests. This means that the goal is not to produce a single common ontology, but to support organisations in interpreting common conceptualisations in their own terms, and feeding back these results. This requires continuous support for so-called co-evolution of ontologies. A continuous alignment of common and organisational ontologies is therefore required.
4. The starting point for each version should be the current insight about the common interest, i.e., common conceptual definitions relevant for the collaborative services for which the interorganisational ontology is going to be used.
5. The end result of each version should be a careful balance of this *proposal* for a common ontology with the various *individual interpretations* represented in the organisational ontologies.

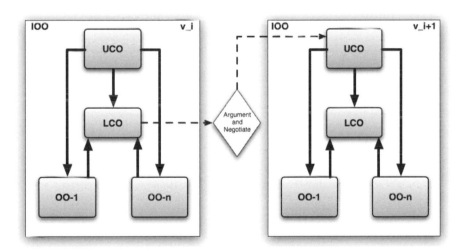

Figure 5-7. A model inter-organisational ontology engineering, inspired by de Moor *et al.* (2006).

The inter-organisational ontology (IOO) model in Figure 5-7 and its assumptions suggests many different types of context dependencies, within and between ontological elements of various levels of granularity, ranging from individual concepts of definitions to full ontologies.

Inter-organisational dependencies: The engineering process starts with the creation (or adoption) of an (existing) upper common ontology (UCO), which contains the conceptualisations and semantic constraints that are common to and accepted by a domain. For example, a domain glossary or thesaurus could frame all future OE activities in a top-down fashion. Each participating organisation contextualises (through e.g., specialisation) this ontology into its own Organisational Ontology (OO), thus resulting in a local interpretation of the commonly accepted knowledge. In the Lower Common Ontology (LCO), a new proposal for the next version of the IOO is produced, selecting and merging relevant material from the UCO and various OOs. The part of the LCO that is accepted by the community then forms the legitimate UCO for the next version of the IOO (dashed arrows, engendering the upward spiral). The performed context-driven ontology engineering processes characterise different dependency types between the sub-ontologies (full arrows).

Intra-organisational dependencies: For each new concept or relationship within an organisational ontology, different OE activities are conducted accordingly. E.g., first a natural language label is chosen to refer to the concept, next it is disambiguated and hooked into the upper common type hierarchy, then it is applied in terms of relationships with other concepts (*differentiae*), and finally axioms constrain the possible interpretations of the genera and differentiae. Again, this results in many dependencies within the individual organisational ontologies that are characterised by ontology engineering processes.

The formal characterisation of context dependency types in terms of applicable change operators depends on the adopted KR model, hence is omitted here. For a technical elaboration of this in the DOGMA KR model, we refer to (De Leenheer et al., 2007: pp. 40). For an elaborated example of context dependency management in a real-world business case, we refer the reader to Chapter 10.

4.4   Argumentation and negotiation

A negotiation process is defined as a specification conversation about a concept (e.g., a process model) between selected domain experts from the stakeholding organisations. For an excellent survey on different conversation models we refer to de Moor (2002).

In order to substantiate their perspectives, domain experts must formulate *arguments*. The most accepted argumentation model is IBIS (Kunz, 1970), which provides a simple and abstract infrastructure for so-called *wicked problems*. Wicked problems are usually not solvable in a fashionable way as there are many social obstacles such as time, money, and people.

By considering ontology negotiation as a wicked problem, Tempich *et al.* (2005), propose DILIGENT, which is an integrated formal argumentation model (based on IBIS) to support ontology alignment negotiations. This ontology supports the process in several ways. In negotiations, it focuses the participants and helps to structure their arguments. In the usage and analysis phases, the exchanged arguments can be consulted to better understand the current version of the model. Moreover, it allows for inconsistency detection in argumentations. Since the ontology covers all aspects of the negotiation activity, namely issue raising, formalisation of the issues, and ultimately decision making, the participants are always informed about the current status of the negotiation and the ontology they are building.

Another ontology engineering methodology that provides similar argumentation support is HCOME (Kotis *et al.*, 2004). However, they emphasise on the distributed and human-centered character of ontology engineering and user interfaces.

4.5   Integration

An important activity in context-driven OE concerns *ontology integration*. This process has been studied extensively in the literature. For a state-of-the-art survey, see Euzenat *et al.* (2004), and Kalfoglou and Schorlemmer (2005). Although different groups vary in their exact definition, ontology integration is considered to consist of four key subactivities (adopting the terminology from Kalfoglou and Schorlemmer (2005)):

1. **Mapping** and
2. **Alignment:** Given a collection of multiple contextualisations, these often need to be put in context of each other, by means of mapping or aligning (overlapping) knowledge elements pairwise.
3. **Schema articulation:** A collection of individual knowledge elements may need to be contextualised, by means of a consensual articulation schema of these (overlapping) elements.
4. **Merging:** A collection of individual knowledge elements may need to be contextualised by means of a consensual merging of these (overlapping) elements[9]. Because merging is an essential activity, we will discuss it in detail here. For mapping and alignment we refer to Chapter 6.

Merging is the activity of integrating changes that have been made in parallel to the same or related artefacts, in order to come to a new consistent system that accommodates these parallel changes. Merging is typically

---

[9] An ontology merging process requires an established articulation schema, which is the result of a successful articulation process. However, in this chapter we do not work out such relations between contextualisations.

needed in a collaborative setting, where different persons can make changes simultaneously, often without even being aware of each other's changes. An excellent survey of a wide variety of different techniques to software merging that have been proposed and used in software engineering can be found in Mens (2002).

The kind of support that is required depends on the particular architecture that is provided. In a *centralised architecture*, each user possesses its own personal working copy that needs to be synchronised from time to time with a central repository. In other words, one ontology is considered to be the central one, and changes are always made to this central ontology and propagated to its depending ontologies. This approach to ontology change management has already gained considerable attention in the research community (Klein *et al.*, 2002; Stojanovic, 2004).

In a *distributed architecture*, such as the World Wide Web, it is unrealistic to assume that there is a central ontology. Instead, each ontology can be subject to changes, which need to be propagated to all depending ontologies. This problem becomes even more complex since such changes to ontologies may be made in parallel, in which case the need arise to merge these changes. Maedche *et al.* (2003) propose a framework for managing evolution of multiple distributed ontologies. This decentralised view is also the main focus of this chapter.

Contemporary tools that support merging can be classified according to whether they support t*wo-way* or *three-way merging.* Two-way merging attempts to merge two versions of a system without relying on the common ancestor from which both versions originated. With *three-way merging*, the information in the common ancestor is also used during the integration process. This makes three-way merging more powerful than its two-way variant, in the sense that more conflicts can be detected.

Yet another distinction can be made between state-based and change-based merging. With *state-based merging,* only the information in the original version and/or its revisions is considered during the merge. In contrast, *change-based merging* additionally uses information about how the changes were performed. Compared to state-based merging, change-based merge approaches can improve detection of merge conflicts, and allow for better support to resolve these conflicts (Feather, 1989; Lippe and van Oosterom, 1992). The underlying idea is that we do not need to compare the parallel revisions entirely; it suffices to compare only the changes that have been applied to obtain each of the revisions (Edwards, 1997; Munson and Dewan, 1994).

5.   CHALLENGES

The key challenge of this chapter was to construct a single framework, based on these mechanisms, which can be tailored for the needs of a particular version environment. Therefore, we performed a comprehensive survey on all ontology evolution activities involved in both single user and collaborative ontology engineering. During our research, however, we have learned and shown that concerning the collaborative aspects, still much can be learned from other domains. This conclusion restrains us from claiming that we would have reached our goals. However, the results of our study did allow us to send a valuable message to the data and knowledge engineering community. Next, we reflect on some future challenges.

5.1   Conflict management

Meaning divergences are inevitable, and the technique of merging can be used to address and resolve their resulting conflicts. Based on the surveys of Conradi and Westfechtel (1998) and Mens (2002), it turns out that the change-based variant of merging is the most powerful. In combination with the idea of operation-based versioning, each revision between two consecutive versions is represented as a sequence of primitive change operations. Merge conflicts can thus be detected by pairwise comparison of these primitive operations that appear as part of the change sequences that need to be merged. Resolution of the conflicts can be achieved by modifying one or both change sequences (e.g., by adding or removing operations in the sequence) in such a way that the merge conflict no longer occurs.

As it turns out, the theory of graph transformation (Ehrig *et al.* 1999) provides a generic formalism to reason about such merge conflicts. Westfechtel (1991) was arguably the first to explore these ideas to support merging of "software documents," whose syntax could be expressed using a formal, tree-structured, language. In his dissertation, Tom Mens (1999, 1999b) built further on these ideas to propose graph transformation as a domain-independent formalism for software merging. In this formalism, the notion of merge conflict corresponds to the formal notion of parallel dependence, and the mechanism of critical pair analysis can be used to detect merge conflicts.

Given that the use of change-based versioning has already been suggested by Maedche *et al.* (2003) in the context of ontologies, and given that it is relatively straightforward to represent ontologies formally as a graph, the idea of graph transformation can also be applied to support evolution and merging of ontologies in a formal way. Some initial experiments that we have carried out in this direction indicate that this is indeed feasible. The idea is that the ontological metaschema (defining the syntax of a well-formed ontology) is expressed as a so-called *type graph*, and that the change operations can be expressed formally as a (sequence of) *graph transformation rules*. A formal (yet automated) dependency analysis then allows us to identify and explore potential conflicts between these change operations. For more details on how this process works, we refer to (Mens *et al.*, 2007), that details the approach in the context of software evolution.

Mens *et al.* (2006) performed a formal and static analysis of mutual exclusion relationships and causal dependencies between different alternative resolutions for model inconsistencies that can be expressed in a graph-based way. This analysis can be exploited to further improve the conflict resolution process, for example by detecting possible cycles in the resolution process, by proposing a preferred order in which to apply certain resolution rules, and so on.

5.2   Towards community-driven ontology evolution

Research in ontology engineering has reached a certain level of maturity, considering the vast number of contemporary methods and tools for formalising and applying knowledge representation models found in main-stream research. Several EU FP6 integrated projects[10] and networks of excellence[11] tested and validated these technologies in a wide variety of applications such as Semantic Web Services. However, there is still little understanding of, and technological support for, the methodological and evolutionary aspects of ontologies as resources. Yet these are crucial in distributed and collaborative settings such as the Semantic Web, where ontologies and their communities of use naturally and *mutually* co-evolve. For managing the evolution of domain vocabularies and axioms by one single dedicated user (or a small group under common authority), established techniques from data schema evolution have been successfully adopted, and consensus on a generic ontology evolution process model has begun to emerge. Much less explored, however, is the problem of operational evolution of inter-organisational or community-shared, yet autonomously maintained ontologies.

There are many additional complexities that should be considered. As investigated in FP6 integrated projects on collaborative networked organisations[12], the different professional, social, and cultural backgrounds among communities and organisations can lead to misconceptions, leading

---

[10] e.g., http://www.sekt-project.com, http://dip.semanticweb.org
[11] e.g., http://knowledgeweb.semanticweb.org
[12] e.g., http://ecolead.vtt.fi/

to frustrating and costly ambiguities and misunderstandings if not aligned properly. This is especially the case in inter-organisational settings, where there may be many pre-existing organisational sub-ontologies, inflexible data schemas interfacing to legacy data, and ill-defined, rapidly evolving collaborative requirements. Furthermore, participating stakeholders usually have strong individual interests, inherent business rules, and entrenched work practices. These may be tacit, or externalised in workflows that are strongly interdependent, hence further complicate the conceptual alignment. Finally, one should not merely focus on the practice of creating ontologies in a project-like context, but view it as a continuous process that is integrated in the operational processes of the community. The shared background of communication partners is continuously negotiated as are the characteristics or values of the concepts that are agreed upon.

Modelling of communities: Successful virtual communities and communities of stakeholders are usually self-organising. The knowledge creation and sharing process is driven by implicit community goals such as mutual concerns and interests. Hence, in order to better capture relevant knowledge in a *community-goal-driven* way, these community goals must be externalised appropriately. They may then be linked to relevant *strategies* underlying the collaborative ontology engineering process and its support. This requires us to model communities completely (i.e., establish their formal semantics) in terms of their intrinsic aspects such as *goals, actors, roles, strategies, workflows, norms*, and *behaviour*, and to so integrate the concept of community as first-class citizen in the knowledge structures of the evolving system. This *holistic* approach is breaking with current practice, where systems are usually reduced to only the non-human parts, with the possible exception of the field of *organisational semiotics* that already involved a few socio-technical aspects of communities such as norms and behaviour in information system specification.

These rapidly evolving community aspects, and the many dependencies they have with the actual knowledge *artefacts* in the knowledge structures, lead to knowledge structures that can be extremely volatile. Hence, research into a special-purpose, disciplined and comprehensive framework will be needed to address the manageable evolution of knowledge structures, taking into account crucial issues such as versioning, dependency management, consistency maintenance, impact analysis, change propagation, trend detection and traceability while respecting the autonomous yet self-organising drives inherent in the community.

Knowledge divergence: Given the diversity of knowledge domains that need to be accommodated, a viable ontology engineering methodology should not be based on a single, monolithic domain ontology maintained by a single knowledge engineer, but should instead support multiple domain experts in the gradual and continuous building and managing of increasingly mature versions of ontological artefacts, and of their diverging and converging interrelationships. Contexts are necessary to formalise and reason about the structure, interdependencies, and evolution of these ontologies, thus keeping their complexity manageable. As already mentioned, the *socio-technical* aspects of the ontology engineering process in complex and dynamic realistic settings are still poorly understood, and introduce new problems in ontology evolution that where so far not described and studied in an integrated fashion. A conceptualisation and unification of the socio-technical aspects of the involved communities, such as the community goals, should drive the continuous evolution (divergence and convergence) of knowledge structures.

Community-grounded negotiation: For defining valuable knowledge structures, a complex socio-technical process of *ontology alignment* and *meaning negotiation* is required. Furthermore, sometimes it is not necessary (or even possible) to achieve context-independent ontological knowledge, as most ontologies used in practice assume a certain professional, social, and cultural perspective of some community.

It is especially interesting to contrast the meaning negotiations with ontology-based business negotiations. Such negotiations enable the negotiators to set an agenda that can be dynamically adapted and to define and clarify terms that are used and concepts of a negotiation ontology used in the negotiation messages and the resulting business contract. Meaning is thus also defined but has a more economically-oriented character.

Human-computer confluence: In general, dynamic communities require tools and systems for interaction and exchange. On the one hand, computer-supported cooperative work (CSCW) aims at supporting groups in their cooperation and collaboration. On the other hand, the ontology engineering within communities requires a different type of system support. Both types need to be integrated into a holistic knowledge-intensive system, of which humans are part, to be both useful for and useable by such dynamic communities.

Humans play an important role in the interpretation and analysis of meaning during the elicitation and application of knowledge. Consider for example the crucial process of externalising subjective tacit knowledge into formal knowledge artefacts, or the iterative incremental process of inconsistency resolution through negotiation. Instead of being frustrated by out-of-control evolution processes, adequate management support for co-evolving (inter-dependent) knowledge structures with their communities of use will allow human experts to focus on these much more interesting "community-grounded" processes of realising the *appropriate* amount of consensus on *relevant* conceptual definitions through *effective* meaning negotiation in an *efficient* manner.

Clearly, many of these processes are intrinsically interactive in nature and require a lot of human intervention. This does not mean, however, that we should rule out other approaches that are fully automated. A careful balance and communication is needed between human, semi-automatic (i.e. requiring human interaction) and automatic approaches for knowledge interpretation and analysis processes. Ultimately, communities will consist of a mix of human and software agents that transparently will communicate and request services from each other in order to maintain the shared knowledge structures appropriately.

Impact analysis: Moving this process and its associated knowledge forward into *real-time* co-evolving, in order to respond to the continuously shifting collaboration requirements, is an additional hard problem. This requires us to be able to analyse the impact the changes will have on the actual situation governed by inherent business rules and entrenched work practices.

6. SOFTWARE AND TOOLS

Although a plethora of ontology engineering tools are available, most of them still lack full support for all activities in the single user ontology evolution process model from Sect 2.2. In this section we give a short overview of state-of-the-art ontology evolution tools. For these tools, we also explore their support for collaborative development.

6.1 Protégé tool suite

Protégé is a free, open source ontology editor and knowledge-base framework. It supports two main ways of modelling ontologies via the Protégé-Frames (based on OKBC (Chaudhri *et al.*, 1998)) and Protégé-OWL editors. Furthermore, Protégé ontologies can be exported into a variety of formats including RDF(S), OWL, and XML Schema. The implementation is based on Java, and provides a plug-and-play environment that makes it a flexible base for rapid prototyping and application development. Plessers (2006) provides plug-ins supporting versioning, change detection and inconsistency checking. Diaz (2005) developed a plugin that supports evolution activities in a collaborative setting.

6.2   KAON

The KAON[13] tool suite is a workbench integrating different tools for different ontology engineering activities. It uses the Ontology Instance KR model, or *OI-model*. The evolution facilities in KAON are basically the implementation of the work proposed in (Stojanovic, 2004) and (Maedche *et al.*, 2003), including following features:

- **Change representation,** including complex and compound change operators.
- **Configurable evolution strategies:** Users are allowed to set up preferences for ontology evolution strategies. When the user requests a change, the tool presents details to the user for approval. The change request could generate a cascade of changes based on the defined evolution strategies in order to maintain the consistency of the ontology. The KAON API also computes sequences of additional changes when it is necessary to maintain the consistency of an ontology after performing a modification. It also provides the necessary interfaces to provide access to this functionality from external applications (Gabel *et al.*, 2004).
- **Dependent ontology evolution** is intended to support distributed ontology engineering, where ontology reuse through extension is motivated, which results in many dependencies that lead to significant changes to all dependent artefacts.

Currently, KAON does not support versioning identification and storage. It also does not provide facilities to assure backward compatibility.

6.3   WSMO Studio

WSMO Studio is Semantic Web Service modelling environment for the Web Service Modeling Ontology (Roman *et al.*, 2005). It includes the Ontology Management Suite[14] which supports the management of Web Services Modeling Language (WSML) ontologies (de Bruijn *et al.*, 2006). The featured single user WSML ontology versioning tool (De Leenheer *et al.*, 2006) has the following features:

- **Ontology versioning API:** This API allows the user to start a new version of an ontology, to go back to the previous version, and to commit (finalise) a version. Further, the user of this API has full control

---

[13] http://kaon.semanticweb.org/
[14] http://www.omwg.org/tools/dip/oms/

over the version identifier of a committed version. Versions are persistently stored in triple stores[15], the latter for which the interface is facilitated through the ORDI (Kiryakov *et al.*, 2002) repository middleware.

- **Formulating change requests:** In order to enable Semantic Web Services in performing their goals, requests for defining new semantics can be published. This is supported by an on-line auditing and reporting tool.

- **Version identification and metadata:** The API contains interfaces and classes for versioned WSMO API identifiers, and for version metadata containing version comment, date of creation, etc.

- **Version change log functionality:** During the creation of a new version, the significant changes are logged and when a version is committed, this change log is available to the application.

- **Partial version mapping:** From the change log a partial mapping is generated for mediation between the old and the new version. This partial mapping is an input to a human designer who can complete it as appropriate.

- **Alternative evolution strategies:** A wizard guides the user through resolving the impact of changes like concept removal, whose instances and subconcepts can be handled in different ways depending on the intent of the change.

6.4 DOGMA Studio

DOGMA[16] Studio is the tool suite behind the DOGMA ontology engineering approach (Spyns *et al.*, 2002, De Leenheer *et al.*, 2007). It contains both a Workbench and a Server. The Workbench is constructed according to the plug-in architecture in Eclipse. There, plug-ins, being loosely coupled ontology viewing, querying or editing modules support the different ontology engineering activities and new plug-ins continuously emerge. This loose coupling allows any arbitrary knowledge engineering community to support its own ontology engineering method in DOGMA Studio by combining these plug-ins arbitrarily. Such a meaningful combination of view/edit/query plug-ins is called a "perspective" in Eclipse. The DOGMA Server is an advanced J2EE application running in a JBoss server which efficiently stores Lexons and Commitments in a PostgreSQL Database. DOGMA Studio is complemented by a community layer in which the DOGMA collaborative ontology engineering processes are grounded in

---

[15] triple stores are databases for (meta-)data that are expressed in triples characterised by three elements, viz. object, property, subject
[16] http://starlab.vub.ac.be/website/dogmastudio

communities of use. This layer is implemented by the DOGMA-MESS[17] methodology and system. For an in-depth elaboration on DOGMA studio and -MESS in the context of a business use case, we refer to Chapter 12.

ADDITIONAL READING

Model driven architecture and ontology development: Defining a formal domain ontology is generally considered a useful, not to say necessary step in almost every software project. This is because software deals with ideas rather than with self-evident physical artefacts. However, this development step is hardly ever done, as ontologies rely on well-defined and semantically powerful AI concepts such as description logics or rule-based systems, and most software engineers are largely unfamiliar with these. Gašević *et al.* (2006) tries to fill this gap by covering the subject of MDA application for ontology development on the Semantic Web.

Software evolution: As repeatedly mentioned in this chapter, ontology evolution has many relationships and overlaps with software evolution research. Madhavji *et al.* (2006) explore what software evolution is and why it is inevitable. They address the phenomenological and technological underpinnings of software evolution, and it explain the role of feedback in software maintenance. Mens and Demeyer (2007) present the state-of-the-art and emerging topics in software evolution research.

ACKNOWLEDGMENTS

We would like to thank our colleagues Robert Meersman and Stijn Christiaens in Brussels for the valuable discussions about theory and case, and for reviewing the text during the preparation of this document.

REFERENCES

Andany, J., Léonard, M., and Palisser, C. (1991) Management of Schema Evolution in Databases. In Proc. of the 17th Int'l Conf. on Very Large Data Bases (Barcelona, Spain), Morgan-Kaufmann, pp. 161–170

Aschoff, F.R., Schmalhofer, F., van Elst, L. (2004) Knowledge mediation: A procedure for the cooperative construction of domain ontologies. In Proc. of Workshop on Agent-Mediated Knowledge Management at the 16th European Conference on Artificial Intelligence (ECAI'2004) (Valencia, Spain), pp. 20–28

---

[17] http://www.dogma-mess.org

Bachimont, B., Troncy, R., Isaac, A. (2002) Semantic commitment for designing ontologies: a proposal. In Gómez-Pérez, A., Richard Benjamins, V., eds.: Proc. of the 13th Int'l Conf. on Knowledge Engineering and Knowledge Management. Ontologies and the SemanticWeb (EKAW 2002) (Siguenza, Spain), Springer Verlag, pp. 114–121

Banerjee, J., Kim, W. Kim, H., and Korth., H. (1987) Semantics and implementation of schema evolution in object-oriented databases. Proc. ACM SIGMOD Conf. Management of Data, 16(3), pp. 311–322

Bennett, K. and Rajlich, V. (2000) Software Maintenance and Evolution: A Roadmap. In: Finkelstein, A. (ed.) The Future of Sotware Engineering, Finkelstein, ACM Press.

Boehm, B. W. (1988). A spiral model of software development and enhancement. IEEE Computer 21(5), IEEE Computer Society Press, pp. 61–72

Bouaud, J., Bachimont, B., Charlet, J., and Zweigenbaum, P. (1995) Methodological Principles for Structuring an "Ontology." In Proc. IJCAI95 Workshop on Basic Ontological Issues in Knowledge Sharing" (Montreal, Canada)

Bohner, S. and Arnold, R. (1996) Software change impact analysis. IEEE Computer Society Press

Brachman, R., McGuiness, D., Patel-Schneider, P., Resnik, L., and Borgida, A. (1991) Living with classic: When and how to use a KL-ONE-like language. In Sowa, J., ed.: Principles of Semantic Networks, Morgan Kaufmann, pp. 401–456

Chikofsky, E.J. and Cross, J.H. (1990) Reverse engineering and design recovery: A taxonomy. IEEE Software 7(1), pp. 13–17

Chaudhri, V.K., Farquhar, A., Fikes, R., Karp, P.D, and Rice, J.P. (1998) OKBC: A Programmatic Foundation for Knowledge Base Interoperability. In Proc. AAAI'98 Conference (Madison, WI), AAAI Press

Clarke, E.M., Grumberg, O., and Peled, D.A. (2000) Model Checking, MIT Press.

Codd, E. (1972) Further Normalisation of the Database Relational Model. In Rustin, R. (ed.) Database Systems, Prentice-Hall, pp. 33–74

Conradi, R. and Westfechtel, B. (1998) Version Models for Software Configuration Management. ACM Computing Surveys 30(2): 232–282

de Bruijn, J., Lausen, H., Pollares, A., and Fensel, D. (2006) The Web Service Modeling Language WSML: An Overview. In Proc. 3rd European Semantic Web Conference (ESWC 2006). LNCS 4011, Springer

De Leenheer, P. (2004) Revising and Managing Multiple Ontology Versions in a Possible Worlds Setting. In Proc. On The Move to Meaningful Internet Systems Ph.D. Symposium (OTM 2004) (Agia Napa, Cyprus), LNCS 3292, Springer-Verlag, pp. 798–818

De Leenheer, P., de Moor, A. (2005) Context-driven disambiguation in ontology elicitation. In Shvaiko, P., Euzenat, J., eds.: Context and Ontologies: Theory, Practice, and Applications. Proc. 1st Context and Ontologies Workshop, AAAI/IAAI 2005 (Pittsburgh, USA), pp. 17–24

De Leenheer, P., de Moor, A., and Meersman, R. (2007) Context Dependency Management in Ontology Engineering: a Formal Approach. Journal on Data Semantics VIII, LNCS 4380, Springer-Verlag, pp. 26–56

De Leenheer, P., Kopecky, J., Sharf, E., and de Moor, A. (2006) A Versioning Tool for Ontologies. DIP EU Project (FP6-507483) WP2: Ontology Management, Deliverable nr. D2.4

de Moor, A. (2002) Language/action meets organisational semiotics: Situating conversations with norms. Information Systems Frontiers, 4(3):257–272

de Moor, A. (2005) Ontology-guided meaning negotiation in communities of practice. In Mambrey, P., Gräther, W., eds.: Proc. Workshop on the Design for Large-Scale Digital Communities, 2nd Int'l Conf. Communities and Technologies (C&T 2005) (Milano, Italy) de Moor, A., De Leenheer, P., and Meersman, R. (2006) DOGMA-MESS: A meaning evolution support system for interorganisational ontology engineering. In Proc. 14th Int'l Conf. Conceptual Structures (ICCS 2006) (Aalborg, Denmark), LNAI 4068, Springer Verlag, pp 189–203

de Moor, A. and Weigand, H. (2007) Formalizing the evolution of virtual communities. Inf. Syst., 32(2):223–247

De Troyer, O. (1993) On Data Schema Transformation, PhD Thesis, University of Tilburg, Tilburg, The Netherlands.

Diaz, A. (2005) Supporting Divergences in Knowledge Sharing Communities. PhD Thesis, Univesité Henry Poincarè, Nancy I, France.

Edwards, W.K. (1997) Flexible Conflict Detection and Management in Collaborative Applications, Proc. Symp. User Interface Software and Technology, ACM Press

Ehrig, H., Kreowski, H.-J., Montanari, U., and Rozenberg G. (1999) Handbook of Graph Grammars and Computing by Graph Transformation, Volume 3, World Scientific

Euzenat, J., Le Bach, T., Barrasa, J., et al. (2004) State of the art on ontology alignment. Knowledge Web deliverable KWEB/2004/d2.2.3/v1.2

Feather, M.S. (1998) "Detecting Interference when Merging Specification Evolutions," Proc. 5th Int'l Workshop Software Specification and Design, ACM Press, pp. 169–176.

Fellbaum, C., ed. (1998) Wordnet, an Electronic Lexical Database. MIT Press

Franconi, E., Grandi, F., and Mandreoli, F. (2000) A Semantic Approach for Schema Evolution and Versioning in Object-oriented Databases. In Proc. 6th Int'l Conf. Rules and Objects in Databases (DOOD 2000) (London, UK), Springer-Verlag, pp. 1048–1060

Fogel, K. and Bar, M. (2001) Open Source Development with CVS. The Coriolis Group, 2nd edition

Gabel, T., Sure, Y., and Voelker, J. (2004) KAON — Ontology Management Infrastructure. SEKT deliverable D3.1.1.a

Gaševic, D., Djuric, D., and Devedžic, V. (2006) Model Driven Architecture and Ontology Development, Springer

Gómez-Pérez, A., Manzano-Macho, D. (2003) A survey of ontology learning methods and techniques.OntoWeb Deliverable D1.5

Gray, J. (1981). The transaction concept: Virtues and limitations. Proc. 7th Int'l Conf. Very Large Data Bases, pp. 144–154

Gruber, T.R. (1993) A translation approach to portable ontologies. Knowledge Acquisition 5(2):199–220

Guarino, N. (1998) Formal Ontology and Information Systems. In Guarino, N. (ed.), Proc. 1st Int'l Conf. Formal Ontologies in Information Systems (FOIS98) (Trento, Italy), pp. 3-- 15, IOS Press

Haase, P., Sure, Y., and Vrandečić, D. (2004) Ontology Management and Evolution: Survey, Methods, and Prototypes. SEKT Deliverable D3.1.1

Haase, P. and Stojanovic, P. (2005) Consistent evolution of OWL ontologies. Proc. 2nd European Conf. Semantic Web: Research and Applications. LNCS 3532, Springer, pp. 182–197

Halpin, T. (2001) Information Modeling and Relational Databases (From Conceptual Analysis to Logical Design). Morgan Kauffman

Heflin, J. (2001) Towards the SemanticWeb: Knowledge Representation in a Dynamic, Distributed Environment. PhD thesis, University of Maryland, Collega Park, MD, USA

Hepp, M., Van Damme, C., and Siorpaes, K. (2007) Folksontology: An integrated approach for turning folksonomies into ontologies. In Proc. of the ESWC Workshop "Bridging the Gap between Semantic Web and Web 2.0" (Innsbruck, Austria). Springer

Hepp, M. (2007) Possible Ontologies: How Reality Constrains the Development of Relevant Ontologies. In Internet Computing 11(1):90–96

Holsapple, C., and Joshi, K. (2002) Collaborative Approach in Ontology Design, Communications of the ACM 45(2), ACM Press, pp. 42–47

Hunt, J. W., McIllroy, M.D. (1976) An Algorithm for Differential File Comparison, Technical Report 41, AT&T Bell Laboratories Inc.

Jackson, D., and Ladd, D. A. (1994) Semantic Diff: A tool for summarizing the effects of modifications. In Proc. Of the Int'l Conf. on Software Maintenance (ICSM), pp. 243–252, IEEE Computer Society

Jarrar, M., Demey, J., Meersman, R. (2003) On reusing conceptual data modeling for ontology engineering. Journal on Data Semantics 1(1):185–207

Jarrar, M. (2006) Position paper: towards the notion of gloss, and the adoption of linguistic resources in formal ontology engineering. In Proc WWW 2006. ACM Press, pp. 497–503

Kalfoglou, Y., Schorlemmer, M. (2005) Ontology mapping: The state of the art. In Proc. Dagstuhl Seminar on Semantic Interoperability and Integration (Dagstuhl, Germany).

Katz, R.H. (1990) Toward a Unified Framework for Version Modeling in Engineering Databases. ACM Computing Surveys 22(4):375–408, ACM Press

Kim, W. and Chou, H. (1988) Versions of Schema for Object-oriented Databases. In Proc. 14th Int'l Conf. Very Large Data Bases (VLDB88) (L.A., CA.), Morgan Kaufmann. pp. 148–159

Kiryakov, A., Ognyanov, D., and Kirov, V. (2004) A Framework for Representing Ontologies Consisting of Several Thousand Concepts Definitions. DIP Project Deliverable D2.2.

Klein, M., Kiryakov, A., Ognyanov, D., and Fensel, D. (2002) Ontology Versioning and Change Detection on the Web. Proc. 13th European Conf. Knowledge Engineering and Knowledge Management, pp. 192–212

Klein, M. and Noy, N. (2003) A Component-based Framework for Ontology Evolution. In Proc. Workshop on Ontologies and Distributed Systems, IJCAI 2003 (Acapulco, Mexico).

Klein, M. (2004) Change Management for Distributed Ontologies. PhD Thesis, Vrije Universiteit Amsterdam, Amsterdam, The Netherlands

Kotis, K., Vouros, G.A., Alonso, J.P. (2004) HCOME: tool-supported methodology for collaboratively devising living ontologies. In Proc. of the 2nd Int'l Workshop on Semantic Web and Databases (SWDB 2004), Springer

Kunz, W., Rittel, H.W.J. (1970) Issues as elements of information systems. Working Paper 131, Institute of Urban and Regional Development, University of California

Lerner, B. and Habermann, A. (1990) Beyond Schema Evolution to Database Reorganization. In Proc. Joint ACM OOPSLA/ECOOP 90 Conf. Object-Oriented Programming: Systems, Languages, and Applications (Ottawa, Canada), ACM Press, pp. 67–76.

Lerner, B. (2000) A model for compound type changes encountered in schema evolution. ACM Transactions on Database Systems (TODS), 25(1):83{127, ACM Press, New York, NY, USA.

Lippe, E. and van Oosterom, N. (1992) Operation-Based Merging. In Proc. 5th ACM SIGSOFT Symp. Software Development Environments, ACM SIGSOFT Software Engineering Notes, Vol. 17, No. 5, pp. 78–87.

Littlejohn, S.W. (1992) Theories of human communication (4th ed.). Belmont, CA: Wadsworth Publishing Company

Madhavji, N.H.,, Fernandez-Ramil, J. and Perry, D.E. (2006) Software evolution and feedback: Theory and practice. Wiley

Maedche, A., Motik, B. and Stojanovic, L. (2003) Managing multiple and distributed ontologies on the Semantic Web. VLDB Journal 12, Springer, pp. 286–302

McCarthy, J. (1993) Notes on formalizing context. In Proc. 15th Int'l Joint Conf. Artificial Intelligence (IJCAI93) (Chambry, France), 555–560. Morgan Kaufmann.

Meersman, R. (1999) The use of lexicons and other computer-linguistic tools in semantics, design and cooperation of database systems. In Proc. Conf. Cooperative Database Systems (CODAS99), Springer Verlag, pp. 1–14.

Mens, T. (1999) Conditional Graph Rewriting as a Domain-Independent Formalism for Software Evolution. Proc. Int'l Conf. Agtive 1999: Applications of Graph Transformations with Industrial Relevance. Lecture Notes in Computer Science 1779, Springer-Verlag, pp. 127–143

Mens, T. (1999) A Formal Foundation for Object-Oriented Software Evolution. PhD Thesis, Department of Computer Science, Vrije Universiteit Brussel, Belgium

Mens, T. (2002) A State-of-the-Art Survey on Software Merging. Transactions on Software Engineering 28(5): 449–462, IEEE Computer Society Press

Mens, T., Van Der Straeten, R., and D'hondt, M. (2006) Detecting and resolving model inconsistencies using transformation dependency analysis. In Proc. Int'l Conf. MoDELS/UML 2006, LNCS 4199, Springer, pp. 200–214

Mens, T., Taentzer, G., and Runge, O. (2007) Analyzing Refactoring Dependencies Using Graph Transformation. Journal on Software and Systems Modeling, September, Springer, pp. 269–285

Mens, T. and Demeyer, S. (2007) Software Evolution. Springer

Munson, J.P. and Dewan, P. (1994) A flexible object merging framework. In Proc. ACM Conf. Computer Supported Collaborative Work, ACM Press, pp. 231–241

Nguyen, G. and Rieu, D. (1989) Schema Evolution in Object-Oriented Database Systems. Data and Knowledge Engineering 4(1):43–67

Nonaka, I. and Takeuchi,, H. (1995) The Knowledge-Creating Company : How Japanese Companies Create the Dynamics of Innovation. Oxford University Press

Noy, N.F., Klein, M.: Ontology evolution: Not the same as schema evolution. Knowledge and Information Systems 6(4) (2004) 428–440

Noy, N.F. and Musen, M. A. (2002). PromptDiff: A Fixed-Point Algorithm for Comparing Ontology Versions. In the Proc. 18th National Conf. Artificial Intelligence (AAAI–2002) (Edmonton, Alberta), AAAI Press

Nuseibeh, B., Easterbrook, S., and Russo, A. (2000) Leveraging inconsistency in software development. IEEE Computer, 33(4):24–29

Oliver, D., Shahar, Y., Musen, M., Shortliffe, E. (1999) Representation of change in controlled medical terminologies. AI in Medicine 15(1):53–76

Parsia, B., Sirin, E., and Kalyanpur, A. (2005) Debugging OWL ontologies. Proc. 14th Int'l Conf. World Wide Web, ACM Press, pp. 633–640

Penney, D. and Stein, J. (1987) Class Modification in the GemStone Object-oriented DBMS. In Proc. Int'l Conf. Object-Oriented Programming Systems, Languages, and Applications (OOPSLA) (Orlando, FL), pp. 111–117.

Peters, R. and Özsu, M. (1997) An Axiomatic Model of Dynamic Schema Evolution in Objectbase Systems. ACM Transactions on Database Systems 22(1):75–114.

Plessers, P. and De Troyer, O. (2006) Resolving Inconsistencies in Evolving Ontologies. In Proc. 3rd European Semantic Web Conference (ESWC 2006), Springer, pp. 200–214

Plessers, P. (2006) An Approach to Web-based Ontology Evolution. PhD Thesis, Department of Computer Science, Vrije Universiteit Brussel, Brussel, Belgium

Proper, H.A. and Halpin, T.A. (1998) Conceptual Schema Optimisation: Database Optimisation before sliding down the Waterfall. Technical Report 341, Department of Computer Science, University of Queensland, Australia

Putnam, L. and Poole, M. (1987) Conflict and Negotiation. In Porter, L. (ed.) Handbook of Organizational Communication: an Interdisciplinary Perspective, pp. 549–599, Newbury Park: Sage

Ra, Y. and Rundensteiner, E. (1997) A Transparant Schema-evolution System Based on Object-oriented view technology. IEEE Trans. of Knowledge and Data Engineering, 9(4):600–623

Rajlich, V. (1997) A model for change propagation based on graph rewriting. Proc. Int'l Conf. Software Maintenance, IEEE Computer Society Press, pp. 84–91

Ramil, J. F. (2003) Continual Resource Estimation for Evolving Software. PhD Thesis, Department of Computing, Imperial College, London, United Kingdom

Reinberger, M.L., Spyns, P. (2005) Unsupervised text mining for the learning of DOGMA-inspired ontologies. In: Buitelaar P., Handschuh S., and Magnini B.,(eds.), Ontology Learning and Population, IOS Press

Roddick, J., Craske, N., and Richards, T. (1993) A Taxonomy for Schema Versioning Based on the Relational and Entity Relationship Models, In Proc. the 12th Int'l Conf. on Conceptual Modeling / the Entity Relationship Approach (Dallas, TX), Springer, pp 143–154

Roddick, J. (1995) A Survey of Schema Versioning Issues for Database Systems, in Information and Software Technology 37(7):383–393

Roman, D., Keller, U., Lausen, H., de Bruijn, J., Lara, R., Stollberg, M., Polleres, A., Feier, C., Bussler, C., and Fensel, D. (2005) Web Service Modeling Ontology. In Journal of Applied Ontology 1(1):77–106, IOS Press

Sanderson, D. (1994) Cooperative and collaborative mediated research. In Harrison, T. and Stephen, T. (eds.) Computer networking and scholarly communication in the twenty-first century, State University of New York Press, pp. 95–114

Skarra, A.H. and Zdonik, S.B. (1986) The Management of Changing Types in an Object-oriented Database. In Proc. Int'l Conf. on Object-Oriented Programming Systems, Languages, and Applications (OOPSLA 1986) (Portland, Oregon), pp. 483–495

Sneed, H. (1995) Estimating the Costs of Software Maintenance Tasks. In Proc. Int'l Conf. Sotware Maintenance (ICSM), pp. 168–181

Sowa, J. (1984) Conceptual Structures: Information Processing in Mind and Machine. Addison-Wesley

Schoop, M., de Moor, A., Dietz, J. (2006) The pragmatic web: A manifesto. Communications of the ACM 49(5)

Simperl, E., Tempich, C., and Mochol, M. (2007) Cost estimation for ontology development: applying the ONTOCOM model. In Abramowicz, W. and Mayr, H. Technologies for Business Information Systems, Springer, pp. 327–339

Spanoudakis, G. and Zisman, A. (2001) Inconsistency management in software engineering: Survey and open research issues. Handbook of software engineering and knowledge engineering, World Scientific, pp. 329–390

Spyns, P., Meersman, R., Jarrar, M. (2002) Data modelling versus ontology engineering. SIGMODRecord 31(4):12–17

Stamper, R. (1992) Linguistic Instruments in Knowledge Engineering, chapter Language and Computing in Organised Behaviour, Elsevier Science Publishers, pp. 143–163

Stojanovic, L., Maedche, A., Motik, B., and Stojanovic, N. (2002) User-driven ontology evolution management. Proc. 13th European Conf. Knowledge Engineering and Knowledge Management. pp. 285–300

Stojanovic, L. (2004) Methods and tools for ontology evolution. PhD Thesis, University of Karlsruhe, Karlsruhe, Germany

Tempich, C., Pinto, S., Sure, Y., and Staab, S. (2005) An Argumentation Ontology for Distributed, Loosely-controlled and evolving Engineering processes of ontologies . In Proc. of the 2nd European Semantic Web Conference (ESWC, 2005), LNCS 3532, Springer, pp. 241–256

Verheijen, G., Van Bekkum, J. (1982) NIAM, an information analysis method. In: Proc. IFIP TC-8 Conf. Comparative Review of Information System Methodologies (CRIS 82), North-Holland

Wang, H., Horridge, M., Rector, A., Drummond, N., and Seidenberg, J. (2005) Debugging OWL-DL ontologies: A heuristic approach. Proc. 4th Int'l Conf. Semantic Web. Springer-Verlag

Westfechtel, B. (1991) Structure-Oriented Merging of Revisions of Software Documents. Proc. Int'l Workshop on Software Configuration Management. ACM Press, pp. 68–79

Chapter 6

ONTOLOGY ALIGNMENTS
An Ontology Management Perspective

Jérôme Euzenat[1], Adrian Mocan[2], and François Scharffe[2]

[1]*INRIA Rhône-Alpes & LIG, 655 avenue de l'Europe, F-38330 Montbonnot Saint-Martin, France, Jerome.Euzenat@inrialpes.fr;* [2]*Innsbruck Universität, 21a Technikerstrasse, A-6020 Innsbruck, Austria, Adrian.Mocan@deri.at, Francois.Scharffe@deri.at*

Abstract: Relating ontologies is very important for many ontology-based applications and more important in open environments like the Semantic Web. The relations between ontology entities can be obtained by ontology matching and represented as alignments. Hence, alignments must be taken into account in ontology management. This chapter establishes the requirements for alignment management. After a brief introduction to matching and alignments, we justify the consideration of alignments as independent entities and provide the lifecycle of alignments. We describe the important functions of editing, managing and exploiting alignments and illustrate them with existing components.

Key words: alignment management; alignment server; mapping; ontology alignment; ontology matching; ontology mediation

1.   RELATING ONTOLOGIES: FROM ONTOLOGY ISLANDS TO CONTINENT

In many applications, ontologies are not used in isolation. This can be because several ontologies, representing different domains have to be used within the same application, e.g., an ontology of books with an ontology of shipping for an on-line bookstore, or because different ontologies are encountered dynamically, e.g., different ontologies from different on-line bookstores to choose from.

These ontologies must be related together for the ontology-based application to work properly. In the context of ontology management, these relations may be used for composing at design time the different ontology parts that will be used by the applications (either by merging these ontologies or by designing data integration mechanisms), for dealing with different versions of ontologies that may be found together at design time, or for anticipating the need for dynamically matching encountered ontologies at run time.

We call "ontology matching" the process of finding the relations between ontologies and we call alignment the result of this process expressing declaratively these relations.

In an open world in which ontologies evolve, managing ontologies requires using alignments for expressing the relations between ontologies. We have defended elsewhere the idea that for that purpose the use of alignments is preferable to using directly mediators or transformations (Euzenat, 2005). We go one step further here by proposing that ontology management involves alignment management.

In the remainder we first briefly present what ontology matching is and where it is used (Section 2). Then, we consider some requirements and functions for alignment management addressing the alignment lifecycle (Section 3). Following this lifecycle we present in more details how to address these requirements in what concerns alignment editing (Section 4), alignment storing and sharing (Section 5) and finally alignment processing (Section 6). We then consider existing systems that feature to some extent ontology management capabilities (Section 7).

2.   ONTOLOGY MATCHING AND ALIGNMENTS

We present in deeper details what is meant by an alignment and provide some vocabulary as it will be used in this chapter (Section 2.1). Then we discuss the different applications that can take advantage of matching ontologies (Section 2.2). We identify some characteristics of these applications in terms of exploitation of the alignments. Finally, we provide an overview of the various matching techniques available (Section 2.3). Complete coverage of these issues can be found in (Euzenat and Shvaiko, 2007).

When we talk about ontologies, we include database schemas and other extensional descriptions of data which benefit from matching as well.

2.1   Alignments for expressing relations

The ontology matching problem may be described in one sentence: given two ontologies each describing a set of discrete entities (which can be classes, properties, rules, predicates, or even formulas), find the correspondences, e.g., equivalence or subsumption, holding between these entities. This set of correspondences is called an alignment.

Given two ontologies o and o', alignments are made of a set of correspondences (called mappings when the relation is oriented) between (simple or complex) entities belonging to o and o' respectively. A correspondence is described as a quadruple $<e, e', r, n>$ such that:

- e and e' are the entities, e.g., formulas, terms, classes, individuals, between which a relation is asserted by the correspondence.
- r is the relation declared to hold between e and e' by the correspondence. This relation can be a simple set-theoretic relation (applied to entities seen as sets or their interpretation seen as sets), a fuzzy relation, a probabilistic distribution over a complete set of relations, a similarity measure, etc.
- n is a degree of confidence associated with that correspondence (this degree does not refer to the relation r, it is rather a measure of the trust in the fact that the correspondence is appropriate — "I trust 70% the fact that the correspondence is correct, reliable, etc." — and can be compared with the certainty measures provided by meteorological agencies). The trust degree can be computed in many ways, including user feedback or log analysis.

So, the simplest kind of correspondence (level 0) is:

$$URI_1 = URI_2$$

while a more elaborate one could be:

$$employee(x,y,z) <=_{.85} empno(x,w) \ \& \ name_3(w,concat(y,'\ ',z))$$

The first one expresses the equivalence ($=$) of what is denoted by two URIs (with full confidence). These URI can be the denotations of classes, properties or instances. The second one is a Horn-clause expressing that if there exists a w such that $empno(x,w)$ — w's identifier is x — and $name(w,concat(y,'\ ',z))$ — the name of w is the result of the concatenation of string y, '$\ $' and z — are true in one ontology then $employee(x,y,z)$ must be true in the other one (and the confidence is here quantified with a degree equal to .85). Of course, in this last example, functions and predicates can also be identified by URIs.

As can be observed from these two examples, alignments in themselves are not tied to a particular language. But in order to use complex alignments like the second one, systems must be able to understand the language in which formulas and relations are expressed. This is supported through the definition of a particular subtype of alignment.

Since everyone does not share the same terminology, we define below, according to (Euzenat and Shvaiko, 2007), the various terms used in this chapter:

- **alignment** is the result of the matching task: it is a set of correspondences;
- **bridge** axioms are formulas in an ontology language that expresses the relations as assertions on the related entities. They are used when merging ontologies.
- **correspondence** is the relation holding (or supposed to hold according to a particular matching algorithm or individual) between two entities of different ontologies. These entities can be as different as classes, individuals, properties or formulas. Some authors use the term "mapping" or "mapping rule" that will not be used here;
- **matching** is the task of comparing two ontologies and finding the relationships between them;
- **mediator** a mediator is a software module (Wiederhold, 1992), providing interoperability between heterogeneous knowledge sources. In query application it is a dual pair of translations that transforms the query from one ontology to another and that translate the answer back.
- **merging** ontologies consists of creating a new ontology out of two or more ontologies. Ontology merging first involves the definition of an alignment between the ontologies to be merged.
- **transformation** is a program that transforms an ontology from one ontology expression language to another;
- **translation** is a program that transforms formulas with regard to some ontology into formulas with regard to another ontology (translation can be implemented by a set of translation rules, an XSLT stylesheet or a more classical program).

2.2   Applications

Several classes of applications can be considered (they are more extensively described in (Euzenat and Shvaiko, 2007), we only summarize them here). They are the following:

---

[1] http://www.foaf-project.org
[2] http://www.w3.org/TR/vcard-rdf

- **Ontology evolution** uses matching for finding the changes that have occurred between two ontology versions. See Chapter 5 of this book.
- **Schema integration** uses matching for integrating the schemas of different databases under a single view;
- **Catalog integration** uses matching for offering an integrated access to on-line catalogs;
- **Data integration** uses matching for integrating the content of different databases under a single database;
- **P2P information sharing** uses matching for finding the relations between ontologies used by different peers;
- **Web service composition** uses matching between ontologies describing service interfaces in order to compose Web services by connecting their interfaces;
- **Multiagent communication** uses matching for finding the relations between the ontologies used by two agents and translating the messages they exchange;
- **Context matching in ambient computing** uses matching of application needs and context information when applications and devices have been developed independently and use different ontologies;
- **Query answering** uses ontology matching for translating user queries about the Web;
- **Semantic Web browsing** uses matching for dynamically (while browsing) annotating Web pages with partially overlapping ontologies.

It is clear, from the above examples, that matching ontologies is a major issue in ontology related activities. It is not circumscribed to one area of ontology, but applies to any application that communicates through ontologies.

These kinds of applications have been analysed in order to establish their requirements with regard to matching systems. The most important requirements concern:

- the type of available input a matching system can rely on, such as schema or instance information. There are cases when data instances are not available, for instance due to security reasons or when there are no instances given beforehand. Therefore, these applications require only a matching solution able to work without instances (here schema-based method).
- some specific behaviour of matching, such as requirements of (i) being automatic, i.e., not relying on user feed-back; (ii) being correct, i.e., not delivering incorrect matches; (iii) being complete, i.e., delivering all the matches; and (iv) being performed at run time.

- the use of the matching result as described above. In particular, how the identified alignment is going to be processed, e.g., by merging the data or conceptual models under consideration or by translating data instances among them.

In particular, there is an important difference between applications that need alignments at design time and those that need alignments at run time.

Ontology evolution is typically used at design time for transforming an existing ontology which may have instances available. It requires an accurate, i.e., correct and complete, matching, but can be performed with the help of users. Schema, catalogue and data integration are also performed off-line but can be used for different purposes: translating data from one repository to another, merging two databases or generating a mediator that will be used for answering queries. They also will be supervised by a human user and can provide instances.

Other applications are rather performed at run time. Some of these, like P2P information sharing, query answering and Semantic Web browsing are achieved in presence of users who can support the process. They are also less demanding in terms of correctness and completeness because the user will directly sort out the results. On the other hand, Web service composition, multiagent communication and context matching in ambient computing require matching to be performed automatically without assistance of a human being. Since, the systems will use the result of matching for performing some action (mediating or translating data) which will be feed in other processes, correctness is required. Moreover, usually these applications do not have instance data available.

The difference between design time and run time is very relevant to ontology management. On the one hand, if alignments are required at design time, then ontology developers will need support in creating, manipulating and using these alignments. They should be supported in manipulating alignments during the whole ontology lifecycle (see Chapter 3 of this book).

On the other hand, if alignments are required at run time, then one way of ensuring timely and adequate response may be to find some existing alignment in an alignment store. Alignments stored there should be carefully evaluated and certified alignments. They thus require alignment management on their own.

2.3   Matching ontologies

The matching operation determines the alignment A' for a pair of ontologies o and o'. There are some other parameters that can extend the definition of the matching process, namely:

1. the use of an input alignment A, which is to be completed by the process;
2. the matching parameters, p, e.g., weights, thresholds; and
3. external resources used by the matching process, r, e.g., common knowledge or domain specific thesauri.

So, the matching process can be seen as a function f which, from a pair of ontologies o and o', an input alignment A, a set of parameters p and a set of resources r, returns an alignment A' between these ontologies:

$$A' = f(o, o', A, p, r)$$

There have already been many reviews of ontology matching algorithms (Rahm and Bernstein, 2001; Wache *et al.*, 2001; Kalfoglou and Schorlemmer, 2003, Euzenat and Shvaiko, 2007)[3] so we will be brief and refer the reader to these presentations.

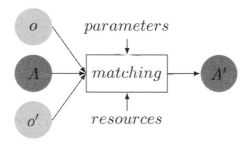

Figure 6-1. The ontology matching process: it establishes an alignment (A) from two ontologies (*o* and *o'*) and optionally an input alignment (A'), parameters and external resources.

Ontology matching consists of generating an alignment from two (or more) ontologies. There are many different features of ontologies that are usually used for providing matching:

- **terminological techniques** are based on the text found within ontologies for identifying ontology entities (labels), documenting them (comments) or other surrounding textual sources (related element labels). These techniques come from natural language processing and information retrieval. They can use the string structure themselves, e.g., string distances, the ontology as corpus, e.g., statistical measures based on the

---

[3] In fact, the ontology matching builds on previous research done in databases and information integration.

frequency of occurrence of a term, or external resources, such as dictionaries.

- **structural techniques** are based on the relations between ontology entities. These can be relations between entities and their attributes, including constraints on their values, or relations with other entities. These techniques take advantage of type comparison techniques or more elaborate graph techniques, e.g., tree distances, path matching, graph matching.

- **extensional techniques** compare the extension of entities. These extensions can be made of other entities, e.g., instances, as well as related resources, e.g., indexed documents. They differ depending on if the two ontologies share resources, e.g., they index the same set of documents, or not (in which case a similarity between the extensions may be established). These techniques can come from data analysis and statistics.

- **semantic techniques** are based on the semantic definition of ontologies. They use extra formalised knowledge and theorem provers for finding consequences of a particular alignment. This can be used for expanding the alignment or, on the contrary, for detecting conflicting correspondences.

Of course, most of the systems combine several techniques in order to improve their results. The techniques can be combined by aggregating distance results (Van Hage, 2005), by using selection functions for choosing which one to use in the present case (Jian *et al.*, 2005; Tang *et al.*, 2006), or by deeply involving them all in global distance computation (Euzenat and Valtchev, 2004, Melnik *et al.*, 2002).

Moreover, there is a difference when training sets are available or not (this is most often useful when a matching algorithm is needed for recognising instances). When available, one can apply machine learning techniques such as Bayes learning, vector support machines or decision trees.

As a conclusion, many applications need ontology matching for many different purposes. Ontology matching can, in turn, be obtained by many different techniques that can be combined in many different ways. Currently, matching systems are not usable automatically on real scale ontologies. Their results loss in accuracy as the ontologies gain in size, complexity and heterogeneity. They are usable in particular contexts such as databases for which common identifiable data exists or evolutionary versions of ontologies. Consequently, matching systems are currently used interactively or semi-automatically so that users control and improve the quality of the result. In this context, the help of matching algorithms is as powerful as the ontologies grow in size and complexity.

Current scale of using such systems is not known otherwise than from their providers. However, some commercial systems are available, especially in the area of database and directory integration showing serious interest. A good way to approach the performances of matching algorithms is to follow the yearly Ontology Alignment Evaluation Initiative campaigns[4].

This difficulty of obtaining usable alignments calls for proper alignment management beside ontology management. We consider this in the next section.

3. TOWARDS ALIGNMENT MANAGEMENT

We first identify why alignments should be considered in isolation (Section 3.1). We then present what should be an alignment lifecycle from the standpoint of ontology management (Section 3.2) and elicit the requirements for supporting this lifecycle (Section 3.3). Finally we describe a set of services and tools that can be provided for fulfilling these requirements (Section 3.4). The further sections will present in more details possible implementations of these services.

3.1 Why supporting alignments?

The reasons for supporting alignments have been provided in Section 2: many applications use them for different purposes using various matching algorithms combined in multiple ways.

As hetcrogeneous ontologies are a global problem for many applications, this calls for an infrastructure able to help these diffcrent applications to deal with it. In such a way, the effort of interoperating ontologies does not need to be solved for each kind of use.

Moreover, given the difficulty of the matching task, there are few algorithms available and when good alignments are available, they are worth sharing.

Supporting alignments has notable advantages over supporting other kind of matching results such as transformations, mediator implementations or merged ontologies. There are several reasons for this:

- **Sharing matching algorithms**: Many different applications have matching needs. It is thus appropriate to share the solutions to these problems, the matching algorithms and systems, across applications.

---

[4] http://oaei.ontologymatching.org

- **Sharing alignments**: Alignments are quite difficult to provide. There is no magic algorithm for quickly providing a useful alignment. Once high quality alignments have been established — either automatically or manually — it is very important to be able to store, share and reuse them.
- **Sharing exploitation means**: Matching results, once expressed as alignments, may be used for different purposes. Hence, a good matching algorithm does not have to be reimplemented for merging ontologies or for transforming new data: the same implementation will be reused together with mediator generators for exploiting the alignment in different mediation scenarios.
- **Combining matchers**: If one wants to combine several matching systems in a particular application, this is easier if all the systems can exchange their results in a pivot language. This is illustrated in Figure 6-2.

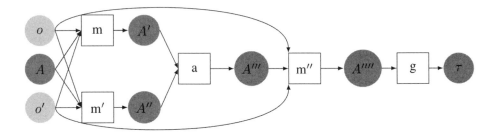

Figure 6-2. Alignment passing from tools to tools. Two matchers (m and m') are first run in parallel from the given ontologies, their resulting alignments are aggregated (a) resulting in another alignment which will be improved by another method (m'') before generating (g) a transformation program from it.

So, considering ontology alignments as first class citizens, has several benefits:

- from a software engineering point of view, as alignments can be passed from a program to another.
- from an ontology engineering and management point of view, as they will evolve together with the ontology lifecycle.

3.2   The alignment lifecycle

Like ontologies, alignments have their own lifecycle (see Figure 6-3). They are first *created* through a matching process (which may be manual). Then they can go through an iterative loop of *evaluation* and *enhancement*. Again, evaluation can be performed either manually or automatically, it consists of assessing properties of the obtained alignment. Enhancement can be obtained either through manual change of the alignment or application of refinement procedures, e.g., selecting some correspondences by applying thresholds. When an alignment is deemed worth publishing, then it can be *stored* and *communicated* to other parties interested in such an alignment. Finally, the alignment is transformed into another form or interpreted for *performing* actions like mediation or merging.

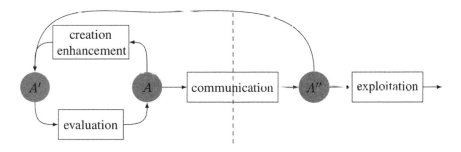

Figure 6-3. The ontology alignment lifecycle.

To this first independent cycle is added the joint lifecycle that can tie ontologies and alignments. As soon as ontologies evolve, new alignments have to be produced for following this evolution. This can be achieved by recording the changes made to ontologies and transforming these changes into an alignment (from one ontology version to the next one). This can be used for computing new alignments that will update the previous ones. In this case, previously existing alignments can be replaced by the composition of themselves with the ontology update alignment (see Figure 6-4).

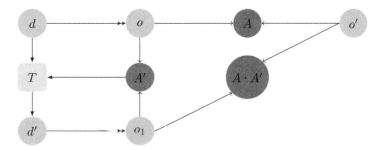

Figure 6-4 Evolution of alignments. When an ontology o evolves into a new version o_1, it is necessary to update the instances of this ontology (d) and the alignments (A) it has with other ontologies (o'). To that extent, a new alignment (A') between the two versions can be established and it can be used for generating the necessary instance transformation (T) and updated alignments ($A \bullet A'$).

Taking seriously ontology management requires to involve alignment management with ontology management. However, so far very few tools offer support for alignment management, let alone, joint ontology-alignment support.

3.3   Requirements for alignment support

Ontology alignments , like ontologies, must be supported during their lifecycle phases by adequate tools. These required functions can be implemented by services. The most notable services are:

- **Matching two ontologies** possibly by specifying the algorithm to use and its parameters (including an initial alignment).
- **Storing an alignment** in persistent storage.
- **Retrieving an alignment** from its identifier.
- **Retrieving alignment metadata** from its identifier can be used for choosing between specific alignments.
- **Suppressing an alignment** from the current alignment pool.
- **Finding (stored) alignments** between two specific ontologies.
- **Editing an alignment** by adding or discarding correspondences (this is typically the result of a graphic editing session).
- **Trimming alignments** over a threshold.
- **Generating code** implementing ontology transformations, data translations or bridge axioms from a particular alignment.
- **Translating a message** with regard to an alignment.
- **Finding a similar ontology** is useful when one wants to align two ontologies through an intermediate one.

For instance, someone wanting to translate a message expressed in ontology o to ontology o'' can ask for matching the two ontologies and for a translation of the message with regard to the obtained alignment. A more extreme scenario involves (1) asking for alignments between o and o'', maybe resulting in no alignment, (2) asking for an ontology close to o'' which may result in ontology o' , (3) asking for the alignments between o and o', which may return several alignments $a,$ a' and a'', (4) asking for the metadata of these alignments and (5) choosing a' because it is certified by a trusted authority, (6) matching o' and o'' with a particular algorithm, (7) trimming the result over a reasonable threshold for this algorithm, (8) editing the results so that it seems correct, (9) storing it in the server for sharing it with other people, (10) retrieving alignment a' and this latter one as data translators, (11) finally applying these two translations in a row to the initial message.

Most of these services correspond to primitives provided by the Alignment API (Euzenat 2004). They require, in addition, several features extending traditional matching frameworks:

- The ability to store alignments, whether they are provided by automatic means or by hand;
- Their proper annotation in order for the clients to evaluate the opportunity to use one of them or to start from it (this starts with the information about the matching algorithms, and can be extended to the justifications for correspondences that can be used in agent argumentation);
- The ability to generate knowledge processors such as mediators, transformations, translators, rules as well as to apply these processors if necessary;
- The possibility to find similar ontologies and to contact other such services in order to ask them for operations that the current service cannot provide by itself.

There is no constraint that the alignments are computed on-line or off-line, i.e., they are stored in the alignment store, or that they are processed by hand or automatically. This kind of information can however be stored together with the alignment in order for the client to be able to discriminate among them.

3.4 Example scenario: data mediation for Semantic Web services

The remainder of this chapter presents in more depth the functions of editing (Section 4), communicating (Section 5) and processing (Section 6) alignments. We will neither consider the alignment creation which has been the subject of much literature, nor the evaluation. Each of these functions will be illustrated through a common example related to Semantic Web services.

Web services represent one of the areas where data mediation is the most required. Services are resources usually developed independently which greatly vary from one provider to another in terms of the used data formats and representation. By adding semantics to Web services, heterogeneity problems do not disappear but require more intelligent dynamic and flexible mediation solutions. Ontologies which carry most of these explicit semantics become the crucial elements to support the identification and capturing of semantic mismatches between models.

Web Services Execution Environment (WSMX) is a framework that enables discovery, selection, invocation and interoperation of Semantic Web services (Mocan *et al.*, 2006a). Ontology-based data mediation plays a crucial role in enabling all the above mentioned service operations. Different business actors use ontologies to describe their services internal business logic, and, more importantly in this case, their data. Each of these actors uses its own information system, e.g., WSMX, and tries to interact with other actors, part of other (probably more complex) business processes (Figure 6-5). A specialized component or service is needed to transform the data expressed in terms of a given ontology (the source ontology) in the terms of another ontology (target ontology), allowing the two actors to continue using their own data representation formats. Being part of a run time process the data (i.e. instances) transformation has to be performed completely automatically. Also, due to the fact that such a mediator has to act in a business environment, the result of the mediation process has to be correct and complete at all time.

In order to achieve these three requirements (automation, correctness and completion), the whole process is split in two phases: a design time phase which covers the correctness and completion by involving the human domain expert and the run time phase when the mediation is performed in an automatic manner based on the alignments established at design time.

We will provide further details on these two phases in Section 4 and Section 6; Section 5 will consider the management of the alignments between these two phases.

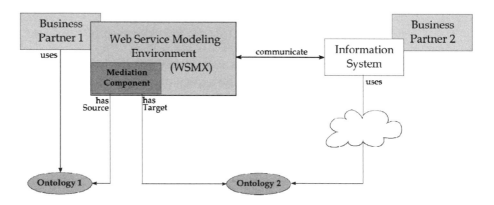

Figure 6-5. Instance transformation scenario.

4.   DESIGN TIME ALIGNMENT SUPPORT

The first place where ontology heterogeneity can be found is while designing an application. Ontology management environments (see Chapter 3 of this book) must support users in obtaining alignments and manipulating them. We provide some requirements for such an environment and detail further the Web Service Modeling Toolkit from this point of view.

4.1   Requirements

Design time alignment support requires first the ability to obtain an alignment between two ontologies. This can be achieved by retrieving an existing alignment, running a matching algorithm or creating an alignment manually.

Retrieving an alignment requires that alignments are stored and accessible somewhere. This can be done within the current ontology management environment, either from the local disk or from a remote server. If alignments are to be of good quality, it is preferable that the environment provides access to remote servers storing alignments. We will come back to this point in Section 6.

Running a matching algorithm requires the availability of such an algorithm. Having several such algorithms available in an ontology management environment seems highly desirable. Some tools provide support for finding the correspondences, like Protégé through the Prompt suite (Noy and Musen, 2003).

An often overlooked functionality of matching algorithms is their ability to provide explanation for the provided alignments. Explanations can be obtained by interacting with the matcher or by accessing metadata about a stored alignment. (Shvaiko *et al.*, 2005) explores the first alternative.

These alignments may also need to be manipulated. Most common manipulations involve trimming correspondences under a threshold or aggregating several alignments obtained on the same two ontologies.

Finally, creating an alignment manually requires an alignment editor. The same alignment editor can be used for manipulating more precisely the obtained alignments. They should provide a convenient display of the currently edited alignments and the opportunity to discard, modify or add correspondences. Ideally, from the alignment editor, all the design time functions should be available. Since ontologies and alignments can be very large, it is very challenging to offer intuitive alignment editing support.

The VisOn tool, developed by University of Montréal, is such a tool that can be used for editing alignments in the Alignment API format. Prompt also offers such facilities. Other tools developed for database schema matching could be adapted.

The Web Service Modeling Toolkit is an Integrated Development Environment (IDE) for Semantic Web services which also provides ontology engineering capabilities. Among other capabilities, WSMT offers a set of tools for creating, editing and storing ontology alignments. In the following section these WSMT features will be described in more details.

4.2   Example design-time tool: Web Service Modeling Toolkit

As mentioned above, data mediation within a semantic environment such as WSMX is a semi-automatic process where alignments between two ontologies are created at design time and then applied at run time in order to perform instance transformation in an automatic manner. Approaches for automatic generation of ontology alignments do exist but their accuracy is usually unsatisfactory for business scenarios and it is necessary for business to business integration to have an engineer involved in creating and validating the correspondences between ontologies. This is a non-trivial task and the user should be guided through the process of creating these alignments and ensuring their correctness.

Web Service Modeling Toolkit (WSMT) (Kerrigan *et al.*, 2007) is a Semantic Web service and ontology engineering toolkit, also featuring tools capable of producing alignments between ontologies based on human user inputs. It offers a set of methods and techniques that assist domain experts in their work such as different graphical perspectives over the ontologies, suggestions of the most related entities from the source and target ontology, guidance throughout the matching process (Mocan *et al.*, 2006b). The tools and the domain expert work together in an iterative process that involves cycles consisting of suggestions from the tool side and validation and creation of correspondences from the domain expert side.

Within WSMT, alignments are expressed by using the Abstract Mapping Language (AML) (Scharffe and de Bruijn, 2005) which is a formalism-neutral syntax for ontology alignments. WSMT includes several tools and editors meant to offer all the necessary support for editing and managing such ontology alignments:

Alignment Validation: WSMT provides validation for the AML syntax useful especially when alignments created in various tools need to be integrated into the same application.

Alignment Text Editor: It provides a text editor for the human readable syntax of AML. It provides similar features to that of a programming language editor, e.g., a Java editor, including syntax highlighting, in line error notification, content folding and bracket highlighting. This editor enables the engineer to create or modify correspondences through textual descriptions. Such a tool is normally addressed to experts familiar with both the domain and the alignment language.

Alignment View-based Editor: The View-based Editor provides graphical means to create correspondences between ontologies. Such a tool is addressed to those experts that are capable of understanding the problem domain and who can successfully align the two heterogeneous ontologies but they are not specialists in logical languages as well. Additionally, even if domain experts have the necessary skills to complete the alignment by using a text editor, a graphical mapping tool would allow them to better concentrate on the heterogeneity problems to be solved and in principle to maximize the efficiency of the overall mapping process. All the advantages described above, have been acknowledged by other approaches as well (Maedche *et al.*, 2002; Noy and Musen, 2003). The View-based Editor includes some of well-established classical methods, e.g. lexical and structural suggestion algorithms, iterative alignment creation processes. Additionally, this particular approach provides several new concepts and strategies aiming to enhance the overall automation degree of the ontology matching tool (Mocan and Cimpian, 2005). Three of the most important features of this tool (*views*, *decomposition* and *contexts*) are presented below.

A *view* (also referred to as a *perspective* in (Mocan *et al.*, 2006b)) represents a viewpoint in displaying the entities defined in a particular ontology, each view displays entities from the ontology in a two-level tree structure. The graphical viewpoint adopted to visualize the source and the target ontologies is important to simplify the design of the correspondences according to their type. By switching between combinations of these views on the source and the target ontologies, certain types of correspondences can be created using the same operations, combined with mechanisms for ontology traversal and contextualized visualization strategies.

Each view specifies what ontological entities should appear as roots or as children in these trees, by switching the focus between various relationships existing in the ontology. Views can be defined and grouped in pairs in such a way to solicit specific skill sets, offering support for users profiling. Currently, three types of views are available, namely *PartOf* (concepts as roots and their attributes as children), *InstanceOf* (concepts as roots and their attributes together with the values they can take as children) and *RelatedBy* (attributes as roots and their domain or range as children); Figure 6-6 illustrates the creation of alignments by using combinations of these perspectives.

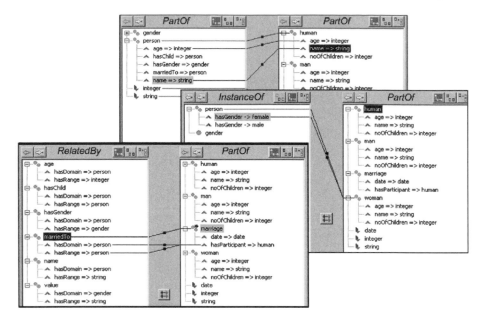

Figure 6-6 Mapping views in the AML View-Based Editor.

Decomposition is the process of bringing into focus the descriptive information of the root items presented in the view tree by exploring their children. A successful decomposition is followed by a *context* update. That is, instead of displaying the whole ontology at a time, only a subset (the one determined by decomposition) can be presented. Such subsets form the source and target contexts. If views can be seen as a vertical projection over ontologies, contexts can be seen as a horizontal projection over views. Decomposition and contexts aims to improve the effectiveness of the matching process by keeping the domain expert focused on the exact heterogeneity problem to be solved and by assuring that all the problem-related entities have been explored.

Mappings Views: The Mappings Views provide a light overview on the alignment created either by using the Text Editor or the View-based Editor. Instead of seeing the full description of an alignment (as quadruples in AML syntax or grounded rules in an ontology language) the domain expert can choose to see a more condensed version of this information: which are the entities in the source and in the target that are matched and if there are some special conditions associated with them.

Once a satisfying alignment has been designed, it can be stored and managed so that it is available to whoever needs it.

5. ONTOLOGY ALIGNMENT MANAGEMENT AND MAINTENANCE

As mentioned in our requirements, the alignments should be stored and shared adequately. In particular, if alignments between widely accepted ontologies are required, they will have to be found over and over again. An infrastructure capable of storing the alignments and of providing them on demand to other users would be useful.

Alignment support can be implemented either as a component of an ontology management tool and even being specific to each particular workstation (see Section 7). However, in order to optimize sharing, which is an important benefit of using alignments, it is better to store the alignments in an independent alignment server. Such a server can be either used for sharing alignments among a particular organization or open to the semantic Web at large.

5.1 Alignment server for storing

Alignment servers are independent software components which offer a library of matching methods and an alignment store that can be used by their clients. In a minimal configuration, alignment servers contribute storing and communicating alignments. Ideally, they can offers all the services identified in Section 3 and in particular alignment manipulation.

Alignment servers serve two purposes: for design time ontology matching, they will be components loosely coupled to the ontology management environment which may ask for alignments and for exploiting these alignments. For run time matching, the alignment servers can be invoked directly by the application. So, alignment servers will implement the services for both design time and run time matching at once.

These servers are exposed to clients, either ontology management systems or applications, through various communication channels (Agent communication messages, Web services) so that all clients can effectively share the infrastructure. A server may be seen as a directory or a service by Web services, as an agent by agents, as a library in ambient computing applications, etc.

Alignment servers must be found on the Semantic Web. For that purpose they can be registered by service directories, e.g., UDDI for Web services. Services or other agents should be able to subscribe some particular results of interest by these services. These directories are useful for other Web services, agents, peers to find the alignment services.

In addition, servers can be grouped into an alignment infrastructure which supports them in communicating together. They can be able to exchange the alignments they found and select them on various criteria. This can be useful for alignment servers to outsource some of their tasks. In particular, it may happen that:

- they cannot render an alignment in a particular format;
- they cannot process a particular matching method;
- they cannot access a particular ontology;
- a particular alignment is already stored by another server.

In these events, the concerned alignment server will be able to call other servers. This is especially useful when the client is not happy with the alignments provided by the current server, it is then possible to either deliver alignments provided by other servers or to redirect the client to these servers.

Moreover, this opens the door to value-added alignment services which use the results of other servers as a pre-processing for their own treatments or which aggregates the results of other servers in order to deliver a better alignment.

5.2   Sharing alignments

The main goal of storing alignments is to be able to share them among different applications. Because, these applications have diverse needs and various selection criteria, it is necessary to be able to search and retrieve alignments on these criteria. Alignment metadata used for indexing alignments are thus very important. So far, alignments contain information about:

- the aligned ontologies;
- the language in which these ontology are expressed;
- the kind of alignment it is (1:1 or n:m for instance);
- the algorithm that provided it (or if it has been provided by hand);
- the confidence in each correspondence.

This information is already very precious and helps applications selecting the most appropriate alignments. It is thus necessary that ontology matchers be able to generate and alignment servers be able to store these metadata. Oyster (Palma and Haase, 2005), a peer-to-peer infrastructure for sharing metadata about ontologies that can be used in ontology management, has been extending for featuring some metadata about alignments.

However, metadata schemes are extensible and other valuable information may be added to alignment format, such as:

- the parameters passed to the generating algorithms;

- the properties satisfied by the correspondences (and their proof if necessary);
- the certificate from an issuing source;
- the limitations of the use of the alignment;
- the arguments in favor or against a correspondence (Laera *et al.*, 2007).

All such information can be useful for evaluating and selecting alignments and thus should be available from alignment servers.

5.3 Evolving and maintaining ontology alignments

Like ontologies, alignments are not cast in stone once and for all. In particular, as ontologies evolve, it is necessary to evolve alignments accordingly. However, it can be quite hard for the engineer to be aware of the effects that these constant changes have. It is thus particularly important to provide support for alignment evolution and maintenance in alignment management environments.

Some tools, such as PrompDiff (Noy and Musen, 2003), are already particularly good at finding alignments between versions of ontologies. When such an alignment is made available, it is possible, as displayed in Figure 6-4, to provide by composition new versions of the alignment tied to the previous version and to migrate data.

WSMT offers a MUnit Testing View for the Abstract Mapping Language which gives the engineer support to ensure that instances are being correctly transformed. Users can define pairs of sources and targets, specifying that the result of transforming the sources, using the existing alignments, should be the targets. These tests can then be incrementally run by engineers when alignment validation is required.

6. ALIGNMENT PROCESSING

Finally, once alignments are obtained, either using a graphical tool, as the output of a matching algorithm, or retrieved from an alignment store, they can be processed in concrete mediation scenarios. The following techniques all require an alignment between the source and target ontologies in order to be achieved.

- **Query rewriting**: a query addressed to a source ontology needs to be rewritten in terms of a query for a target ontology.
- **Instance transformation**: a set of instances described under a source ontology needs to be transformed into terms of a target ontology.

- **Ontology merging**: a set of source ontologies need to be merged into a one ontology.

The scenario determines the operation that must be processed: a Web service data mediator, as the one presented in Section 3.5, requires transformation of instances, while on-line catalog integration may require query rewriting in order to query the various catalogs.

When applying instance transformation or query rewriting, the resulting sets of instances may contain duplicates. For example, two similar products sold by different vendors. In the case of ontology merging, it might also be necessary to merge instances described by the merged ontologies. Again, duplicates have to be identified in order to avoid their duplication in the newly created ontology. The technique of merging similar instances is known as *instance identification* and *unification.*

We describe these techniques in detail in the remaining of this section. Their application often requires preprocessing of the alignment in order to make it executable for the mediation system. Section 6.3 presents how alignments are transformed between various formats, motivating the use of a common alignment format for exchange between applications, algorithms and tools.

6.1   Query rewriting and instance transformation

Applying query rewriting techniques consists, as the name suggests, of rewriting a query in terms of a source ontology O_s into terms of a target ontology O_t. The rewriting engine takes as input the original query q_s, the alignment between O_s and O_t, and returns a query q_t in terms of O_t. Figure 6-7 illustrates this process. Query rewriting has been largely studied in database integration (Dushka and Genesereth, 1997).

Once the rewritten query addressed to the target ontology, the instances eventually returned are described in terms of O_t. They might have to be transformed to instances of O_s in order to be further processed by the system.

Instance transformation is done by taking a set of instances described under a source ontology O_s, and transforming it to instances of a target ontology O_t using the alignment between the two ontologies. New instances of O_t classes are described, and attribute values are transformed (Scharffe and de Bruijn, 2005) according to the alignment. This process may lead to the creation of multiple target instances for one source instance, or, inversely, to combine some source instances into one target instance. Instance transformation, illustrated in Figure 6-7, is used in the example scenario in Section 3.5.

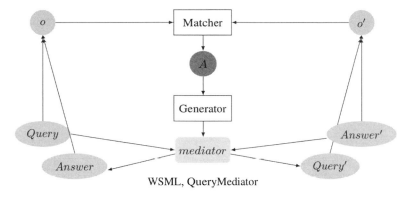

Figure 6-7. Query mediation (from (Euzenat and Shvaiko, 2007)). From two matched ontologies *o* and *o'*, resulting in alignment *A*, a mediator is generated. This allows the transformation of queries expressed with the entities of the first ontology into a query using the corresponding entities of a matched ontology and the translation back of the results from the second ontology to the first one.

The two former techniques result in two sets of instances described according to a single ontology. The different origin of these instances may lead to duplicates. For instance, in a Web application integrating various on-line catalogs, each described as an ontology, once the catalogs queried and the results adapted to the reference ontology, it is likely that some products are sold by many vendors. Similar products have to be identified in order to be presented under the same one (eventually with the different prices kept separated). Instance unification techniques are used to merge similar instances by analyzing their attributes values, as well as the relations they share with other instances.

Instance unification is also necessary after two ontologies have been merged into one. Instances of the source ontologies then also need to be merged, and duplicates removed. The next section presents the ontology merging technique.

6.2 Merging

There are cases where the ontologies are not kept separate but need to be merged into a single new ontology. As an example, we can consider the case of one vendor acquiring another; their catalog will probably be merged into a single one. Ontology merging is realized by taking the two ontologies to be merged and an alignment between these two ontologies. It results in a new ontology combining the two source ontologies. The ontology merging process can be fully automatized if an adequate alignment is provided (Scharffe, 2007), but usually requires human intervention in order to solve conflicts and choose a merging strategy. Figure 6-8 illustrates the ontology merging process.

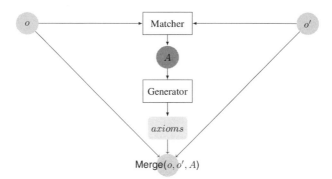

Figure 6-8. Ontology merging (from (Euzenat and Shvaiko, 2007)). From two matched ontologies *o* and *o'*, resulting in alignment *A*, articulation axioms are generated. This allows the creation of a new ontology covering the matched ontologies.

The techniques presented in the previous two subsections require only the alignment as an input (they interpret it). As we will see in the next section, this alignment may require a further step in order to be usable. This step is tightly linked to the format in which the alignment is expressed.

6.3   Semantic data mediation

The mediation of the heterogeneous semantic data can be achieved through instance transformation. Data represented by ontology instances has to be transformed either by the sender or transparently by a third party in the format required by the receiver, i.e., instances expressed in the target ontology.

In order to accommodate such a mediation scenario, the alignments generated by using the techniques described in Section 4 have to be processed by an engine able to perform instance transformation. If the alignments are expressed in an abstract form, e.g., using AML, an extra step has to be performed: the correspondences in the alignment must be expressed in a concrete ontology specification language which can be interpreted.

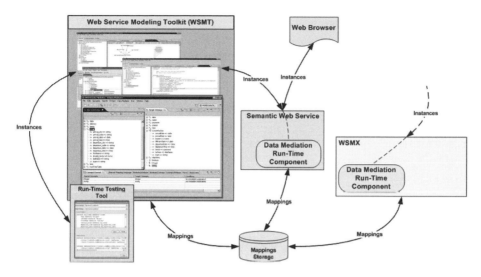

Figure 6-9. Run time Data Mediator Usage Scenario (from (Mocan and Cimpian, 2007)).

Figure 6-9 shows how such an instance transformation engine (the Data Mediation Run-Time Component in WSMX) can be deployed and used in various scenarios. A straightforward way is to integrate it in an Information System (in this case WSMX) which needs mediation support in order to facilitate the exchange of heterogeneous data.

Another possibility is to encapsulate this engine in a (Semantic) Web service and to allow external calls having as inputs the source instances and optionally the alignments to be applied. As output, the corresponding target instances are returned.

Additionally, such an engine can be used for testing the correctness of the alignments been produced, either by using it as a test module in the design-time matching tool (see the WSMT MUnit) or by providing a Web interface that would allow domain experts to remotely send source instances to be transformed in target instances.

7. SOFTWARE AND TOOLS

Most of the work on general organisation of alignments is tied to some kind of application, e.g., C-OWL for peer-to-peer applications, WSMX for Web services, Edutella for emerging semantics. There are, however, a few systems which are autonomous enough for being used as independent alignment management support.

Model management has been promoted in databases for dealing with data integration in a generic way. It offers a high-level view to the operations applied to databases and their relations. Rondo[5] is such a system (Melnik *et al.*, 2002). It offers operators for generating the alignments, composing them and applying them as data transformation. It is currently a standalone program with no editing functions.

MAFRA[6] (Mädche *et al.*, 2002) proposes an architecture for dealing with "semantic bridges" that offers many functions such as creation, manipulation, storing and processing such bridges. MAFRA has transformations associated with bridges: it does not record alignments in a non processable format. MAFRA does not offer editing or sharing alignments.

Protégé is an ontology edition environment (see Chapter 3 of this book) that offers design time support for matching. In particular it features Prompt[7] (Noy and Musen, 2003), an environment that provides some matching methods and alignment visualisation. Since alignments are expressed in an ontology, they can be stored and shared through the Protégé server mode. Prompt can be extended through a plug-in mechanism.

Foam[8] (Ehrig, 2007) is a framework in which matching algorithms can be integrated. It mostly offers matching and processor generator. It does not offer on-line services nor alignment editing, but is available as a Protégé plug in and is integrated in the KAON2 ontology management environment.

COMA++ is another standalone (schema) matching workbench that allows integrating and composing matching algorithms. It supports matching, evaluating, editing, storing and processing alignments.

The Alignment Server, associated with the Alignment API[9] (Euzenat, 2004), offers matching ontologies, manipulating, storing and sharing alignments as well as processor generation. It can be accessed by clients through API, Web services, agent communication languages ot HTTP. It does not support editing.

WSMT[10], which has been taken as example within these pages is a design time alignment creator and editor. It manipulates the AML format and can generate WSML rules. It also works as a standalone system.

The NeOn[11] project ambitions to produce a toolkit for ontology management which features run time and design time ontology alignment support.

---

[5] http://infolab.stanford.edu/~modman/rondo/

[6] http://mafra-toolkit.sourceforge.net

[7] http://protege.stanford.edu/plugins/prompt/prompt.html

[8] http://www.aifb.uni-karlsruhe.de/WBS/meh/foam/

[9] http://alignapi.gforge.inria.fr

[10] http://wsmt.sourceforge.net

[11] http://www.neon-project.org

8.   CONCLUSIONS

Applications using ontologies face the problem of ontology heterogeneity whenever they want to communicate with each others or evolve. Hence, ontology management must take ontology heterogeneity into account. Dealing with ontology heterogeneity involves finding the alignments, or sets of correspondences, existing between ontology entities and using them for reconciling the ontologies.

Because, this problem occurs in many applications and is solved in many different ways, it is better dealt with in a general way. This involves managing alignments together with ontologies.

We have presented alignment management through the lifecycle of alignments and the associated support functions: creating, selecting, editing, maintaining, sharing and processing alignments. We have presented a few systems which implement part of this alignment support and in particular the notion of alignment server which can be used for storing and sharing alignment at both run time and design time.

Alignment management is not as advanced as ontology management and much remains to be developed for fully supporting and sharing alignments on a wide scale. Challenges for alignment management include adoption challenges and research problems. The important challenge is to have a natural integration of alignment management with most of the ontology engineering and ontology management systems. If alignment sharing and management is to become a reality, then there should not be one proprietary format with each tool that cannot be handled by other tools. Another challenge is the easy finding of available alignments. For this purpose, proper alignment metadata and Web-wide search support have to be set up.

There remains difficult research problems in the domain of alignment management such as:

- The identification of duplicate alignments or evolutions from a particular alignment;
- Aggregating, composing and reasoning usefully with a massive number of alignments;

The design of ever better user interaction systems for both interacting with matching systems and editing alignments.

ADDITIONAL READING

The topic of alignment management is relatively new so there is no specifically dedicated publications. A recent extensive reference on ontology matching is (Euzenat and Shvaiko, 2007). ontologymatching.org is a Web site collecting information about ontology matching.

ACKNOWLEDGEMENTS

This work has been partly supported by the European network of excellence Knowledge Web (IST-2004-507482). The first author has also been supported by the European integrated project NeOn (IST-2005-027595) and the RNTL project WebContent.

The first author thanks Pavel Shvaiko for many fruitful discussions related to this chapter.

REFERENCES

Christoph Bussler, Dieter Fensel, and Alexander Mädche. A conceptual architecture for Semantic Web enabled Web services. *ACM SIGMOD Record*, 31(4):24–29, 2002.

Oliver Duschka and Michael Genesereth. Infomaster - an information integration tool. In *Proceedings of the International Workshop on Intelligent Information Integration*, Freiburg, Germany, 1997.

Marc Ehrig. Ontology Alignment: Bridging the Semantic Gap. Semantic Web and Beyond: Computing for Human Experience. Springer, New-York (NY US), 2007.

Jérôme Euzenat and Petko Valtchev. Similarity-based ontology alignment in OWL-Lite. In *Proceedings of 16th European Conference on Artificial Intelligence (ECAI)*, Valencia (ES), pages 333–337, 2004.

Jérôme Euzenat. Alignment infrastructure for ontology mediation and other applications. In *Proceedings of the 1st ICSOC International Workshop on Mediation in Semantic Web Services*, pages 81–95, Amsterdam, Netherlands, December 2005

Jérôme Euzenat. An API for ontology alignment. In *Proceedings of the 3rd International Semantic Web Conference (ISWC-2004)*, pages 698–712, Hiroshima, Japan, 2004

Jérôme Euzenat and Pavel Shvaiko. Ontology matching. Springer Verlag, Berlin, 2007

Michael Genesereth, Arthur Keller, and Oliver Duschka. Infomaster: An Information integration system. In *Proceedings of the ACM SIGMOD International Conference on Management of Data*, Tucson, 1997.

Ningsheng Jian, Wei Hu, Gong Cheng, and Yuzhong Qu. Falcon-AO: Aligning ontologies with Falcon. In *Proceedings of K-CAP Workshop on Integrating Ontologies*, pages 87–93, Banff, CA, 2005.

Yannis Kalfoglou and Marco Schorlemmer. Ontology mapping: the state of the art. *The Knowledge Engineering Review*, 18(1):1–31, 2003

Mike Kerrigan, Adrian Mocan, Martin Tanler, Dieter Fensel: The Web Service Modeling Toolkit - An Integrated Development Environment for Semantic Web Services. In

Proceedings of the 4th European Semantic Web Conference (ESWC), System Description Track, June 2007, Innsbruck, Austria.

Loredana Laera, Ian Blacoe, Valentina Tamma, Terry Payne, Jérôme Euzenat, and Trevor Bench-Capon. Argumentation over Ontology Correspondences in MAS. *In Proceedings of the 6th International conference on Autonomous Agents and Multiagent Systems (AAMAS)*, Honolulu , USA, 2007

Holger Lausen, Jos de Bruijn, Axel Polleres, and Dieter Fensel: WSML — A Language Framework for Semantic Web Services. *W3C Workshop on Rule Languages for Interoperability*, April 2005

Aexander Mädche, Boris Motik, Nuno Silva, and Raphael Volz: MAFRA — A Mapping Framework for Distributed Ontologies. In *Proceedings of the 13th European Conference on Knowledge Engineering and Knowledge Management (EKAW-2002)*, pages 235–250, Siguenza, Spain, September 2002.

Sergey Melnik, Erhard Rahm, and Philip Bernstein. Rondo: A programming platform for model management. *In Proceedings of the 22nd International Conference on Management of Data (SIGMOD)*, pages 193–204, San Diego (CA US), 2003

Adrian Mocan and Emilia Cimpian: Mapping creation using a view based approach. In *Proceedings of the 1st International Workshop on Mediation in Semantic Web Services (Mediate-2005), volume 168, pages 97–112, Amsterdam, The Netherlands*, December 2005.

Adrian Mocan, Matthew Moran, Emilia Cimpian, and Michal Zaremba. Filling the Gap - Extending Service Oriented Architectures with Semantics. In *Proceedings of the IEEE International Conference on e-Business Engineering (ICEBE-2006)*, pages 594–601, Shanghai, China, October 2006.

Adrian Mocan, Emilia Cimpian, and Mike Kerrigan: Formal Model for Ontology Mapping Creation. In *Proceedings of the 5th International Semantic Web Conference (ISWC-2006)*, pages 459–472, Athens, Georgia, USA, November 2006.

Natalia F. Noy and Mark A. Musen: The PROMPT Suite: Interactive Tools for Ontology Merging And Mapping. *International Journal of Human-Computer Studies*, 6(59):983–1024, 2003.

Raúl Palma, Peter Haase, Oyster: Sharing and re-using ontologies in a peer-to-peer community. In *Proceedings of the 4th International Semantic Web Conference*, pages 1059–1062, Galway, Ireland, 2005

Erhard Rahm and Philip Bernstein. A survey of approaches to automatic schema matching. *The VLDB Journal*, 10(4):334–350, 2001

François Scharffe and Jos de Bruijn: A language to specify mappings between ontologies. In *Proceedings of the IEEE Conference on Internet-Based Systems SITIS6*, Yaounde, Cameroon, December 2005.

François Scharffe: Dynamerge: A Merging Algorithm for Structured Data Integration on the Web. In *Proceeedings of the DASFAA 2007 International Workshop on Scalable Web Information Integration and Service (SWIIS 2007)*, 2007.

Pavel Shvaiko, Fausto Giunchiglia, Paulo Pinheiro da Silva, and Deborah McGuinness. Web explanations for semantic heterogeneity discovery. In *Proceedings of the 2nd European Semantic Web Conference (ESWC)*, pages 303–317, Hersounisous, Greece, May 2005

Jie Tang, Juanzi Li, Bangyong Liang, Xiaotong Huang, Yi Li, and Kehong Wang. Using Bayesian decision for ontology mapping. *Journal of Web Semantics*, 4(1):243–262, 2006

Willem Robert van Hage, Sophia Katrenko, Guus Schreiber. A Method to Combine Linguistic Ontology-Mapping Techniques. In *Proceedings of the 4th International Semantic Web Conference (ISWC-2005)*, pages 732–744, Galway, Ireland, 2005

Holger Wache, Thomas Voegele, Ubbo Visser, Heiner Stuckenschmidt, Gerhard Schuster, Holger Neumann, and Sebastian Hübner. Ontology-based integration of information — a survey of existing approaches. In *Proceedings of the IJCAI Workshop on Ontologies and Information Sharing*, pages 108–117, Seattle, USA, 2001

Gio Wiederhold. Mediators in the architecture of future information systems. *IEEE Computer*, 25(3), 1992.

Chapter 7

THE BUSINESS VIEW: ONTOLOGY ENGINEERING COSTS

Elena Simperl[1] and York Sure[2]

[1]Digital Enterprise Research Institute (DERI), University of Innsbruck, Technikerstrasse 21a, A-6020 Innsbruck, Austria, elena.simperl@deri.at; [2]SAP Research, Vincenz-Priessnitz-Str. 1, D-76131 Karlsruhe, Germany, york.sure@sap.com

Abstract: A core requirement for the take-up of ontology-driven technologies at industry level is the availability of proved and tested methods which allow an efficient engineering of high-quality ontologies, be that by reuse, manual building or automatic knowledge acquisition methods. This includes in equal measure feasible technological support, which is provided by the methodologies, methods and tools emerged in the last decades in the field of ontology management, and the economics of ontology engineering projects, in particular issues of cost effectiveness and profitability. This chapter presents and discusses approaches for reliably assessing the costs of building ontologies and the usage of cost-related information to quantifiably support a wide range of decisions arising during the lifecycle of an ontology. We account for the similarities and differences between software and ontology engineering in order to establish the appropriateness of applying methods, which have a long-standing tradition in this adjacent engineering field, to ontologies. Building upon the results of this analysis we introduce ONTOCOM as the first parametric cost model for ontologies and discuss means to improve its accuracy and extend its applicability for a wide range of ontology engineering projects at public and corporate level.

Keywords: business view; cost estimation; ontology costs; ontology engineering; parametric method

1.   INTRODUCTION

Though ontologies and associated ontology management tools have become increasingly popular in the last decades, the dissemination of ontologies and ontology-based applications as envisioned by the Semantic

Web community requires fine-grained methodologies which are able to deal with both technical and economic challenges of ontology engineering. In order for ontologies to be built and deployed at a large scale and with sufficient efficiency and effectiveness one needs not only technologies and tools to assist the development process, but also proved and tested means to control the overall engineering process. A wide range of ontology engineering methodologies have emerged in the Semantic Web community. Apart from minor differences in the level of detail adopted for the description of the process stages they define ontology engineering as an iterative process, which shows major similarities to the neighbored research field of software engineering. However existing methodologies do not cover a crucial aspect of the engineering process, which has gained significant attention in adjacent engineering areas because of its importance in real-world business contexts: the costs estimation using pre-defined cost models (Hepp,2007).

In order to precisely estimate the costs related to the ontology engineering process, there is a need for empirically tested cost models which exploit the results already achieved with respect to this issue in related engineering fields. At the same time a cost model for ontologies should take into account the critical factors and particularities of the ontology engineering process. With ONTOCOM we present the first existing approach in this new emerging field of ontology engineering. Estimating costs for ontology engineering is similar to estimating costs for software engineering as it requires the consideration of economic aspects for generic products and the processes they result of. Therefore, our approach largely benefits from the experiences made in estimating costs for software engineering. By using expert interviews we identified the most relevant cost drivers for a wide class of ontology engineering projects. In a large user study we acquired relevant data from a large number of already existing ontology engineering projects and calibrated the model with promising results. Combing the two we were able to identify dimensions for further research and development in order to create a methodology for the creation of any kind of cost estimation model for ontologies, independently of the ontology lifecycle or the organizational setting it might be employed.

The outline of this chapter is as follows. We start by motivating the need for cost-related information in ontology engineering and elaborating on the most relevant methods for cost estimation which are likely to be suited for this purpose in **Section 2**. In **Section 3** we present the ONTOCOM model based on the previously identified most promising methods for cost estimation. We show the various parts of ONTOCOM such as a parametric formula to estimate costs and relevant cost drivers. We show how the generic ONTOCOM model can be broken down for concrete industrial projects by instantiation of the various parameters and analyze the critical issues which are required in order to design a methodology for the design of flexible, customized cost models for ontologies which best fit specific organizational and technological constraints. Next, **Section 4** gives an outline of the software tool support which can ease the usage of ONTOCOM or other cost models by ontology engineers. **Section 5** gives an overview of related work, and finally **Section 6** summarizes the conclusions and lessons learned from our research and the planned future work.

2. COST ESTIMATION FOR ONTOLOGY ENGINEERING

Cost estimation can be defined as the art of predetermining the lowest realistic price of an item or activity which assures a normal profit. Independently of the sector in which it is performed, cost estimation produces probabilistic assessments of the expected effort (usually expressed in person months rather than monetary units) and/or the elapsed time. Concretely, cost estimation methods generate predictions which indicate at different levels of accuracy the most likely values, as well as upper and lower bounds on the values of the aforementioned parameters. In the case of Ontology Engineering cost estimation aims at predicting the costs related to activities performed during the lifecycle of an ontology.

Estimates of effort and duration are required throughout the entire lifecycle of a product, be that software, ontologies or any other type of merchandise. In an early stage of a project, they are essential for determining the feasibility of the project, or for performing cost-benefit analysis to choose among alternative methods to achieve the project goals. The inaccuracy of such estimates is, however, relatively high, because of the lack of detailed knowledge on the project or its planned outcomes characteristic for this stage. Nevertheless, initial estimates can be updated once the project evolves. They are used for controlling purposes, as an instrument to check the current status of a project against its final objectives.

Compared to other engineering disciplines, the goal of estimating the costs of an ontology is related to a series of challenges, which can be traced back to the particularities of ontology engineering projects and to the current state of the art in the field. First, and by contrast to other industry sectors which design a new product and produce it multiple times, ontology engineering is about building new ontologies, using different methods and tools. This problem also applies for software. However, in the latter case it is alleviated by

- a deeper knowledge on typical cost drivers resulting from the long-standing tradition of the IT industry,
- the wide range of cost estimation methods which can be applied complementarily to overcome limitations at individual method level, and
- the comparatively high amounts of historical project data available to adjust and improve them.

This should not mean that cost estimation for ontologies can not be performed at a feasible level of accuracy. Due to the inherent similarities between software and ontologies, many of the achievements, experiences and lessons learned for the former are likely to be applicable for the latter, and hence form a viable basis to start developing ontology-specific prediction methods. However, ontology engineering is a comparatively young field of research and development whose economic aspects require additional investigation. In the following we study possible approaches to the question of ontology development costs before introducing the ONTOCOM method, as a first attempt to cope with this problem

2.1.1   Cost estimation methods

Estimating costs for engineering processes can be performed according to several methods. Due to their limitations with respect to certain classes of situations these methods are often used in conjunction during the estimation phase.

- **Expert judgment/Delphi method** The Delphi Method is based on a structured process for collecting and distilling knowledge from a group of human experts by means of a series of questionnaires interspersed with controlled opinion feedback. The involvement of human experts using their past project experiences is a major advantage of the approach. Its most extensive critique point is related to the difficulties to explicitly state the decision criteria used by the contributing experts and to its inherent dependency of the availability of experts to carry on the process.
- **Analogy method** The main idea of this method is the extrapolation of available data from similar projects to estimate the costs of the proposed project. The method is suitable in situations where empirical data from previous project is available and trustworthy, and depends on the accuracy in establishing real differences between completed and current projects.
- **Decomposition method** This involves generating a work breakdown structure, i.e. breaking a product into smaller components or a project into activities and tasks in order to produce a lower-level, more detailed

description of the product/project at hand, which in turn allows more accurate cost estimates. The total costs are calculated as average values, possibly adjusted on the basis of the complexity of the components/tasks considered. The successful application of the method depends of the availability of necessary information related to the work breakdown structure.

- **Parametric/algorithmic method** This method involves the usage of mathematical equations based on research and historical data from previous projects. The method analyzes main cost drivers of a specific class of projects and their dependencies and uses statistical techniques to refine and customize the corresponding formulas. As in the case of the analogy method the generation of a proved and tested cost model using the parametric method is directly related to the availability of reliable and relevant data to be used in calibrating the initial core model.

Orthogonally to the aforementioned methods we mention two core approaches to cost estimation (cf. Table 7-1).

- **Bottom-up estimation** This methodology involves identifying and estimating costs of individual project components separately and subsequently summing up the outcomes to produce an estimation for the overall project.
- **Top-down estimation** In contrast to the bottom-up approach the top-down method relies on overall project parameters. For this purpose, the project is partitioned into lower-level components and lifecycle phases beginning at the highest level. The approach produces are total project estimates, in which individual process tasks or product components are responsible for a proportion of the total costs.

The decomposition method is based on a bottom-up approach. Estimation by expert judgment, analogy or parametric equations can be carried in a top-down or a bottom-up fashion, also depending of the stage of the project in which the estimates need to calculated. Top-down estimation is more applicable to early cost estimates when only global properties are known, but it can be less accurate due to the less focus on lower-level parameters and technical challenges — usually predictable later in the process lifecycle, at most. The bottom-up approach produces results of higher-quality, provided a realistic work breakdown structure and means to estimate the costs of the lower-level units the product/project has been decomposed into.

In addition to effort estimates in terms of person months several cost models also provide means to estimate the duration of projects, whilst the two values are usually assumed to depend of each other according to a specific mathematical function. The most prominent examples of duration estimation methods are parametric (e.g. the Putnam model (Putnam, 2003) or the COCOMO model (Boehm, 1981) in software engineering).

Table 7-1. Methods and approaches to cost estimation

	Bottom-up estimation	Top-down estimation
Expert judgment method	Experts estimate the costs of low-level components or activities.	Experts estimate the total costs of a product or a project
Analogy method	Costs are calculated using analogies between low-level components or activities	Costs are estimated using a global similarity function for products or projects
Decomposition method	Costs are calculated as an average sum of the costs of lower-level units, whose development effort are known in advance	
Parametric method	Costs are calculated using a statistic model which predicts the costs of lower-level units on the basis of historical data about the costs of developing such units.	Costs are calculated using a statistic model which is calibrated using historical data about, and predicts the current value of the total development costs

2.1.2 Applicability to ontology engineering

The applicability of the mentioned cost estimation methods to ontology engineering depends of course on the process- and product-driven characteristics of ontology engineering. In the following we examine the advantages and disadvantages of each of these approaches given these characteristics and the current state of the art in the field:

- **Expert judgment/Delphi method** The expert judgment method seems to be appropriate for our goals since large amount of expert knowledge with respect to ontologies is already available in the Semantic Web community, while the costs of the related engineering efforts are not. Experts' opinion on this topic can be used to compliment the results of other estimation methods.
- **Analogy method** The analogy method requires knowledge about the features of an ontology, or of an ontology development process, which are relevant for cost estimation purposes. Further on it assumes that an accurate comparison function for ontologies is defined, and that we are aware of cost information from previous projects. While several similarity measures for ontologies have already been proposed in the Semantic Web community, no case studies on ontology costs are currently available. There is a need to perform an in-depth analysis of

the cost factors relevant for ontology engineering projects, as a basis for the definition of such an analogy function and its customization in accordance to previous experiences.

- **Decomposition method** This method implies the availability of cost information with respect to single low-level engineering tasks, such as costs involved in the conceptualization of single concepts or in the instantiation of the ontology. Due to the lack of available information the decomposition method can not be applied yet to ontology engineering.

- **Parametric/algorithmic method** Apart from the lack of costs-related information which should be used to calibrate cost estimation formula for ontologies, the analysis of the main cost drivers affecting the ontology engineering process can be performed on the basis of existing case studies on ontology building, representing an important step toward the elaboration of a predictable cost estimation strategy for ontology engineering processes. The resulting parametric cost model has to be constantly refined and customized when cost information becomes available. Nevertheless the definition of a fixed spectrum of cost factors is important for a controlled collection of existing real-world project data, a task which is fundamental for the subsequent model calibration. This would also be useful for the design and customization of alternative prediction strategies, such as the aforementioned analogy approach.

Given the fact that cost estimation has been marginally explored in the Semantic Web community so far, and that little is known about the underlying cost factors, a bottom-up approach to the previously introduced methods is currently not practicable, though it would produce more accurate results. In turn, expert judgment, analogy and parametric cost estimates could be obtained in a top-down fashion, if the corresponding methods are clearly defined and customized in the context of ontology engineering. An overview of the results of this feasibility study is depicted in Table 7-2. Due to the incompleteness of the information related to cost issues, a combination of the three is likely to overcome certain limitations of single methods.

Table 7-2. Cost estimation methods and approaches currently applicable to Ontology Engineering

	Bottom-up estimation	Top-down estimation
Expert judgment method		
Analogy method		
Decomposition method		
Parametric method		

Duration estimates can be defined analogously for parametric models. For this purpose one can assume a similar function defining the correlation between staff efforts and time within ontology engineering projects as in other engineering disciplines. This function needs to be customized to the particularities of ontology engineering projects.

In the following we introduce the ontology cost model ONTOCOM, which is a first attempt to apply the parametric method to ontology engineering, and discuss ways to improve its prediction quality.

3.   THE ONTOLOGY COST MODEL ONTOCOM

ONTOCOM is a generic cost model for ontology engineering. The model is generic in the sense that it assumes a sequential ontology lifecycle, according to which an ontology is conceptualized, implemented and evaluated, after an initial analysis of the requirements it should fulfill (see below). By contrast ONTOCOM does not consider alternative engineering strategies such as rapid prototyping or agile methods, which are based on different lifecycles. This limitation is issued in Section 3.5, which describes among other things how the generic model could be customized to suit such scenarios.

The cost estimation model is realized in three steps. First a top-down work breakdown structure for ontology engineering processes is defined in order to reduce the complexity of project budgetary planning and controlling operations down to more manageable units (Boehm, 1981). The associated costs are then elaborated using the parametric method. The result of the second step is a statistical prediction model (i.e. a parameterized mathematical formula). Its parameters are given start values in pre-defined intervals, but need to be calibrated on the basis of previous project data. This empirical information complemented by expert estimations is used to evaluate and revise the predictions of the initial a-priori model, thus creating a validated a-posteriori model.

3.1   The work breakdown structure

The top-level partitioning of a generic ontology engineering process can be realized by taking into account available process-driven methodologies in this field (Gomez et al, 2004, Sure et al, 2006). According to them ontology building consists of the following core steps (cf. Figure 7-1):

1. Requirements Analysis. The engineering team consisting of domain experts and ontology engineers performs a deep analysis of the project setting with respect to a set of predefined requirements. This step might also include knowledge acquisition activities in terms of the re-usage of

existing ontological sources or by extracting domain information from text corpora, databases etc. If such techniques are being used to aid the engineering process, the resulting ontologies are to be subsequently customized to the application setting in the conceptualization /implementation phases. The result of this step is an ontology requirements specification document (Sure et al, 2006). In particular this contains a set of competency questions describing the domain to be modeled by the prospected ontology, as well as information about its use cases, the expected size, the information sources used, the process participants and the engineering methodology.

2. Conceptualization. The application domain is modeled in terms of ontological primitives, e. g. concepts, relations, axioms.

3. Implementation. The conceptual model is implemented in a (formal) representation language, whose expressivity is appropriate for the richness of the conceptualization. If required reused ontologies and those generated from other information sources are translated to the target representation language and integrated to the final context.

4. Evaluation. The ontology is evaluated against the set of competency questions. The evaluation may be performed automatically, if the competency questions are represented formally, or semi-automatically, using specific heuristics or human judgment. The result of the evaluation is reflected in a set of modifications/refinements at the requirements, conceptualization or implementation level

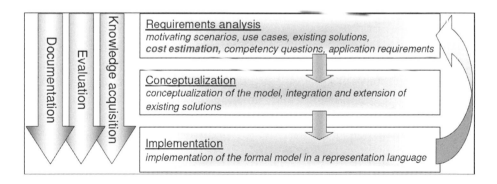

Figure 7-1. Ontology Engineering Process

Depending on the ontology lifecycle underlying the process-driven methodology, the aforementioned four steps are to be seen as a sequential workflow or as parallel activities. Methontology (Gomez et al, 2004), which applies prototypical engineering principles, considers knowledge acquisition, evaluation and documentation as being complementary support activities performed in parallel to the main development process. Other methodologies, usually following a classical waterfall model, consider these support activities as part of a sequential engineering process. The OTK-Methodology (Sure et al, 2002) additionally introduces an initial feasibility study in order to assess the risks associated with an ontology building attempt. Other optional steps are ontology population (also called instantiation) and ontology evolution and maintenance. The former deals with the alignment of concrete application data to the implemented ontology. The latter relate to modifications of the ontology performed according to new user requirements, updates of the reused sources or changes in the modeled domain. Further on, likewise related engineering disciplines, reusing existing knowledge sources — in particular ontologies — is a central topic of ontology development. In terms of the process model introduced above, ontology reuse is considered a knowledge acquisition task.

The parametric method integrates the efforts associated with each component of this work breakdown structure to a mathematical formula as described below.

3.2   The parametric equation

ONTOCOM calculates the necessary person-months effort using the following equation:

$$PM = A * Size^\alpha * \Pi\ CD_i \qquad\qquad\qquad (1)$$

According to the parametric method the total development efforts are associated with cost drivers specific for the ontology engineering process and its main activities. Experiences in related engineering areas (Boehm, 1981; Korotkiy, 2005) let us assume that the most significant factor is the size of the ontology (in kilo entities) involved in the corresponding process or process phase. In Equation 1 the parameter Size corresponds to the size of the ontology i.e. the number of primitives which are expected to result from the conceptualization phase (including fragments built by reuse or other knowledge acquisition methods).

The possibility of a non-linear behavior of the model with respect to the size of the ontology is covered by parameter α. The constant A represents a baseline multiplicative calibration constant in person months, i.e. costs which occur "if everything is normal" when building an ontology with 1000 ontological primitives. The cost drivers CD_i have a rating level (from *Very low* to *Very high*) that expresses their impact on the development effort. For the purpose of a quantitative analysis each rating level of each cost driver is associated to a weight (effort multipliers EM_{ij}). The productivity range PR_i of a cost driver is an indicator for the relative importance of a cost driver for the overall estimation (Boehm, 1981). It is calculated as the ratio between the highest and the lowest effort multiplier of a cost driver:

$$PR_i = \max(EM_{ij}) / \min(EM_{ij}) \qquad\qquad (2)$$

3.3   The ONTOCOM cost drivers

The core of the parametric method to estimate costs are the cost drivers, which are associated to features of the product or project at hand, which are likely to have an impact on the total development efforts. The relevance and impact of each cost driver to the overall estimate is subject to continuous adjustments based on the analysis of existing project data.

In order to generate a preliminary list of potential cost drivers for ontology engineering, and implicitly for the ONTOCOM model, we performed a comprehensive study of the literature in the field, conducted and analyzed various case studies, and interviewed several experts.

The resulting cost drivers can be roughly divided into three categories:

1. Product-related cost drivers account for the impact of the characteristics of the product to be engineered (i.e. the ontology) on the overall costs. The most important ontology features with this respect are the complexity of the modeled domain, the complexity of the conceptual model and its implementation, the complexity of the instantiation and the complexity of the evaluation procedure.
2. Personnel-related cost drivers emphasize the role of the team experience, ability and continuity with respect to the effort invested in the engineering process. In this category we mention the capability of ontology engineering and domain experts, their experience in developing ontologies or in working with ontology languages and tools as well as the personnel turnover.
3. Process-related cost drivers relate to characteristics of the global ontology engineering process and their impact on the total costs. The current version of ONTOCOM uses two project-related cost drivers: the availability of tools and technology to speed-up certain phases of an ontology development process and the multi-site development to mirror the usage of the communication support tools in a location-distributed team.

For each cost driver we specified in detail the decision criteria which are relevant for the model user in order for him to determine the concrete rating of the driver in a particular situation. For example for the cost driver CCPLX — accounting for costs produced by a particularly complex conceptualization — we pre-defined the meaning of the rating levels as depicted in Table 7-3. The appropriate rating should be selected during the cost estimation procedure and used as a multiplier in Equation 1. The concrete values of the effort multipliers have been determined during the calibration of the model, which is described in (Paslaru et al, 2006). Some of the values are depicted in Table 7-4 for exemplification purposes.

Table 7-3. The cost driver CCPLX (complexity of the conceptualization), its rating levels and associated effort multipliers.

Rating level	Effort multiplier	Description
Very low	0.28	The conceptual model is a concept list
Low	0.64	The conceptual model is a taxonomy. A high number of patterns supporting the creation of the taxonomy are available. No special modeling constraints are imposed through application requirements.
Nominal	1.0	The model contains a taxonomical structure and domain properties. Again, modeling patterns are available, while the application setting imposes some simple constraints which produce additional modeling overload.
High	1.36	The model contains in addition to the previous case axioms. By contrast the engineering team can not resort to a feasible number of modeling patterns to ease the conceptualization task. In the same time, the number of application-driven constrains increases.
Very high	1.72	The conceptual model is an axiomatized ontology containing both schema and instance data. In turn, there are few to no modeling patterns to support the conceptualization task, while the number of application-driven constrains is considerably high.

The decision criteria associated with a cost driver are typically more complex than in the previous example and might be sub-divided into further sub-categories, whose impact is aggregated to the final effort multiplier of the corresponding cost driver by means of normalized weights.

3.4   Using the ONTOCOM model

Starting from a typical ontology-building scenario, in which a domain ontology is created from scratch by the engineering team, we simulate the cost estimation process according to the parametric method underlying ONTOCOM. Given the top-down nature of our approach this estimation can be realized in the early phases of a project. In accordance to the process model introduced above the prediction of the arising costs can be performed during the feasibility study or, more reliably, during the requirements analysis. Many of the input parameters required to exercise the cost estimation are expected to be accurately approximated during this phase: the expected size of the ontology, the engineering team, the tools to be used, the implementation language etc.

The first step of the cost estimation is the specification of the size of the ontology to be built, expressed in thousands of ontological primitives (concepts, relations, axioms and instances): if we consider an ontology with 1000 concepts, 200 relations (including is-a) and 100 axioms, the size parameter of the estimation formula will be calculated as follows:

$$\text{Size} = 1000 + 200 + 100 / 1000 = 1, 3 \qquad (3)$$

The next step is the specification of the cost driver ratings corresponding to the information available at this point (i.e. without reuse and maintenance factors, since the ontology is built manually from scratch). Depending on their impact on the overall development effort, if a particular activity increases the nominal efforts, then it should be rated with values such as *High* and *Very high*. Otherwise, if it causes a decrease of the nominal costs, then it would be rated with values such as *Low* and *Very low*. Cost drivers which are not relevant for a particular scenario, or are perceived to have a nominal impact on the overall estimate, should be rated with the nominal value 1, which does not influence the result of the prediction equation.

Table 7-4. Cost drivers and their concrete values in a project

Cost driver	Effort	Value	Cost drivers	Effort	Value
Product-related drivers			Personnel-related drivers		
DCPLX	High	1.26	OCAP	Low	1.11
CCPLX	Nominal	1	DCAP	High	0.93
ICPLX	Low	1.15	OEXP	Low	1.11
DATA	Nominal	1	DEXP	Very high	0.89
REUSE	Nominal	1	LEXP	Nominal	1
DOCU	Nominal	1	TEXP	Nominal	1
OE	Nominal	1	PCON	Very High	1.2
Process-related drivers					
TOOL	Very low	1.7	SITE	Nominal	1

Assuming that the ratings of the cost drivers are those depicted in Table 7-4 these ratings are replaced by numerical values. The value of the DCPLX cost driver was computed as an equally weighted, averaged sum of a high-valued rating for the domain complexity, a nominal rating for the requirements complexity and a high effort multiplier for the information sources complexity (for details of other rating values see (Simperl et al., 2006)). According to the formula 1 the development effort of 11.44PM would be calculated as follows:

$$PM = 2.92 * 1.3 * (1.26 * 1.15 *$$
$$1.11 * 0.93 * 1.11 * 0.89 * 1.2 * 1.7) \tag{4}$$

The constant A has been set to 2.92 after the calibration of the model, while the economies of scale are so far not taken into consideration.

In order to increase the quality of the produced predictions in a particular project or organizational setting the generic model should however be subject to further calibrations or even extensions and revisions based on local data definitions. These issues are elaborated in the next section.

3.5   Applying the ONTOCOM model to arbitrary ontology engineering projects

ONTOCOM provides a generic model for predicting the costs arising in ontology engineering projects. In order to increase its real-world applicability it should be further extended and revised according to several dimensions:

- Support for the entire ontology lifecycle. The model briefly introduced in this chapter considers solely those projects in which ontologies are built manually without reusing existing knowledge resources. Cost drivers reflecting the impact of ontology reuse, or more generally knowledge acquisition, on the overall costs should be defined in order to cope with this limitation. A second aspect which is not addressed in the presented model is its usage in the target application context. With this respect one should extend the product- and process-related cost drivers with support for integration (how much does it cost to integrate the built ontology into its application system) and maintenance.
- Support for alternative ontology engineering methodologies. As explained in Section 3.1 the generic ONTOCOM model assumes a sequential ontology lifecycle which contains only the most important management, development and support activities (Gómez-Pérez et al., 2004). In case the model is applied to a different setting, the relevant cost drivers are to be aligned (or even re-defined) to the new sub-phases and activities, while the parametric equation needs to be adapted to the new activity breakdown.
- Refinements of the parametric method. The current release of the ONTOCOM model addresses two issues which are an integral part of

the parametric method solely marginally. First, the model should further investigate the need and determine an appropriate value for the economies of scale parameter in Equation 1. This can be achieved in a similar manner as in classical parametric models in the software engineering field such as COCOMO. This popular model, as well as other prominent approaches for software systems seems to agree upon a value of around 1 for this parameter (Barker and Kemerer, 2003). Second, the model needs to be extended with a means to estimate the duration of an ontology engineering project in addition to the person months efforts. In adjacent engineering disciplines it has been shown that duration can be predicted in close relationship to development efforts.

- Improvement of the prediction quality of the generic model. This can be achieved in several ways, which are not necessarily specific to the field of ontology engineering, but are related to the very nature of the parametric method:

  o Calibration with larger amounts of data. As the model is based on statistical analysis (e.g. using multi-linear regression, Bayes analysis or both, cf. (Paslaru et al, 2006)) its prediction quality is directly proportional to the number of data points used for the calibration.

  o Calibration with more accurate data. The quality of the obtained predictions equally depends on the quality of the collected historical data and on its representativeness for the present project. In this context calibrating the model using local data is likely to produce further improvements of the prediction quality.

  o Accurate input parameters: A prediction model, no matter how accurately calibrated, will not produce accurate values if the input parameters employed in the parametric equation are inexact. As the model is applied in an early stage of an ontology engineering project, it is likely that some of the required input parameters are not known in advance and need to be estimated by the engineering team. The most prominent example in this category is the size of the prospected ontology. In order to alleviate this problem, one could apply group decision methods to allow a more precise estimation of the size parameter. In addition, the analogy method could provide an alternative instrument for calculating this value.

4.   SOFTWARE AND TOOLS

Software tools are required for various types of tasks in the context of cost estimation models, in particular ONTOCOM.

On the one side the customization of a model to particular needs (expressed in terms of historical project data describing these needs implicitly through cost drivers) should be supported by tools for data collection and calibration. Depending on the estimation method applied the data collection can be systematically undertaken through face-to-face interviews, or structured questionnaires in a variety of forms (from Excel to Word documents and online tools). The calibration of the method requires statistical tools to perform the regression or the Bayes analysis (Devnani-Chulani, 1999). Figure 7-2 depicts a screenshot of the online questionnaire used for data collection for the ONTOCOM model.[1]

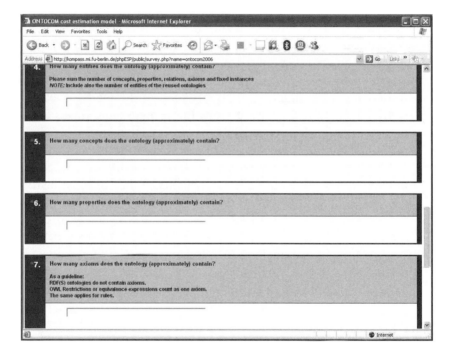

Figure 7-2. Online questionnaire used for data collection in ONTOCOM

Once the model can be viably applied to a project environment there is a need for tools which automatically calculate estimates using actual value inputs provided by the user. In their simplest form such tools can be specially designed Excel sheets or client applications with sophisticated user interfaces. Figure 7-3 gives an example of a tool we developed for the usage of the analogy method in ontology engineering.

---

[1] The questionnaire is available at http://kompass.mi.fu-berlin.de/phpESP/public/survey.php?name=ontocom2006.

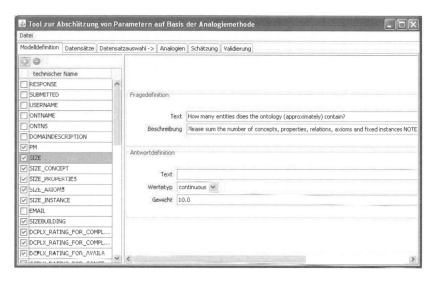

Figure 7-3. Tool for the usage of the analogy method

5. STATE OF THE ART AND RELATED WORK

Cost estimation methods have a long-standing tradition in more mature engineering disciplines such as software engineering or industrial production (Boehm, 1981, Kemerer, 1987, Putnam, 2003, Stewart, 1995). Although the importance of cost issues is well-acknowledged in the community, as to the best knowledge of the authors, no cost estimation model for ontology engineering has been published so far. Analogue models for the development of knowledge-based systems, e.g., (Felfernig, 2004) implicitly assume the availability of the underlying conceptual structures. (Menzies, 1999) provides a qualitative analysis of the costs and benefits of ontology usage in application systems, but does not offer any model to estimate the efforts. (Cohen et al, 1999) presents empirical results for quantifying ontology reuse. (Korotkiy, 2005) adjusts the cost drivers defined in a cos estimation model for Web applications with respect to the usage of ontologies. The cost drivers, however, are not adapted to the requirements of ontology engineering and no evaluation is provided.

6. SUMMARY AND CONCLUSIONS

Reliable methods for cost estimation are a fundamental requirement for a wide-scale dissemination of ontologies in business contexts. However, though the importance of cost issues is well-recognized in the community, no cost estimation model for ontology engineering is available so far. Starting from existing cost estimation methods applied across various engineering disciplines, we identify relevant cost drivers having a direct impact on the effort invested in the main activities of the ontology lifecycle and propose a parametric cost estimation model for ontologies based on the results. We explain how this model can be used and adapted in order to suit a wide range of ontology engineering projects at corporate level.

In the near future we intend to continue the data collection procedure in order to improve the quality of the generic model and its customizations. Much work needs to be done by many people, thus we see ONTOCOM as a seed for an urgently needed field of research, the cost estimation for ontologies. Any significant improvement in this field will substantially facilitate the uptake of semantic technologies for industrial projects. A second direction of research is related to the design and development of tools which allow an appropriate usage of the model, be that in terms of user-friendly applications for using the current model, or through alternative methods for the estimation of critical input parameters such as the size of the prospected ontology.

REFERENCES

Banker, R. D. and Kemerer, C. F., 1989, Scale economies in new software development. *IEEE Transactions of Software Engineering*, **15**(10):1199–1206.

Boehm, B. W., 1981, *Software Engineering Economics*. Prentice-Hall.

Cohen, P. R., Chaudhri, V. K., Pease, A. and Schrag, R., 1999 Does prior knowledge facilitate the development of knowledge-based systems? In *Proceedings of the AAAI/IAAI*, pp. 221–226.

Devnani-Chulani; S., 1999, Bayesian analysis of the software cost and quality models. *PhD thesis*, Faculty of the Graduate School University of Southern California.

Felfernig, A., 2004, Effort estimation for knowledge-based configuration systems. In *Proceedings of the 16th International Conference of Software Engineering and Knowledge Engineering SEKE04.*

Gómez-Pérez, A., Fernández-Lopez, M. and Corcho, O., 2004, *Ontological Engineering — with Examples from the Areas of Knowledge Management, e-Commerce and the Semantic Web*. Springer Verlag.

Hepp, M., 2007, Possible ontologies: How reality constrains the development of relevant ontologies, *IEEE Internet Computing*, **11**:90-96.

IEEE Computer Society, 1996, IEEE Standard for Developing Software Life Cycle Processes. IEEE Std 1074-1995.

Kemerer, C. F., 1987, An empirical validation of software cost estimation models. *Communications of the ACM*, **30**(5).

Korotkiy, M., 2005, On the effect of ontologies on Web application development effort. In *Proceedings of the Knowledge Engineering and Software Engineering Workshop.*

Menzies, T., 1999, Cost benefits of ontologies. *Intelligence*, **10**(3):26–32.

Paslaru-Bontas Simperl, E., Tempich, C. and Sure, Y., 2006. ONTOCOM: A cost estimation model for ontology engineering. In *Proceedings of the International Semantic Web Conference ISWC2006*, Springer Verlag.

Putnam, L. H. and Myers, M. W., 2003. *Five Core Metrics : the Intelligence Behind Successful Software Management*. Dorset House Publishing.

Stewart, R. D., Wyskida, R. M. and Johannes, J. D., 1995, *Cost Estimator's Reference Manual*.Wiley.

Sure, Y., Staab, S. and Studer, R., 2002, Methodology for development and employment of ontology based knowledge management applications. *SIGMOD Record*, **31**(4).

Sure, Y., Tempich, C. and Vrandecic, D., 2006, Ontology engineering methodologies. In *Semantic Web Technologies: Trends and Research in Ontology-based Systems*. Wiley

Tempich, C., Pinto, H. S. and Staab, S., 2006, Ontology engineering revisited: an iterative case study with diligent. In *Proceedings of the 3rd European Semantic Web Conference ESWC 2006*, pp. 110–124, Springer Verlag.

IV. EXPERIENCES

Chapter 8

ONTOLOGY MANAGEMENT IN E-BANKING APPLICATIONS
Integrating Third-Party Applications within an e-Banking Infrastructure

José-Manuel López-Cobo[1], Silvestre Losada[1], Laurent Cicurel[1], José Luis Bas[2], Sergio Bellido[2], and Richard Benjamins[3]
[1]Intelligent Software Components S.A., C/ Pedro de Valdivia 10, 28006, Madrid, Spain; [2]Bankinter, Paseo de la Castellana 29, 28046, Madrid, Spain; [3]Telefónica Investigación y Desarrollo SAU, Emilio Vargas 6, 28029, Madrid, Spain

Abstract: In this chapter we introduce how ontologies, semantic technologies in general, and Semantic Web Services in particular boost productivity in software and service development, by discovering new ways to extend the added value of applications in that domain. Two different applications have been developed between Bankinter, a Spanish bank with a strong innovation tendency and iSOCO, a leading company in the development of applications based on semantic technologies. We demonstrate the importance of semantic technologies for commercial banking applications and share experiences in working with ontologies and Semantic Web Services.

Keywords: mortgage application; ontology management; Semantic Web; Semantic Web Services; stock brokering; WSMO

1. INTRODUCTION

The Internet represents a real revolution that is here to stay: Millions of people access the Web to extract information, do some shopping, get entertained or just learn. From its early stages, the Web has provided a magnificent opportunity for anyone: persons, businesses or communities that want worldwide exposure.

However, communication between machines has not been developed deeply enough. The Internet currently does not allow for fluent communication between machines to do anything more but searching for words, whereas they should be exchanging information about the transactions they perform.

Overcoming, or at least lowering, existing barriers to a more efficient and automatic human-machine communication is at the forefront of research and development efforts. Although this may sound pretentious, we could be talking about a second revolution of the information society, just like in the past we knew the first and the second industrial revolutions caused by the steam machine and chain production, respectively. Analogously, we could be talking about the Internet for persons as the first revolution of the information society and the Internet for machines as the second one.

Nevertheless, as it happened with the steam machine or chain production, scientific innovations are useless if they are not reflected in economic activity and society. On one hand, the Internet has a role in showing information to the user. On the other hand, the most frequent commercial activity on Internet is based on services, especially in information-intensive sectors, maybe as providers, as intermediaries or transporters.

Given the online access that banks and financial institutions provide to their customers and business partners, banks can adopt several strategies regarding technology evolution. Orlikowski (1992) pointed out three possible roles for technology. The first one assumes that technology is a force external to the company with deterministic impacts on it. The second is a "softer" determinant and considers some moderating role of the company on this force. Finally, the third one sees technology as a product of shared interpretations or interventions. This leads us to distinguish among three types of banks:

- Technological leaders. Profile: medium-size banks that focus their strategy on technology and consider the Internet as an opportunity to improve their markets.
- Follower banks. Profile: big or medium size banks (there may be some exceptions) that first considered the Internet like a threat. When the market matured, they changed their strategy from a defensive position to a competitive attitude towards those who were first leaders.
- Non believer banks. The third group of banks did not invest in Internet because of their small size, strategy or other reasons. However, they are a minority in terms of market share.

2.   SEMANTIC WEB SERVICES FOR E-BANKING

Bankinter, one of Spain's leaders in the first group has always been aggressive in its online offerings and, consequently, is continuously looking for improvements. As we will argue later, ontologies and semantic technologies are among the most important opportunities for its strategy as they can significantly improve the efficiency of the processes[1] in a bank. Processes in a bank can be classified in three categories:

- Inter-banking processes: These processes are created to exchange documents and monetary entries (cheques, receipts, international and national transfers) between banks.
- Processes between a bank and its providers: This refers to basic supplies common to any industrial sector and to information providers that are specific to the financial business. The setting up of such processes requires many resources, in some case due to the development costs and in others due to the necessity of using a certain amount of intelligence to make them compatible with the banking system.
- Processes between a bank and its customers: This refers to product sales processes and the use of the services that the bank makes available through different channels.

Although there is room for big improvements in inter-banking processes, it is in the second and third type of processes where a bank can make a big difference with a significant use of ontologies. The data exchange of a bank with its customers and providers can be automated, reducing cost and time, so that the bank can provide better and more complex services to its customers. This has been the path travelled by Bankinter and iSOCO and is the goal of this chapter.

Bankinter is currently offering a free service that presents data about mortgages from a set of banks in Spain. Bank employees obtain this data manually, by browsing Web pages (when available) or by calling each bank to gather the information. The use of Semantic Web Services (SWS) technology can offer to replace the manual work and therefore improve the bank's resource utilization. If business partners such as mortgage providers develop, deploy and expose Semantic Web Services for public use, bank applications can discover them and utilize them automatically, thus reducing the dependency on human input.

Consequently, more services (product price comparators, information broker, deposits, etc.) can be offered by banks due to their low cost, since

---

[1] Read process in the generic sense of communication mechanism. This is not limited to Web Services, for example.

less human interaction is required to discover and invoke new available SWS once the application is launched. Some of the advantages of SWS over state-of-the-art Web service technology can be named.

When facing standard Web Service registries, such as the Universal Description, Discovery and Integration (UDDI), with a large number of exported Web Services, the lookup (discovery) becomes a serious problem. There is no standard for service goals or capabilities in current Web Service Description Language (WSDL) which prevents automatic service discovery. For example, a bank offering a mortgage information Web service only for fixed interest rates and with a maximum period of 20 years will not be able (or will have many difficulties) to publish such constraints in UDDI registries. External parties looking for services that match those characteristics will not be able to know in advance whether the service is providing this information according to those constraints.

When the discovered services have been defined according to a set of heterogeneous models, discrepancies may occur in the execution of those services. This is summarized as follows by Gartner Research (February 28, 2002): "Lack of technologies and products to dynamically mediate discrepancies in business semantics will limit the adoption of advanced Web services for large public communities whose participants have disparate business processes." Thus, the possibilities of better discovery and mediation are the main advantages of SWS technology over current Web service technology in the context of the described financial application.

Bankinter offers services to consult different kinds of stock market information (news, charts, index variations, stock prices), services to sell and buy stocks, services to send alerts and others. These services allow operating on the continuous stock market using a complete service delivery platform based on Web Service technology.

The StockBroker prototype took advantage of the technology that has been developed inside the European Research Project called DIP (automatic service discovery, service composition and service mediation), to construct complex operations working on different formats and driven by the final user requests. It uses a natural language interface to define the user goal and to construct and invoke the services. In order to build an SWS based solution of the prototype several Semantic Web Services were developed. As the StockBroker prototype uses Semantic Web Services, this prototype contributed to one of DIP's main goals. The application of Semantic Web Services as an infrastructure in real world scenarios within an organization and between organizations and its customers provided a use case for the use of WSMO (Web Service Modelling Ontology) in the description of the SWS involved in an application, and for the use of the SWS architecture defined in the context of the project.

The content of the chapter is structured as follows; first, we will look at existing standards on financial institutions and how they have been used in the applications developed. After that, we will provide evidence of the use of ontologies in e-Banking applications, highlighting lessons learned and making some practical remarks.

3. REUSING EXISTING CONSENSUS

Standardisation efforts in the banking domain are very slow. Efforts made by several organizations, such as the Mortgage Industry Standards Maintenance Organization, Inc. (MISMO) or the Society for Worldwide Interbank Financial Telecommunication (SWIFT), did not succeed in deploying standard world wide and the produced vocabularies can hardly be considered as references, at least in the Spanish bank domain.. Innovation-oriented banks like Bankinter prefer creating innovative products on their own, so that they have some competitive advantage during a short period (usually around half a year) leading the way for financial institutions that mimic its innovations. That is, we strongly believe that a bank like Bankinter will adopt its own conceptual model and then, if successful, this model will be progressively adopted by other banks.

This is well documented by a Forrester Research business report (2001) , in which the process of ontology adoption in business is explained: The financial domain is very dynamic, new products appear on a weekly basis and some of them cannot be categorised a priori. There is a high complexity in the current financial standards, such as IFX (International Financial eXchange[2]), and reaching agreement between different financial entities is difficult as well, as mentioned earlier.

There are also strong reasons to develop a new ontology (based on existing ontologies and standardisation initiatives) instead of directly applying already existing ones:

- In a mature market, such as the financial one, the only advantage competitors have is their expertise and a technology approach. Therefore, standardisation proposals usually result in long projects. In these projects, the strongest banks usually impose their own criteria on the rest, while small banks try to find a way to make things slightly (or completely) different, in order to contend where their big competitor cannot. In that business frame, a descriptive but not-too-complex ontology makes the standardization process easier and faster. It also

---

[2] IFX Forum, http://www.ifxforum.org/home

allows each bank to model its own complexity while maintaining a certain degree of differentiation within a common framework.

- Most of the existing ontologies that we have studied model the financial domain from a customer point of view, and do not sufficiently cover the internal processes that a bank must follow to deploy a mortgage contract or to extract information from the stock market.

We have focused on those parts of the ontology that are applicable to our specific needs. The resulting ontology would cover the requirements of the aforementioned prototype. The ontologies we have built cover in broad terms the financial domain and more specifically those concepts that are more relevant for the application of mortgage loans and for the Stock Market environment and covers almost all the concepts required to semantically describe these markets.

We have established relationships between all the concepts available from the same point of view, with special attention to the possible combinations of information that a stock market service can perform.

Studying the actual standards, however, provides us with the opportunity to gather the necessary vocabulary in order to better model our ontology.

- For developing semantic e-Banking applications, we tried to adapt the standard Interactive Financial eXchange (IFX), which is an XML-based, financial messaging protocol, built by financial industry and technology leaders, designed for interoperability of systems seeking to exchange financial information internally and externally. IFX is built with the recognition that no single financial transaction stands on its own, but is an integral part of the relationship among all of the communicating parties; a payment is not complete until a remittance is sent, an ATM withdrawal is not complete until a consumer's account has been debited, and so forth.

- XBRL (Extensible Business Reporting Language) is the closest standard to the stock market that we have found. We have analysed it to develop the specific Stock Market Ontology. XBRL[3] taxonomy focused on *"financial exchange of information in the reception and diffusion of the periodic public information (quarterly and semester information) that the listed societies with shares admitted to quotation must send to the supervisor"*[4]. Thus, this taxonomy is used to report the periodic information of companies to the stock market authorities and therefore we have used it for reference and to pick up several useful terms.

---

[3] http://www.xbrl.org
[4] http://www.xbrl.org.es/english/english.html

The ontologization of these standards could have been a solution, since the translation of XML documents to an ontology language could be automatized and enhanced further, in order to profit from the semantic expressivity of ontology languages. However, we clearly noticed, from the very beginning, that trying to adapt and ontologize IFX or XBRL would be a paramount effort (that was beyond the scope of the prototypes we were building). Furthermore, the target of those standards was mainly oriented to the exchange of messages between financial institutions and not directly addressing the relationship of a bank with its customers (at least not for the two scenarios we have foreseen: mortgage loans and stock brokerage). The level of IFX was too detailed for the purpose of the prototypes and would need extension and customization as well for the specifics of the mortgage loans and stock brokerage.

Other sources we have studied and adapted include:

- A financial ontology[5] developed by Teknowledge that extends the SUMO (Suggested Upper Merged Ontology) upper-level ontology and provides some top-level terms in the financial domain.
- Mortgage information publicly provided by Web sites from twelve Spanish banks, including the leaders in the mortgage market[6], which are: BBVA[7], Santander[8], Caja Madrid, La Caixa[9], Banco Popular[10], iBanesto[11], Patagon[12], Bankinter[13], Banco Pastor[14], Banco Sabadell, and BBK.
- To detect the most common terms used in the stock market, we have taken a broad vision of the market for this ontology. To make it more powerful, we have included in our research Spanish and worldwide independent stock market services (i.e.: Yahoo Finances[15], Reuters[16], Xignite[17] and Invertia[18]), since they are increasingly used by costumers and, usually, offer more detailed information than banks.

---

[5] http://einstein.teknowledge.com:8080/download/register.jsp?fileType=.tar&fileName=FinancialOnt.tar
[6] An unofficial ranking of Spanish banks with respect to their position on the mortgage market is available at http://tinyurl.com/2evmq3
[7] BBVA: http://tinyurl.com/2ds76a
[8] Santander: http://tinyurl.com/2chesp
[9] La Caixa: http://tinyurl.com/2bw72c
[10] Banco Popular: http://www.bancopopular.es/simuladores/simula.asp
[11] Banesto: http://www.ibanesto.com
[12] Patagon: http://tinyurl.com/2b3y6b
[13] Bankinter: http://tinyurl.com/267zbm
[14] Banco Pastor: http://www.bancopastor.es/d30/d3020/3020_stage2.html
[15] Yahoo! Finance: http://finance.yahoo.com/
[16] Reuters UK: http://uk.reuters.com/home
[17] Xignite: http://preview.xignite.com/
[18] Invertia: http://www.invertia.com

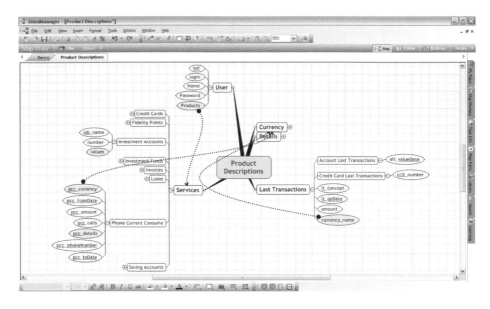

Figure 8-1. Mind map taken in a brainstorm session with domain experts

In our experience, the most fruitful stage of the conceptualization is when some ontology engineer meets with domain experts. Depending on the size and complexity of the Domain, we usually apply METHONTOLOGY (Fernández et al., 1997) or DILIGENT (Pinto et al., 2004). As a first step, we try to capture as much information as possible, using some tool for mind maps as MindManager[19]©, FreeMind[20] or MindMeister[21] (for a shared online conceptualization) as shown in the figure above.

4.   EDITING AND BROWSING

As we have said, previously we have considered the use of a general-purpose tool as a mind mapping tool for the first steps of knowledge acquisition, allowing a shared and distributed editing of concepts and relationships between the experts on the domain (usually bank employees) and knowledge engineers (employees from iSOCO). Once a first draft of the conceptualization is released, a deeper conceptualization is needed for the creation of the set of ontologies needed for the applications we have made.

---

[19] http://www.mindjet.com. Mind Manager is a comercial solution and provides a 30 days trial

[20] http://freemind.sourceforge.net/wiki/index.php/Main_Page#Download_and_install .
    FreeMind is an free software under the GPL license.

[21] http://www.mindmeister.com/ MindMeister provides free or Premium access. It allows
    collaborative online mind mapping.

For that purpose, we have used a couple of tools that have proved to be effective and useful: Protégé[22] and WSMO Studio[23]. The use of one tool or other has been decided based upon the final use of the ontologies created with them. For all the ontologies not directly related to Semantic Web Services, like those connected more to the use and exploitation of Natural Language Processing (NLP) needed for the applications, we have used Protégé because of the support it provides for formalisms such as RDF (Resource Description Framework) and OWL (Web Ontology Language) — given that our suite for Intelligent Access to Information uses them. All the ontologies that dealt with ontology learning for banking purposes thus were described in RDF. Within this category, we can mention the Ontology for Financial Products as the main input for product recognition in the NLP component (Knowledge Access[24]). Other ontologies that were written in RDF within Protégé were the Semantic Pattern Matching Ontology, used to discover goals and further translated into WSMO Goals.

The combination of machine-processable semantics facilitated by the Semantic Web with current Web Service technologies has coined the term Semantic Web Services. Semantic Web Services offer the means to achieve a higher level of value-added services by adding dynamism to the task driven assembly of inter-organization business logics. They have the potential to make the Internet a global, common platform where agents (organizations, individuals, and software) communicate with each other to carry out various activities. Semantic Web Services represent an extension to current Web Services technology. They broaden the Web from a distributed source of information to a distributed source of services (Lara et al., 2003), where software resources can be assembled on the fly to accomplish user goals.

In order to allow the usage and complete integration of Web Services, their capabilities need to be semantically marked up, and their interfaces need to provide the means to understand how to consume their functionality. Furthermore, the exchange of documents requires describing the meaning of the content in a way that can be understood and communicated independently of some particular domain knowledge.

---

[22] Protègè: http://protege.stanford.edu/ . Protègè is available as free software under the open-source Mozilla Public License
[23] WSMO Studio: http://www.wsmostudio.org. WSMO Studio is available under LGPL license.
[24] Knowlegde Access Suite: http://isoco.com/en/solutions/customer.html

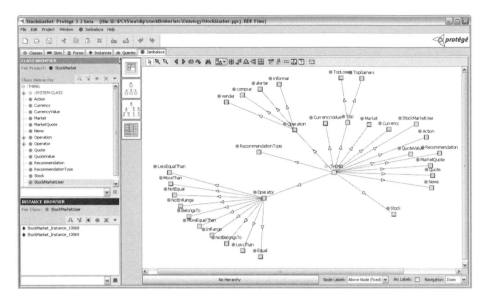

Figure 8-2. Glimpse of the StockMarket ontology and the Jambalaya plug-in for Protégé

WSMO[25] tries to alleviate these problems by defining the modeling elements for describing several aspects of Semantic Web Services. WSMO is a formal ontology and language for describing the various aspects related to Semantic Web Services. It represents the backbone for the development of the Web Service Modelling Language (WSML[26]) and the Web Service Modelling Execution Environment (WSMX[27]). The conceptual grounding of WSMO is based on the Web Service Modeling Framework (WSMF) (Fensel and Bussler, 2002), wherein four main components are defined:

Ontologies provide the formal semantics of the information used by all other components. Ontologies (1) are used to express goals in a machine processable and understandable language; (2) permit enhancing Web Services so they can be matched against goals; and (3) interconnect the different elements with each other by means of mediators.

Goals specify objectives that a client may have when consulting a Web Service. They provide the means to express a high-level description of a concrete task.

Web Services represent the functional part which must be semantically described in order to allow their semi-automated use.

Mediators used as connectors provide interoperability facilities among the rest of components. Currently the specification defines four different

---

[25] WSMO: http://www.wsmo.org

[26] WSML: http://www.wsmo.org/wsml

[27] WSMX: http://www.wsmx.org

types of mediators, which are classified in two main classes: refiners (ggMediators and ooMediators) and bridges (wgMediators and wwMediators). While refiners are used to define new components as a specialization of an existing one, bridges help to overcome interoperability problems by enabling components to interact with each other.

Given that our applications were designed to work with Semantic Web Services, we have defined Ontologies, Goals, Services and Mediators in WSML, to be executed within WSMX. For the definition of those, we have used WSMO Studio, a Semantic Web Service modelling environment for WSMO that has been built as a set of Eclipse[28] plug-ins that can be further extended by third parties.

The environment of WSMO Studio allows the creation of WSMO concepts in two ways:

- Using the WSMO Editor. This editor allows you to conceptually describe the different elements of WSMO. For each element, contextual information can be provided in the form of properties, capabilities in the form of axioms and many other things.
- Using the Text WSML Editor. The editor supports syntax highlighting and extending the list of predefined WSML keywords by the user.

Figure 8-3. Describing a WSMO Goal with WSMO Studio

---

[28] Eclipse: http://www.eclipse.org

Sometimes is easier to use the form-wise structure of the WSMO Editor (i.e., when creating the concept hierarchy or defining the choreography interface), however on other occasions is wiser to write directly in the WSML Editor (we have found that writing axioms in the Text WSML Editor is the best way to finish them).

Once you have created your WSML files describing your Ontologies, Goals and Services and, if needed, Mediators, you need to ground them in order to make them reachable. For our StockBroker application we made use of WSMX, the execution environment for WSMO. In WSMX, there are a number of components that help you to create applications and other elements that need to be extended in order to be used. Among the former, we can find the QoS Discovery and Selection component, which allows semantic matching of goals and services, as well as the Choreography engine and the Invocation component. The architecture of WSMX allows the creation of specific adapters to integrate an application within WSMX, by using the Adapter Framework.

Figure 8-4. Writing an axiom using the Text WSML Editor

As we can see above in the conceptual architecture of the StockBroker, and its relationship with WSMX, we will describe WSMX components and how they were used in our prototype.

- Discovery: The WSMX Discovery component is concerned with finding Web Service descriptions that match the goal specified by the service requester. WSMO descriptions of the goal represent what a user wishes to achieve (described in terms of a desired capability with preconditions, assumptions, effects and post-conditions) and is matched with WSMO descriptions of Web Services known to WSMX (described in terms of offered capabilities). The Discovery component returns a list of Web Service descriptions from various service providers.

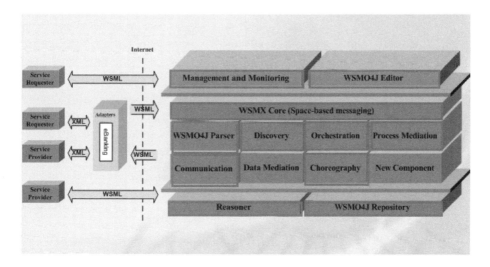

Figure 8-5. Integration of the Stockbroker within WSMX

- Orchestration / Choreography. This component is responsible for making service compositions. A WSMX Choreography (Figure 8-5) defines how to interact with a Web Service in terms of messages exchanged by means of communication patterns. A WSMX Orchestration (Figure 8-5) describes how the service makes use of other services in order to achieve its capability.
- Process Mediator / Mediation Process: A WSMX Process Mediator has the role of reconciling the public process heterogeneity that can appear during the invocation of Web Services. That is, it is to ensure that the public processes of the invoker and the invoked Web Service match. Since both the invoker and the Web Service publish their public processes as choreographies, and the public processes are executed by sending/receiving messages, the Process Mediator Component will deal with reconciliation of message exchange patterns based on choreography.
- Resource Manager: This component is necessary to manage the persistent storage WSMO objects it will be provided with by other components within WSMX. The component implementing this interface

is responsible for storing all data. WSMO4J[29] provides a set of Java interfaces that can be used to represent the domain model defined by WSMO.

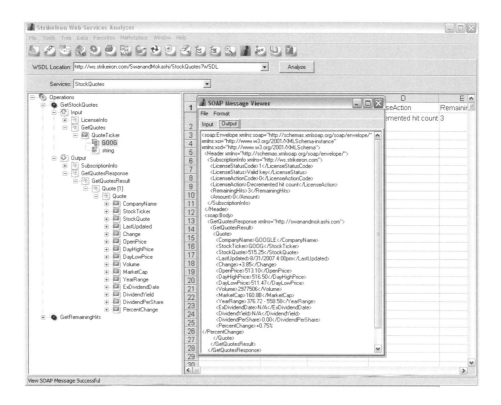

Figure 8-6. Testing Web Service invocation with StrikeIron Analyzer

- **Communication Manager:** This component is necessary to manage the interaction with the system. The Communication Manager accepts the message and handles any transport and security protocols used by the message sender. The Communication Manager is responsible for dealing with the protocols for sending and receiving messages to and from WSMX. A specific e-Banking Adapter performs this work by connecting the StockBroker outgoing messages with the WSMX incoming messages. The importance of this adapter is paramount when integrating third party services, as you need to create specific WSML to XML translators for them and vice versa. For the testing of the *delicate* task of grounding Semantic Web Services, we have used a tool for inspecting Web Services. As one of the providers of third party services

---

[29] WSMO4J: http:// wsmo4j.sourceforge.net

we were using was StrikeIron, we used its StrikeIron Web Service Tools Suite[30]. When using Web Services that have not been designed to work with your application, a *smooth integration* is more a myth than an industrial reality. For that reason, we use the StrikeIron Analyzer, jointly with the output of the e-Banking Adapter to test and tune the XML to the WSML translator.

Our experience has told us that the integration of ontologies and other semantic technologies with commercial deployed services is far from the promised *"seamless integration."* However, the results have been satisfactory for the goals we have in mind. There is still work to be done in fields like Service Grounding, that will help us to automate the connection between a semantically enhanced service and its mapped Web Service.

We have opened the path for future e-Banking applications where the need for automation and an overall and shared vision of information is so important.

5.   CONCLUSIONS

We have presented some experiences with dealing with semantic technologies and Semantic Web Services within the financial domain. Based on these experiences, we can formulate some lessons learned with regard to choosing the application field, implementing the technology, and analyzing benefits of the SWS approach.

The e-Banking application field described in this chapter can be characterized by three features, which in our opinion rationalize the additional effort required by a solution based on SWS. Firstly, the environment is distributed. There are many actors involved in the process of offering a mortgage to the final customer or several providers in competition to offer their resources in the StockBroker prototype, and many information sources influencing the decision taking process. This feature ensures that the potential of semantically enhanced discovery and composition can be utilized.

Secondly, the market is dynamic. The circumstances change, the products evolve and the partners come and go. This feature of the environment ensures that a one-time investment will pay off in the long term. The loose coupling enforced by separating goals and Web service descriptions enables SWS-based applications to continue working even if some of the Web Services used in application stop working, provided that an alternative Web Service can be dynamically discovered and invoked.

---

[30] StrikeIron WS Analyzer: http://www.strikeiron.com/tools/tools_analyzer_windows.aspx

Thirdly, our application field is profitable, but not mission critical. These two characteristics should be a general guideline for introducing new technologies, as the initial costs of adopting new technologies are influenced by the need of training the personnel, which can pay off in the longer term. New technologies bear risks, however, which can be minimized when they are deployed in an iterative process, starting with low-risk areas. With respect to the characteristics of markets described above, we have shown how SWS can bring benefit in B2B and B2C application integration scenarios. In the financial domain, the benefits focus on the automatic discovery and invocation of third party services provided by Semantic Web Services. We expect that with the ongoing work on these functionalities, as well as on composition and mediation, these benefits will be boosted further, so that SWS will become a common artefact in enterprise IT landscapes.

REFERENCES

Fensel, D. and Bussler, C., 2002, The Web Service Modeling Framework WSMF, *Electronic Commerce Research and Applications*, **1**(2)

Fernández, M., Gómez-Pérez, A., and Juristo, N., 1997, METHONTOLOGY: From Ontological Art Towards Ontological Engineering, in: *Spring Symposium Series, Stanford*, pp. 33-40.

Forrester Research, 2001, How the X Internet will Communicate. Available at http://tinyurl.com/yp732s.

Lara, R., Lausen, H., Arroyo, S., de Bruijn, J., and Fensel, D., 2003, Semantic Web Services: description requirements and current technologies, in: *International Workshop on Electronic Commerce, Agents, and Semantic Web Services, In conjunction with the Fifth International Conference on Electronic Commerce (ICEC 2003), Pittsburgh, PA, 2003.*

Orlikowski, W.J., 1992, The Duality of Technology: Rethinking the Concept of Technology in Organizations, *Organization Science*, **3**, pp. 398-427.

Pinto, H., Staab, S. and Tempich, C., 2004, DILIGENT: Towards a fine-grained methodology for DIstributed, Loosely-controlled and evolvInG Engingeering of oNTologies, in: *Proceedings of the 16th European Conference on Artificial Intelligence (ECAI 2004), August 22nd–27th, 2004, Valencia, Spain.*

Chapter 9

ONTOLOGY-BASED KNOWLEDGE MANAGEMENT IN AUTOMOTIVE ENGINEERING SCENARIOS

Jürgen Angele, Michael Erdmann, and Dirk Wenke
ontoprise GmbH, Amalienbadstraße 36 (Raumfabrik 29), D-76227 Karlsruhe, Germany
{angele | erdmann | wenke}@ontoprise.de

Abstract: Nowadays the increasing complexity of cars has become a major challenge for car manufacturers, especially due to the growing rate of electronic components and software. This trend impacts all phases of the car's lifecycle, e.g. the process of testing cars and components. We describe a project from the automotive industry where a semantics-based approach is employed for improving the process of testing different configurations of cars. Here, ontologies serve two main purposes: (i) representing and sharing knowledge to optimize business processes for testing of cars and (ii) integrating live data into this optimization process. The ontology has been created and is now maintained with OntoStudio®. The ontology has been integrated into the internal order system of the car manufacturer to reduce the communication effort between the engineers for configuring test cars and to avoid misconfigurations of test cars.

Keywords: applications; automotive; engineering; information integration; rules; Semantic Web

1. INTRODUCTION

The automotive industry today is moved by two main trends: the reduction of *time-to-market*, and the increasing demand for *built-to-order*. Time-to-market reflects the reduction of innovation cycles, whereas built-to-order refers to the move from the mass production of cars to a limited-lot-production of individual cars. Both trends require an optimization of processes: the manufacturing process and also earlier steps such as research, development, and testing. Manufacturing *and* development benefit from close collaboration with suppliers. Thus, knowledge sharing between different organizations and between different departments of the car manufacturer is required.

In this chapter we describe an ontology based application for configuring test cars of a car manufacturer. The semantic model is mainly used to make sure that only valid configurations are actually built. The ontology serves two different tasks: (i) representing and sharing knowledge to optimize business processes for the testing of cars, and (ii) integrating live data into this optimization process.

The ontology-based application integrates legacy systems of the manufacturer to access up-to-date information for the test-data-analysis. This data is semantically enriched with background knowledge consisting of a complex domain ontology and inference rules. The enriched model accelerates the configuration of test cars and, thus, reduces time-to-market.

The ontology and rule base were created and are now maintained with OntoStudio®, an ontology editor that has been developed by Ontoprise with five main objectives:

1. Ease of use
2. Ontology development supported by inferencing
3. Development of rules
4. Support for reuse and integration of legacy/non-ontological information sources
5. Extensibility through plug-in structure

This chapter starts with the presentation of a use case for ontology use in the automotive industry (Section 2). It continues with an introduction of the relevant features of OntoStudio and illustrates them based on the use case (Sections 3–5, basic modeling, reasoning support for modeling, and integrating legacy data) before summarizing the benefits of building ontology based applications for the automotive industry.

2.   CASE STUDY: CONFIGURATION OF TEST CARS

Having a look at the shares of vehicle sales in US from 1970 – 2001 (see Figure 9-1) we observe that the big three automobile vendors (Chrysler, Ford, General Motors) considerably lost market shares in that time period. One of the reasons was that before the early nineties the quality of their cars compared to the competitor's cars was very poor. Then the big three started a quality offensive which resulted in a slight market gain until 1994. But after 1994 the big three again lost market shares. The reason for the second loss which lasts until today is the slow innovation in the automotive industry in US. The competitors in Asia and Europe have been able to strongly reduce the time for developing new cars. As a consequence time-to-market is one of the main optimization goals in the automotive industry.

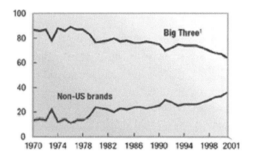

Figure 9-1. Market shares of vehicle sales (source: Wards automotive yearbook)

Another very important trend in consumer oriented production industry is built-to-order. Built-to order means that a product is immediately produced and delivered after the consumer has configured the product according to his wishes. With this strategy Dell edged out a lot of its competitors on the PC market. In contrast to that in the automotive industry cars are first developed and then manufactured in large amounts with a high degree of optimization. Very often the results are huge amounts of cars which cannot be sold and thus produce costs for the investment and for storing them. Finally, these cars must be sold with large sales discounts which again reduce the profit of the manufacturer. Built-to-order avoids all these problems but requires a severe change of logistic and business processes. Built-to-order reduces the mass production of cars to a limited-lot-production. Emphasis for optimization issues moves from the production step to earlier steps such as the collaboration between suppliers and manufacturers in development and delivering. Thus, knowledge has to be shared between different organizations and departments. Therefore, the main emphasis has to be put on optimizing these business processes.

The scenario for this process was given by the business processes around the testing of cars. The car company has a fleet of test cars. These test cars are continuously reconfigured and then tested with this new configuration. Reconfiguration means changing the engine, changing the gear, changing the electric, i.e. changing all kinds of parts. For the changing of parts a lot of dependencies between these parts have to be taken into account. In many cases these dependencies are only known by a few human experts and thus require a lot of communication efforts between different departments of the manufacturer, between the manufacturer and suppliers, and between suppliers. Very often test cars have been configured which did not work or which hampered the measurement of the desired parameters. So making such dependencies exploitable by computers allows for reducing the error rate in configuring test cars with a lower communication effort. This in turn accelerates the development of new cars and enhances the collaboration between manufacturer and suppliers. Thus it reduces time-to-market and supports the built-to-order process.

The resulting system is based on an ontology. This ontology has two major objectives. Firstly it represents the terminology and the complex dependencies between the different car parts. These dependencies are represented as relationships and rules. Secondly the ontology serves as a mediator between data from different sources (Maier et al., 2003), especially to integrate up-to-date data about parts etc. from the legacy systems of the manufacturer.

The ontology has been integrated into the internal order system as a software assistant, which helps the engineer in configuring test cars. The engineer asks the assistant for a reconfiguration and the system answers with the dependencies which have to be taken into account and the contact information for experts in this case. Additionally, the assistant will provide explanations which help the engineer to understand and validate the decision of the assistant.

While in our case the ontology was used to enhance the internal order system the same ontology may be reused for the dynamic configuration of cars in a built-to-order process as well. Restrictions like *"The power of the engine must not exceed the one of the brakes"* need to be checked also during the dynamic configuration of cars.

For the development of the ontology, the ontology modeling environment OntoStudio® was used. During the project it became clear that the following features were very important:

- The ontology is the communication medium between engineers and knowledge engineers. It turned out that graphical means are very well suited for this communication process. This holds especially for complex knowledge representations like rules.
- The ontology must provide immediate feedback, i.e. it is very useful to have it seamlessly integrated with an inference engine which evaluates rules and which creates answers during modeling and validates the model. Also, in this process the immediate feedback from the engineers was crucial. For complex models sophisticated means for debugging and analyzing the models must be provided by the ontology modeling tool.

- In our case a lot of information was stored and maintained in the legacy systems of the car manufacturer, i.e. an important part of the development was reengineering this information and attaching it to the ontology. As this data will further be maintained in the legacy systems it is important to access this information on a real-time basis instead of importing all this information into the ontology system. To be flexible for changes in the legacy systems even this attachment must be supported by graphical means.
- For the run time system the performance of the system is crucial. The ontology tool should support optimization and deployment of the model.
- Finally, the model will no longer be maintained by pure knowledge engineers in future. Instead, the mechanical engineers should be able to maintain and extend it. Thus, the tool should be intuitive enough to be used by them. Again, graphical means are very well suited for this issue.

3.   ONTOLOGY MODELING

The automotive case is a very versatile modeling use case, because many different applications occur. A basic ontology has to be created, existing information has to be integrated, and the expert knowledge of the engineers has to be formalized in a kind of rules. Thus, the modeling process can be divided into four phases:

- the analysis of the domain,
- the construction of the ontology,
- the integration of already existing information in the legacy systems, like in databases, and
- the modeling of the expert knowledge as rules.

This modeling process is described in the subsequent sections.

3.1   Concepts, relations, attributes, instances

The initial step in the modeling process (the *analysis of the domain*) is necessary to exactly define the domain, which is a challenging task because the domain experts in most cases do not know how to develop an ontology and the knowledge engineers do not have sufficient knowledge of the domain. To complete this task knowledge must be transferred from the domain experts to the knowledge engineers.

To initiate this transfer, the OnToKnowledge methodology (Sure and Studer, 2002) was used, where the domain experts fill out competency questionnaires, in which they describe what they expect from the later system and what questions it should be able to answer. The described expectations and stated questions provide a good basis to start the modeling process. Examples for the formulated questions were:

- Is the configuration of the current test-car valid?
- What are the errors of the configuration?
- Which components do not match?
- Which components are connected to the battery?
- Are the brakes sufficient for the power of the engine?

The domain experts provided some hundred of these domain specific questions, which were used afterwards to identify the key terms and properties such as *configuration, component, engine, battery, etc.* After the extraction of the key terms, the modeling phase started. In this step the ontology was formalized using OntoStudio (cf. Figure 9-2). A large amount of concepts was created and arranged in a subsumption hierarchy. Most of them were related to the different parts of the car, e.g. *engine, chassis,* or *gear.*

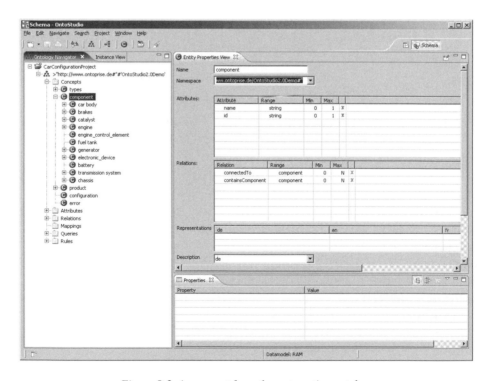

Figure 9-2. An excerpt from the automotive ontology

Attributes have been used for the specific attributes of the different components. Only a small set of relations was needed to describe the relationships between the components, such as the *containsComponent* relation describing that one component is part of another component.

Instances have been added temporarily for testing purposes only. All real instances have later been integrated from different legacy systems by using the integration features of OntoStudio.

3.2   Rules

An ontology without rules describes only simple, structural relationships between concepts like parts being part of components, parts being connected to other parts etc. More complex relationships have to be described by rules and constraints. It is this more complex knowledge which has to be captured by the ontology to help configuring test cars. In the following such constraints are presented:

Constraint 1: For a given configuration the devices connected to the battery must match the amperage of the used battery.

Constraint 2: For a given configuration the maximum power of the motor must not exceed the one of the brakes, i.e. $P_{motor} <= P_{brakes}$

Constraint 3: For a given configuration the filter installed in a catalyst must match with the motor's fuel.

These constraints could easily be modeled by the engineers using OntoStudio's graphical rule editor. It enabled the users to build complex rules using graphical means, thus abstracting from the concrete syntax of the rules. OntoStudio automatically generates the logical syntax out of the rule diagrams and optimizes it for execution.

The graphical representation of constraint 1 is shown in Figure 9-3. The ellipses describe concepts, labeled arrows describe relationships. The squares represent attribute values. Thus, there is a configuration with two components: a battery and a component. The battery is connected to the component. The battery has amperage and the component has amperage and both are not equal. If all these conditions hold, the implication (in green) also holds: the configuration is flagged with an error that has two non-matching components.

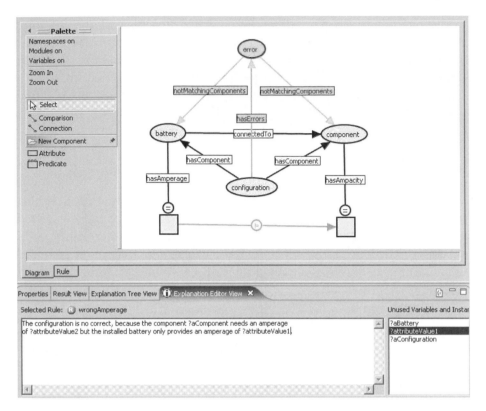

Figure 9-3. Rule diagram for constraint 1 with explanation text in the bottom window.

The experiences in this project have shown that the graphical representation of rules seems to be intuitive enough to serve as a communication medium between the knowledge engineers and the mechanical engineers, i.e. the domain experts understood the model to give valuable feed-back.

3.3   Explanations

If the system detects an error in a given configuration the mechanical engineer still needs the rationale behind it. Thus, the system should be able to generate explanations how it deduced this result. This problem is solved in OntoStudio and OntoBroker® by storing information about the inference process during the evaluation of rules, which can be used to generate explanations for the results.

To obtain readable explanations OntoStudio integrates an explanation editor which allows assigning explanation patterns consisting of readable text for rules. For example, the bottom part of Figure 3 shows the explanation editor for constraint 1. The explanation text contains variables (indicated by a leading "?") which stand for instances of concepts or values of attributes in the rule:

"The configuration is not correct, because the component ?aComponent needs amperage of ?attributeValue2 but the installed battery only provides amperage of ?attributeValue1"

During the inference process the concrete values for all variables are recorded and, thus, an explanation is generated from this text pattern like:

"The configuration is not correct, because the component Controller45a needs amperage of 95Ah but the installed battery only provides amperage of 70Ah".

Because all the dependencies of all used rules are recorded, complex explanations in a hierarchical form can be created to explain the full depth of deduction. The explanation feature is a very useful means for the mechanical engineers to get an insight into the reasoning and validate the model or find incorrect rules.

4. REASONING FOR ENGINEERING

While the ontology evolves and the set of axioms grows, the need to ensure that the ontology together with the rules describe a consistent and correct model of the domain increases. Especially the set of rules and their interrelationships are sometimes complex to survey as a whole. With rules two types of major problems occur:

- Semantic errors in the rule: sometimes the engineers fail in modeling the intended meaning. OntoStudio provides several tools for verifying the ontology which are all based on reasoning:
  - The *Rule Debugger* enables engineers to localize errors in a set of rules.
  - The *Analyzer* allows verifying that the ontology satisfies predefined constraints.
  - The *Regression Test Feature* allows for generating and executing test cases.
- Performance issues: depending on the definition, rules can severely hamper the performance of the resulting system. The inference engine OntoBroker is seamlessly integrated into OntoStudio. This strongly supports a prototyping approach where modified/extended models can immediately be executed in posing appropriate queries. This provides early feedback about the quality and also the performance behaviour of

the model. This allows measuring and displaying performance information and also taking counter measures via choosing different parameters for the inference mechanism such as optimizing the rule set for a specific type of queries.

4.1   Logical foundations

In order to provide a clearly defined semantics for the knowledge model of OntoStudio, its knowledge structures correspond to a well-understood logical framework, viz. F-Logic (cf. (Kifer et al., 1995), "F" stands for "Frames"). F-Logic combines deductive and object-oriented aspects: *"F-Logic [...] is a deductive, object-oriented database language which combines the declarative semantics of deductive databases with the rich data modeling capabilities supported by the object oriented data model."* (Frohn et al., 1996). F-Logic allows for concise definitions with object oriented-like primitives (classes, attributes, object-oriented-style relations, instances) that are reflected by the OntoStudio GUI. Furthermore, it also has Predicate Logic (PL-1) like primitives (predicates, function symbols), that are only partially reflected in the GUI but internally used within the data structures. F-Logic allows for rules and constraints that further constrain the interpretation of the model. F-Logic rules have the expressive power of Horn-Logic with negation.

Normal programs are Horn programs where rules may contain negated literals in their bodies. The semantics defined for these normal programs is the *well-founded semantics* (van Gelder, 1993). In (van Gelder et al., 1995), the alternating fixpoint has been described as a method to operationalize such logic programs. This method has been shown to be very inefficient. Therefore the inference engine realizes dynamic filtering (Kifer and Lozinskii, 1986) which combines top-down and bottom-up inferencing. Together with an appropriate extension to compute the well-founded semantics this method has been proven to be very efficient compared to other Horn-based inference engines (cf. e.g. (Sure et al., 2002b)). For detailed introductions to the syntax and the object model of F-Logic, in particular with respect to the implementation of F-Logic in OntoBroker, we refer to (Erdmann, 2001; Decker, 2002; Ontoprise; 2002).

Our example rule from Figure 3 reads in F-Logic syntax like this:

```
error(?X,?Y):error[notMatchingComponents->>{?X,?Y}] AND
?C[hasErrors->>error(?X,?Y)]
<-
?C:Configuration[hasComponents->>{?X,?Y}] AND
?X:battery[hasAmperage->>?Z1] AND
?Y:component[connectedTo->>?X, hasAmperage->>?Z2] AND
?Z1 != ?Z2.
```

4.2   Debugging rules

Creating explanations and querying for answers is one way of validating an ontology with a complex set of rules. While this method targets the end users of the final system, a more flexible way for validation is needed by ontology engineers.

In the automotive use case the engineers developed some one hundred rules expressing the dependencies of the various components with many of them depending on other rules. If a query is not returning the correct result, this linkage to many rules makes it hard to determine which of the rules actually is the real cause of a wrong result. Thus, the engineers need tools that can show the linkage between the rules and that enable them to investigate the query evaluation process to observe the rules step by step to identify the rule that is not modelled properly.

For these purposes OntoStudio includes a debugging environment that is aligned to the intuitive process of debugging ontologies. Ontology engineers debug queries in an iterative process:

1. Analyze the rule dependencies, i.e. the rule graph.
2. Execute the query/rule body partially to find the part that is not returning the expected results.
3. Detect whether (a) basic facts are missing, or (b) another rule does not infer the expected information.

Thus, the debugging process resembles a drill down process starting at the query looking for the results and then drilling down into rules delivering partial answers, etc. This interactive process is supported by OntoStudio's *Rule Debugger*, which is shown in Figure 4. It contains a visualization of the rule dependencies in the upper left corner, where the user can see whether all rules that should be involved in the execution of the query are correctly involved. If a rule is missing in the rule graph, then the rule does not match the other rules, which might be the cause of the problem.

If all rules are contained in the rule graph, one rule probably does not return the values that are intended. To find this rule, the debugging component allows for the partial execution of the query and rule bodies. The intuitive way to find the defective rule is to remove some conditions in the rule body to find out which conditions are not working. The component for the partial execution of the rule bodies is shown in the upper right part of Figure 9-4.

If the condition is found, it has to be checked whether instance information is missing or whether another rule that should infer information matching this condition is not working properly. In the latter case this rule has to be analyzed in the same way. Iterating these steps finally will determine the defective rule.

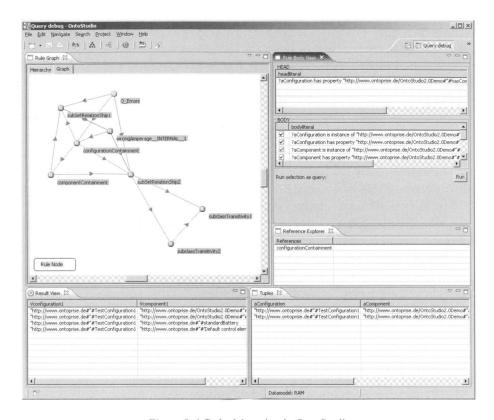

Figure 9-4. Rule debugging in OntoStudio

4.3 Analyzing ontologies

Guidelines for ontology modeling help to ensure coherent ontologies and thus a consistent level of quality. Support for testing the guidelines inherently enhances the quality of collaboratively created models (Sure et al., 2002a).

Integrating guideline checking into ontology engineering environments helps to evaluate the guidelines during modeling time and guarantees immediate feedback for ontology engineers. From our experiences with ontology development and deployment we learned that for different purposes ontologies must have different properties, e.g. for different target applications (Lau and Sure, 2002; Sure and Yosif, 2002; Davies et al., 2003).

Therefore, a flexible way of using and adapting guidelines is needed instead of hard coding them. Guidelines might be used for technology-focussed evaluations, e.g. to ensure that naming conventions are fulfilled (for instance, some inference engines do not allow for white spaces in concept identifiers while others accept them), or for ontology-focussed evaluations. The definition of evaluation methods for such properties must be very flexible and easily maintainable. So it is not convenient to hard code it into the Ontology Engineering Environment itself.

The *OntoAnalyzer* plug-in offers this flexible and modularized checking of formalized guidelines and constraints by making use of inferencing capabilities. Logic is a very comfortable and powerful way to express constraints on a conceptual level. For that purpose, the rule or constraint language must be able to access the ontology itself, i.e. to make statements about classes, relations, subclasses etc. This is possible with F-Logic, e.g. we can formulate that *a concept has at most one super-concept* with the following constraint:

```
! ?C :: ?S1 AND ?C :: ?S2 -> ?S1 == ?S2
```

Further examples for modeling guidelines can be derived from (Noy and McGuinness, 2001). OntoAnalyzer is a tool which applies such constraints to an ontology. It may be loaded with different constraint packages for different purposes. Again, reasoning is used to actually execute the constraint checking.

In the automotive use-case multiple users were involved in the modeling process. In multi-user scenarios it is hard to ensure that the whole model is consistent with respect to guidelines regarding modeling style or ontology structure. In the automotive use-case a project-specific set of guidelines was developed at the beginning of the modeling process. This set was integrated as constraints into OntoAnalyzer and enabled engineers to verify the consistency of the model at any time.

4.4   Regression tests

During the project, a large knowledge base was developed containing many concepts, instances and rules. The larger such a model grows, the higher is the impact of changes on the model and the rules. During the project many changes were applied to the ontology and the rules. Concepts were removed, new ones were added, and the underlying instance base was changed. Additionally, the rules had to be adapted to these changes. The engineers were confronted with the problem, that changes to the model by other engineers influenced the results of their own rules. Additionally created rules sometimes resulted in wrong results as well. Thus, it became a hard task to ensure the stability of the ontology while the ontology evolved.

A fairly simple but feasible approach for this problem is the creation of regression tests. Regression tests are similar to unit tests in Java. These test cases contain a query that shall be evaluated and the results that have to be returned. By running the query and comparing the returned results with the results stored in the test case, the user can easily check the correctness of the current results.

During the project the engineers developed many test cases covering the whole ontology and all rules. For every newly defined rule at least one test case was created. The test suite containing all these regression tests was run regularly to be able to detect failures in the model early. This enabled the engineers to ensure the stability of the ontology and the correctness of the modelled rules during the lifetime of the project.

OntoStudio supports this process by providing graphical means for the definition of these regression tests. New regression tests can be created with a single click and single tests or whole test suites can be run with a single click. If a test fails, the results are interpreted and the differences in the results are highlighted.

5.   INFORMATION INTEGRATION

A major source for the automotive ontology is the *parts breakdown* which is available from a database. For a car around 100,000 parts are stored in such a list. In various workshops, appropriate generalizations of the parts were discussed with the engineers, which finally resulted in the ontology. Although the ontology was developed from scratch, it had to be in sync with the information in the databases.

Ontologies and schema information are relatively stable over time. In contrast, the data in databases can change quite frequently. Usually, operational systems depend on both, schemas and access to *current* data. This raises a couple of questions and challenges, e.g. regarding the connectivity and the lifecycle of ontologies. In the context of semantic information integration, legacy resources might be wrapped locally, while the resulting semantic layer is to be deployed as a service for external access. This allows departments, etc. to publish "their" models in a service-oriented manner.

Ontology servers need to offer integration capabilities as well as a transport layer for distributed models. Engineering environments need support for lifecycle aspects (e.g. versioning) as well as management capabilities for distributed ontologies (storage, registry, etc.). The OntoBroker inference server provides a couple of functionalities for the distributed development and application of ontologies. This includes a Web service-interface, a schema-connector and a schema-import for ontologies.

5.1 Information sources for ontology contents

Besides serving as a common communication language and representing expert knowledge in our scenario, ontologies serve as an integration means of different legacy systems. The ontology is used to reinterpret given information sources in a common language and thus provides a common and single view to different data sources.

In our scenario the components data and the configuration data stems from different departments and different information sources like CAD-, CAE- or CAT-systems or ERP/PPS-applications and databases. All these IT systems accompany the whole PLM-process, beginning with the product design and ending with the product release. Our test configuration system, and thus our ontology system must access this live information to be up-to-date, to avoid inconsistent data and to avoid additional effort.

An ontology could now catch up with these different sources and integrate them in a common logical model. This goes much beyond building just connectors between applications. The goal of integration is to consolidate distributed information intelligently without redundancy and to provide users and applications with easy means to access information without considering the underlying heterogeneity of data structures and systems.

In our case, we already have such a commonly accepted logical model: the automotive ontology. This ontology describes schema information and is not yet populated by instances, which means that there exists a concept e.g. *motor* with attributes *name, cylinders, fuel type* etc. but there is no information about actual *motors* like *TDI V6*, with 6 *cylinders, fuel type super* etc. This information is provided by attaching the ontology to one or more of the existing information sources. In the following we present an example connection to a relational database.

5.2 Database schema import

The first step to connect an ontology to a database is importing the database schema and visualize it in the ontology management environment. The import schema results in a new ontology in which the database tables are represented as concepts and the columns as attributes and relations. In addition to relational database schemas OntoStudio can also import other schemas like RDF or OWL. In our example we will show how to integrate the database table *motor* with the ontology. The database table is displayed in Figure 9-5. It contains information about motors like the *fuel type, power* etc.

2:Daten in Tabelle 'engine' in 'demo' auf 'WALLDORF-NEU'

id	absolute power	fuel	volume flow	engine type
cdi v 6	176	super	124	v
cdi 170	83	diesel	105	v
cdi 160	75	diesel	101	v
boxer	32	normal	80	boxer
stern	450	normal	240	stern

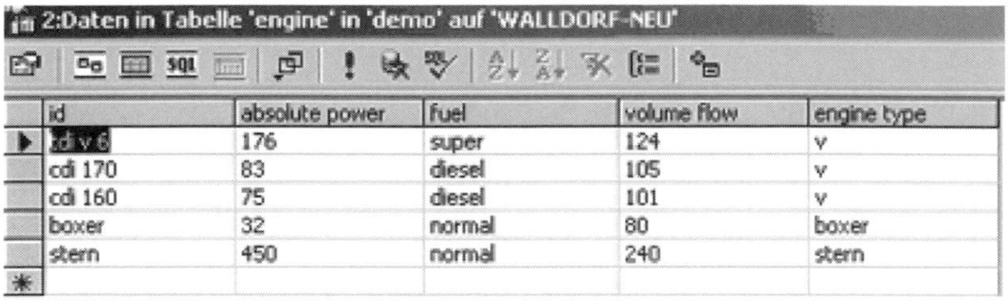

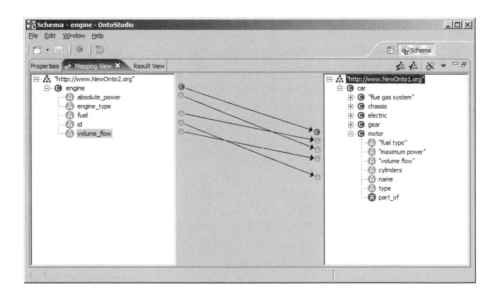

Figure 9-5. Database table "Engine"

5.3 Database mappings

After importing the database schema, the ontology and the schema can be connected. *OntoMap*, a mapping tool included in OntoStudio, supports the fundamental mapping types (i) table-to-concept mapping, (ii) attribute-to-attribute mapping, (iii) attribute-to-concept mapping, and (iv) relation-to-relation mapping.

Figure 9-6. Visualized mappings within OntoStudio

Figure 9-6 shows the imported database schema in the left tree-view and the target ontology in the tree on the right hand side. A table-to-concept mapping connects the table *engine* to the concept *motor* and, additionally, an attribute-to-attribute mapping from *id* in the database to *name* in the ontology. This means that every row in the database corresponds to one object in the ontology. OntoStudio automatically creates a connection to the database via the *dbaccess*-connector (there are various connectors for all kinds of information sources available). This connector automatically creates unique object IDs and is used in rules to retrieve data from the database and make it available via the mapping to the ontology:

```
?X:Motor[name->?NAME,
        maximum_power->?MAXIMUM_POWER,
        volume_flow->?VOLUME_FLOW,
        fuel_type->?FUEL_TYPE]
  <-
dbaccess("engine",?X,
     F("id",?NAME, "absolute power", ?MAXIMUM_POWER,
     "volume_flow", ?VOLUME_FLOW, "fuel", ?FUEL_TYPE),
     "mssqlserver2000",
     "database_motor",
     "server_motordata:1433").
```

Another important mapping type is the mapping of attributes to concepts. It implies that attribute values become unique IDs for ontology instances, e.g. mapping the *ID* of *engine* to the concept *motor* creates an object for every different *ID* in the database. Thus, information about *one* object which is spread across different rows (or tables or even different sources) can always be identified by the same ID and, thus, linked together. In the use case, information about parts had to be integrated from many different sources to yield a consistent and complete part list for the testing scenario.

A query to the integration ontology is, thus, translated at real-time (via the mapping rules) into calls for appropriate built-ins which access the data sources (in case of an RDBMS via SQL queries) and translate the answers back into F-Logic. Thus, a user or an application using the ontology only needs this single ontology view and a single vocabulary to retrieve all necessary information. In our scenario different information sources contribute to the same ontology. E.g. information about electronic parts is stored in other databases than information about mechanical parts. Information about the 3-D geometry of objects is separated from their mechanical properties etc.

It is clear that in practice the different information sources contain redundant or even inconsistent information. For instance in our scenario car types have not been represented in a unique way. The assignment of properties to car types has been described with different keys for one and the same car type, e.g. keys like *A3/A4* have been used to describe common properties of two car types while unique properties have been assigned to the car type by a key *A3*. We again use rules and thus inferencing to solve such integration problems.

```
?X:Car[carType->?Type, has_part->?Part]
<-
dbaccess("car",?X,
    F( "id", ?T, "part", ?Part),
    "mssqlserver2000",
    "car database",
    "server:1433") AND
    tokenize(?T, "/", ?Type).
```

This rule retrieves information from the database via the *dbaccess* predicate but processes the result by extracting the *type* information from the *ID* via another predicate (*tokenize* which extracts *A3* and *A4* separately from *A3/A4*).

Due to the schema import and the mapping rules, the automotive ontology is always populated with the up-to-date instances from the legacy systems. If the inference server is queried for some information (according to the ontology) it results in a set of online (SQL-) queries to the relational databases, thus, serving two important needs: (i) a rich, adequate conceptual model, and (ii) access to the most recently available data.

6.   CONCLUSION

The main role of OntoStudio as an Ontology Engineering Environment is the provision of means to create, modify and navigate ontologies. The modeling of the engineers resulted in an ontology with around 300 concepts, around 200 rules and around 80 explanations. One person-year was spent to develop this ontology and to integrate a first prototype of the application into the internal ordering system of the car manufacturer. Feedback from the domain experts shows that the notion of *ontology* is well understood and the expressiveness of ontologies is appropriate for the modeling task at hand.

Essentially rules represent the main knowledge source in the models. The graphical representation and the support given by the system really help authoring rules. It turned out that the complex dependencies between different car-parts needed to specify constraints could be expressed with rules.

The close integration of the reasoner in the modeling environment esp. via the testing and debugging facilities helps to *bring the knowledge base to life*, which is great feedback for users to foresee the system's behaviour before actually deploying it.

Ontologies were quite successful in integrating different information sources about the configurations and parts of cars which is used to automatically configure test cars. This reduces the communication effort between the mechanical engineers, and reduces the error rate in configuring test cars.

The resulting application, a test car configuration assistant, is based on our ontology run-time environment and inference engine OntoBroker which is based on F-Logic. The assistant embodies the created ontologies and rules, together with the connected legacy sources and accelerates the configuration of test cars for our customer and, thus, accelerates the development of new cars, which finally reduces the time-to-market.

REFERENCES

J. Davies, A. Duke, Y. Sure, 2003, OntoShare – Evaluation of an ontology based knowledge sharing system. Submitted 2003.

S. Decker, 2002, *Semantic Web Methods for Knowledge Management*. PhD thesis, Institute AIFB, University of Karlsruhe.

M. Erdmann, 2001, *Ontologien zur konzeptuellen Modellierung der Semantik von XML*. PhD thesis, Books on Demand.

J. Frohn, R. Himmeröder, P. Kandzia, C. Schlepphorst, 1996, How to write F–Logic programs in FLORID. A tutorial for the database language F–Logic. Technical report, Institut für Informatik der Universität Freiburg, Version 1.0.

I. Horrocks, J. A. Hendler, editors, 2002, *Proceedings of the First International Semantic Web Conference: The Semantic Web (ISWC 2002)*, volume 2342 of Lecture Notes in Computer Science (LNCS), Sardinia, Italy.

M. Kifer, E. Lozinskii, 1986, A framework for an efficient implementation of deductive databases. In *Proceedings of the 6th Advanced Database Symposium*, , Tokyo, August 1986, pp. 109–116.

M. Kifer, G. Lausen, J. Wu, 1995, Logical foundations of object-oriented and framebased languages. *Journal of the ACM*, **42**:741–843.

T. Lau, Y. Sure, 2002, Introducing ontology-based skills management at a large insurance company. In *Proceedings of the Modellierung 2002, Tutzing, Germany, March 2002*, pp. 123–134.

A. Maier, M. Ullrich, H.-P. Schnurr, 2003, Ontology-based Information Integration in the Automotive Industry. Technical report, ontoprise whitepaper series.

R. Meersman, Z. Tari, editors, 2002, *Proceedings of the Confederated International Conferences DOA, CoopIS and ODBASE - On the Move to Meaningful Internet Systems, 2002, Irvine, California, USA*, LNCS 2519.

N. Noy, D. L. McGuinness, 2001, Ontology development 101: A guide to creating your first ontology. Technical Report KSL-01-05 and SMI-2001-0880, Stanford Knowledge Systems Laboratory and Stanford Medical Informatics, March 2001.

Ontoprise, 2002, How to write F–Logic programs — a tutorial for the language F–Logic. Tutorial version 1.9 that covers Ontobroker version 3.5.

Y. Sure, V. Iosif, 2002, First results of a semantic web technologies evaluation. in (Meersman and Tari, 2002).

Y. Sure, R. Studer, 2002, On-To-Knowledge Methodology. In On-To-Knowledge EU IST-1999-10132 Project Deliverable, September 2002.

Y. Sure, M. Erdmann, J. Angele, S. Staab, R. Studer, D.Wenke, 2002a, OntoEdit: Collaborative ontology development for the Semantic Web. In (Horrocks and Hendler, 2002), pp. 221–235.

Y. Sure, S. Staab, J. Angele, 2002b, OntoEdit: Guiding ontology development by methodology and inferencing. In (Meersman and Tari, 2002), pp. 1205–1222.

A. van Gelder, 1993, The alternating fixpoint of logic programs with negation, *Journal of Computer and System Sciences*, **47**(1):185–221.

A. van Gelder, K. A. Ross, J. S. Schlipf, 1991, The well-founded semantics for general logic programs, *Journal of the ACM*, **38**(3):620–650, July 1991.

M. Kifer, A. Bernstein, P.M. Lewis, 2005, *Database Systems, An Application-Oriented Approach*, 2nd Ed., Addison Wesley.

Chapter 10

ONTOLOGISING COMPETENCIES IN AN INTERORGANISATIONAL SETTING

Stijn Christiaens[1], Pieter De Leenheer[1], Aldo de Moor[2], and Robert Meersman[1]

[1]*Semantics Technology & Applications Research Lab, Vrije Universiteit Brussel, Pleinlaan 2, B 1050 BRUSSELS 5, Belgium, stichris@vub.ac.be, pdeleenh@vub.ac.be, meersman@vub.ac.be;* [2]*CommunitySense, Cavaleriestraat 2, 5017 ET Tilburg, the Netherlands, ademoor@communitysense.nl. The work on this paper was done while the author was still at VUB STARLab.*

Abstract: This chapter summarises findings from CODRIVE[1], a large-scale ontology project in the vocational training domain. This competency area is complex, and in order to achieve proper interoperability on the basis of ontologies, all involved stakeholders must participate in interorganisational ontology engineering. In particular, this chapter illustrates the DOGMA-MESS methodology, a community-driven approach to ontology management. It presents practical experiences for the issues addressed in the previous chapters, complementing them with illustrative data and hands-on knowledge.

Keywords: competency modelling; case study; context dependency management; interorganisational ontology engineering; ontology; ontology engineering

1.   INTRODUCTION

Interorganisational ontology engineering (IOO) concerns different organisations that collaboratively build a conceptual common ground of their domain. Ontologies are instrumental in this process by providing formal specifications of shared semantics. Such semantics provide a solid basis for defining and sharing (business) goals and interests, and ultimately for developing useful collaborative services and systems.

---

[1] http://www.codrive.org

Obtaining context-independent ontological knowledge, however, is very difficult, sometimes even impossible as most organisational ontologies used in practice assume a context and perspective of some community (Edgington et al., 2004). Taking this in consideration, it is natural that ontologies co-evolve with their communities of use, and that human interpretation of context in the use and disambiguation of an ontology often plays an important role. We aim to augment human collaboration effectively by appropriate technologies, such as systems for context dependency analysis and negotiation (see also Chapter 5 of this book) during elicitation and application of ontologies for collaborative applications.

In order to make this context-driven co-evolution scalable, it is crucial to capture *relevant* commonalities and differences in a gradual process of meaning negotiation (de Moor, 2005) in order to reach the appropriate amount of consensus. It is important to realize that costly alignment efforts should only be made when necessary for the shared collaboration purpose. In order to effectively and efficiently define shared relevant ontological meanings, clear focus and context are indispensable.

1.1   Competencies as tacit knowledge

In the human resources domain, the (currently) smallest and most important element we can identify is a (human) *competency*. Competencies describe the skills and knowledge individuals should have in order to be fit for particular jobs. Especially in the domain of vocational education, having a central, shared competency model is becoming crucial in order to achieve the necessary level of information exchange, and in order to integrate the existing information systems of competency stakeholders (e.g., schools or public employment agencies). However, none of these organisations have successfully implemented a company-wide "competency initiative," let alone a strategy for interorganisational exchange of competency related information.

For processing purposes, a competency is supposed to be measurable; therefore it is crucial to define it very precisely. Knowledge artefacts are usually induced bottom-up from data or deduced top-down from domain experts, existing schemas and/or upper ontologies.

Competencies, however, are typical examples of knowledge that is merely acquired through *experience*. This is called *tacit* knowledge (Nonaka and Takeuchi, 1995). Polanyi (1967) used the phrase "we know more than we can tell" to describe what he meant by tacit knowledge. Tacit knowledge is a kind of knowledge which is difficult to articulate with formal language because it is either too complex or simply because it is informally internalised in domain experts' minds. Yet it is shared and exchanged in normal social interaction. Furthermore, if we suppose that tacit competency knowledge took an explicit form (e.g., in written documents), a new problem arises: As there currently exists no standard for the representation, the interpretation of such knowledge would require reflection among individuals, which is subjective and ambiguous, hence useless for machine processing. In such cases, the added value of eliciting ontologies through externalising tacit knowledge from domain experts, rather than elicitation via trained knowledge engineers, is considered increasingly important (Nonaka and Takeuchi, 1995; Diaz, 2005).

1.2 A real world case study: the Dutch bakery domain

This chapter summarises findings from CODRIVE, a large-scale ontology project in the area of competencies. CODRIVE aimed at developing a new competency-driven approach to knowledge in vocational education. One goal of this approach was to increase the interoperability of knowledge services between Learning Content Management Systems and public employment service applications. The approach is based on consensual meaning negotiation in the vocational training and public employment domain.

The project consisted of two phases, namely the *elicitation* and *application* of a "Vocational Competency Ontology." The first phase involved the elicitation of an ontology to describe the Dutch bakery domain. Two key issues could be identified. First, *scalability*, since the number of stakeholders in this domain is very large, including representatives (e.g., bakers, teachers) from several bakery organisations in the Netherlands. Second, *terminological specificity*, because the knowledge is very specific and — as usual — unknown to knowledge engineers, even at the linguistic level.

The second phase of the project considered applying the ontology to solve the so-called *gap analysis* problem. Its solution should facilitate matching between competencies, learning objects, and tests. Without the ontology, this would require linking competencies to learning objects and to tests, as well as learning objects to tests. This would lead to a combinatorial explosion of the number of links, which would be hard to manage. The scalability would degrade even further when considering the continuous evolution of the knowledge artefacts involved. The particular problems encountered in the application phase in the project, however, are beyond the scope of this chapter.

This chapter is organised as follows: in **Section 2**, we give a description of our used approach to interorganisational ontology engineering. Next, in

Section 3, we present our use case experiences related to previous theoretical chapters. Finally, in **Section 4**, we conclude with a discussion.

2.   INTERORGANISATIONAL ONTOLOGY ENGINEERING

In our case study we adopted the DOGMA[2] ontology engineering approach. The community layer is provided by the DOGMA-MESS[3] methodology, which is based on the generic model for collaborative ontology engineering, earlier discussed in Chapter 5.

2.1   DOGMA

DOGMA (Spyns et al., 2002, Jarrar et al., 2003, De Leenheer et al., 2007) is an ontology approach and framework that is not restricted to a particular representation language. The approach differs from traditional ontology approaches in that (i) it is grounded in the linguistic representations of knowledge and (ii) it explicitly separates the *conceptualisation* (i.e., lexical representation of concepts and their inter-relationships) from the *axiomatisation* (i.e., semantic constraints). The goal of this separation, referred to as the *double articulation* principle (Spyns et al., 2002), is to enhance the potential for re-use and design scalability. This principle corresponds to an orthodox *model-theoretic* approach to ontology representation and development.

Conceptualisations are materialised in terms of *lexons*. A lexon represents a plausible binary fact-type and is formally described as a 5-tuple <C, term1, role, co-role, term2>, where C is an abstract context identifier, lexically described by a string in some natural language. Intuitively, a lexon may be read as "Within the context C, *term1* may have a relation with *term2* in which it plays a *role*, and conversely, in which term2 plays a corresponding *co-role*."

2.1.1   Language versus conceptual level

Another distinguishing characteristic of DOGMA is the explicit *duality* (orthogonal to double articulation) in interpretation between the *language* level and *conceptual* level. The goal of this separation is primarily to disambiguate the lexical representation of terms in a lexon (on the language

---

[2] acronym for Developing Ontology-Grounded Methods and Applications
[3] acronym for Meaning Evolution Support System

level) into concept definitions (on the conceptual level), which are word senses taken from lexical resources such as WordNet (Fellbaum, 1998). The meaning of the terms in a lexon is dependent on the *context* of elicitation (De Leenheer and de Moor, 2005).

For example, consider a term "capital." If this term were elicited from a typewriter manual, it would have a different meaning (read: concept definition) compared to when elicited from a book on marketing. The intuition that a context provides here is: a context is an abstract identifier that refers to implicit and tacit assumptions in a domain, and that maps a term to its intended meaning (i.e. concept identifier) within these assumptions (Jarrar et al., 2003).

2.1.2   Context dependency types

In (De Leenheer and de Moor, 2005), we distinguished four key characteristics of context: (i) a context packages related knowledge: it defines part of the knowledge of a particular domain, (ii) it disambiguates the lexical representation of concepts and relationships by distinguishing between language level and conceptual level, (iii) it defines context dependencies between different ontological contexts and (iv) contexts can be embedded or linked, in the sense that statements about contexts are themselves in context. Based on this, we identified three different types of context dependencies within one ontology (*intra-ontological*) and between different ontologies (*inter-ontological*): articulation, application, and specialisation.

Context dependencies provide a better understanding of the whereabouts of knowledge elements and their inter-dependencies, and consequently make negotiation and application less vulnerable to ambiguity, hence more practical.

2.2   DOGMA-MESS

Where in the DOGMA methodology efficient and relevant ontology engineering was central, the DOGMA-MESS methodology builds further on these principles and extends them by supporting interorganisational knowledge elicitation and negotiation grounded in communities of use. It is based on the model for interorganisational ontology engineering (IOOE) described in Chapter 5, and also follows the upward spiral knowledge elicitation process. The main focus lies on how to capture *relevant* commonalities and differences in meaning by supporting domain experts in an efficient way by assigning them scalable knowledge elicitation tasks. Differences are aligned insofar necessary through meaning negotiation.

Figure 10-1 illustrates this: DOGMA-MESS was conceived with different actor *roles* and *layers* in mind. The arrows in the diagram indicate different types of dependencies between ontologies that constrain the possible relations between entities and their context. An ontology that is *context-dependent* on another one is called a *contextualisation*. Hence, the contextualisation of ontological definitions might be constrained in different ways. In the following three subsections, we will first explain the roles and the layers, followed by some detail about the process.

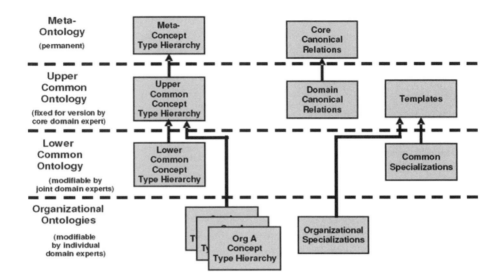

Figure 10-1. DOGMA-MESS meaning layers

2.2.1   Roles

DOGMA-MESS was designed to allow proper and scaleable interorganisational ontology engineering (IOO) in communities of practice. One of its main goals is empowering domain experts to be involved in the ontology engineering process. As this is a complex process, consisting of many different and complex macro- and micro-processes, it is clear that a suitable distribution of complexity is needed. In DOGMA-MESS, we divide the problem into more manageable sub-problems and assign them to three different user roles, the *Knowledge Engineer (KE)*, the *Core Domain Expert (CDE)*, and the *Domain Expert (DE)*.

- In more traditional approaches (e.g., the single-user ontology engineering process model in chapter 5), the Knowledge Engineer (KE) is responsible for creating (and maintaining) knowledge in a formal way. He collects knowledge through cost- and time-consuming interviews (including those for validations and eliminating remaining ambiguities) with domain experts. In DOGMA-MESS, the KE is at the outer boundaries. He defines the system support (e.g., the exact tools, the internal workings, etc.) and the high-level work artefacts (e.g., the Meta Ontology). He assists the other DOGMA-MESS actors by tutoring them in the system, and by analyzing the collected content.

- The Core Domain Expert (CDE) is a domain expert who is recognised as an authority in the domain (e.g., through extensive experience). He is connected with the relevant people involved to whom he can issue detailed requests. He is able to reason about his domain in a more abstract way, and is assisted by the KE in the higher complexity of working at a more generic level (e.g., template construction). The CDE defines the edges of the domain, introducing a necessary (but manageable) amount of structure to the field (templates and type hierarchy). He represents the common interest related to the community.

- The Domain Expert (DE) represents a certain organization (or community). He deals only with domain-specific complexity, namely defining in his owns words how he perceives his part of the domain. In this process, he is both limited and guided by the structure imposed by the KE and by the CDE. The CDE can assign clear tasks in order to guide his Domain Experts in their elicitation.

2.2.2   Layers

DOGMA-MESS consists of four layers, with interlinking dependencies to impose a supporting structure. Each layer is governed by a certain actor role.

- A (permanent) *Meta-Ontology (MO)* is the same for all applications, hence is pre-installed in DOGMA-MESS. It only contains *stable*[4], hence *reusable*, cross-domain concept types like 'Actor,' 'Object,' 'Process,' and 'Quality.' The Meta-Ontology also contains a set of *core canonical relations*, based on the ones described in (Sowa, 1984), such as the 'Agent,' 'Object,' and 'Result'-relations. This layer is governed by the KE.

---

[4] Although considered permanent and stable in this chapter, we do not exclude the possibility this meta-ontology would evolve over time, although to a lesser extent than organisational ontologies, possibly implying considerable effects on the system. We omit this discussion further as it is beyond the scope of this chapter.

- Each domain (in our case the Dutch bakery domain) has its own *Upper Common Ontology (UCO)*, and is maintained by the CDE. It grounds, articulates and organises the (evolving) domain-common concept types in its own *Upper Common Concept Type Hierarchy*, which is a specialisation of the concept type hierarchy of the Meta-Ontology. *Domain canonical relations* specialise core canonical relations in the context of the domain. For instance, whereas 'Agent' is a core canonical relation, in a particular domain this may be translated into 'Person.' The most important type of construct in the UCO is the *template*. A template describes a commonly accepted (i.e. agreed) knowledge definition and acts as an incentive for further relevant knowledge elicitation steered by the current common goals and interests.
- In the *Organisational Ontology (OO)* layer, templates are specialised into *Organisational Specialisations* by the DEs representing the various organisations. To this purpose, domain experts can introduce concept types local to their organisation. The concept types in the *Organisational Concept Type Hierarchy* themselves must specialise the actual concept types in the Upper Common Concept Type Hierarchy.
- The most important layer for meaning negotiation is the *Lower Common Ontology (LCO)*. This is where the target agenda as represented by the UCO and the (often widely differing) organisational interpretations need to be aligned, and the most relevant conceptualisations for the next version need to be selected. The alignment is done by negotiation between the CDE and the (relevant) DEs.

2.2.3   Process

In DOGMA-MESS, ontology engineering is divided in several versions, whereby each version has a part of the domain as its focus. At the beginning of each version, the CDE defines templates that best capture the focus interests of that moment. They are described using concepts from the UCO type hierarchy. When the templates are ready, the CDE assigns tasks to the DEs, asking them to define their organisational specialisations. The DEs build these definitions from concepts in their organisational hierarchy. They can manipulate their hierarchy as they see fit, as long as it specialises the UCO hierarchy. The result of this step is divergence of knowledge. In order to obtain the necessary convergence, the CDE and the DEs perform meaning negotiation on relevant differences. The resulting agreement is stored in the LCO. Any disagreement is left as an organisational difference to be tackled in the next version. This last step marks the end of a version, and all relevant knowledge to be retained is moved to the first step of the next version.

3. EXPERIENCES

In this section we report on the ontology elicitation sessions we have carried out in the bakers' domain using our approach and tools.

3.1 Editing and browsing

The layered and role-based approach of DOGMA-MESS allows the communities to create and maintain their domain description in small, understandable chunks, or *units of knowledge* (e.g., templates). As a result, we were able to provide several ways of targeted editing and browsing functionalities configured for each particular type of user role.

3.1.1 Core Domain Expert (CDE)

The CDE manages the common part in his domain, i.e., the Upper Common Ontology. He does this by browsing and editing his common types in the upper common concept type hierarchy and his templates in the UCO. Figure 10-2 illustrates the introduction of a new term in the upper common ontology, which involves both editing and browsing.

Browsing the type hierarchy: The CDE browses the upper common type hierarchy by scrolling through a drop-down box. The hierarchy level of a type is indicated by the indentation, where higher-level types are preceeded by less white space. The abstract type 'T' is always at the top of the type hierarchy. The use case type hierarchy contained about 200 concept types and contained only single inheritance. Note that the used approach might prove cumbersome with larger hierarchies or those with multiple inheritance.

Introducing a new term: This activity includes language grounding and lexical disambiguation by articulating a term and setting its genus (e.g. add "oven" and make it a subtype of "tool"). For editing the type, one selects the term for the type one will edit from the scroll-down box, and either (i) *renames* the type; (ii) *rehooks* the type to another supertype; (iii) *creates* a new subtype below the selected type by typing the term for the new type; or (iv) *removes* the selected type. Removing a type is currently only possible if it is a leaf in the hierarchy.

Logging the changes: When the CDE has finished editing, a new version is created and the change log is recorded in which he can annotate his change with some plain text comment. This comment will help him (and others) to understand and track all changes to the type hierarchy.

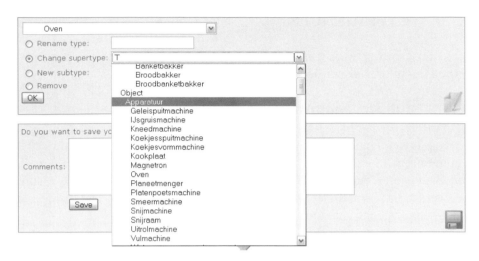

Figure 10-2. Editing the type hierarchy[5]

Managing templates: The CDE can browse and edit the templates that are used in his domain. Browsing is done by showing the CDE a list of the templates in his domain, described by metadata (including author, title, date, and comments). By clicking on one of these templates (or by creating a new one), the CDE enters the edit screen, which is partially displayed in Figure 10-3. In this step, he applies a concept type by specifying it with differentiae. When he commits a new template, an application dependency between the template and the concept is defined (De Leenheer et al., 2007; pp. 42).

The top part of Figure 10-3 displays the template in a visual format. The edit options are displayed at the bottom. From the first drop-down box, the CDE first selects a concept, which corresponds to a concept in the depicted graph. He then chooses one of three actions: (1) *replace* the selected concept by another concept from the type hierarchy (in his domain), (2) *add* another differentia by selection of a relation and a concept from the type hierarchy, or (3) *remove* the concept type from the template. He can then save his changes by providing a name for the template, adding some change comments and pressing the save button (not displayed in this figure).

---

[5] All images used in this chapter display content as it was produced in the use case. We chose to keep the original Dutch labels in order to preserve authenticity and nuance. We will explain figures by an English equivalent term, followed by the Dutch representation in between brackets. In this example, the CDE is changing the supertype of Oven ("Oven") to Equipment ("Apparatuur").

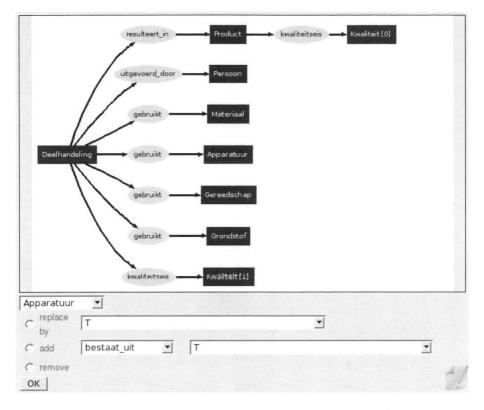

Figure 10-3. Editing the subtask ("Deelhandeling") template[6]

Managing common definitions: The CDE can manage the common definitions (based on templates and the organizational definitions) in the LCO. The steps are similar to those of the managing templates activity.

3.1.2   Domain Expert (DE)

The Domain Expert manages his local organisational ontology. He does this by browsing and editing his organisational types (similar to the CDE activities) in the Organisational Type Hierarchy and his specialisations in the Organisational Specialisations.

---

[6] The displayed template is the Subtask template ("Deelhandeling"), which states that a Subtask ("Deelhandeling") results in ("resulteert_in") a certain Product, which has a quality demand ("kwaliteitseis") of Quality[0] ("Kwaliteit[0]"). The Subtask is performed by ("uitgevoerd_door") a certain Person ("Persoon"), uses ("gebruikt") a certain Material ("Materiaal"), a certain Device ("Apparatuur"), a certain Equipment ("Gereedschap") and a kind of Raw material ("Grondstof"). The Subtask ("Deelhandeling") itself has a quality demand ("kwaliteitseis") of Quality[1] ("Kwaliteit[1]").

Managing definitions: A typical DE activity is building an organisational definition based on a certain template. The editing of a definition is always constrained by the template as this action corresponds to the micro-process specialisation. For instance, if the template specifies a concept "Actor" at a certain position, it is illegal to fill this position with an "Object" type such as "Oven." This constraint is enforced using the conceptual graphs projection operator (Sowa, 1984). We found that it is easiest for the user to constrain editing to allowed choices.

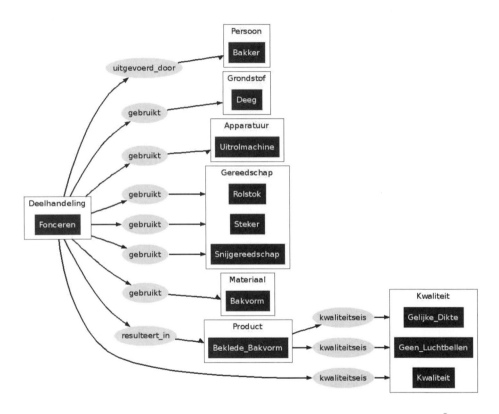

Figure 10-4. Definition of "Fonceren" as a specialisation of the subtask template[7]

As definitions are always based on a template (created and maintained by the CDE), we decided to present both the information from the template

---

[7] "Fonceren" is a kind of Subtask whereby the inside of a baking form is coated with dough as a preparatory process of the baking itself. The inner blue boxes represent the specialized types of the more general, outer white template types. For instance, the quality demands ("kwaliteitseis") for the resulting ("resulteert_in") Coated baking form ("Beklede_Bakvorm") are the qualities Equal thickness ("Gelijke_Dikte") and No airbubbles ("Geen_Luchtbellen").

(outer white boxes) and that from the definition-in-edit (inner dark-grey boxes). We found that this visual clue contributed significantly to understanding the concepts used in the definition (see Figure 10-4).

3.1.3 Knowledge Engineer (KE)

The Knowledge Engineer assists the other DOGMA-MESS actors by tutoring them in the system. Furthermore, he analyses the elicited knowledge artefacts, which are not yet full-fledged ontological commitments. For meaning analysis, the Knowledge Engineer has two main tools at his disposal: the DOGMA-MESS[8] Web front-end we described above, and the DOGMA Studio Workbench[9], which is a plug-in-based architecture (see section 3.4).

Searching graphs: Using the Web front-end, the KE constructs a query graph (which is analogous to defining a template), which is then matched against all available knowledge artefacts (including type hierarchies, templates and definitions) in the ontology server. This functionality allows the KE to detect patterns. For instance, a query could search for all subtask definitions that are performed by a baker using an oven.

Meaning analysis: For further meaning analysis, the KE can rely on the DOGMA workbench, more particularly the T-Lex tool. The main view of this tool is depicted in Figure 10-5. The left pane (LexonBase Explorer) shows an extensive list of contexts identifiers, which represent the multiple contextualisations. The KE selects one of these contexts in order to zoom in on the knowledge collected inside. The tree below the context displays all terms present in the context. The bottom right pane (Lexons) lists all lexons in the currently selected context. The top right pane (T-Lex Lexon Base Browser) shows the NORM-tree browsing approach (Trog et al., 2006). The KE selects one of the concepts in the context as the root of the tree. Starting from that root, he can browse further by exploring all the relations connected. The advantage of this approach is the constant availability of *local context*: all relations connected to the concept in focus are always nearby and in view. Concepts can be displayed more than once, but they are marked in grey to identify them as duplicates.

Furthermore, the KE can also axiomatise definitions by adding semantic constraints (e.g., uniqueness and value constraints) to the paths present in the NORM-tree.

---

[8] http://www.starlab.vub.ac.be/website/dogma-mess
[9] http://www.starlab.vub.ac.be/website/dogmastudio

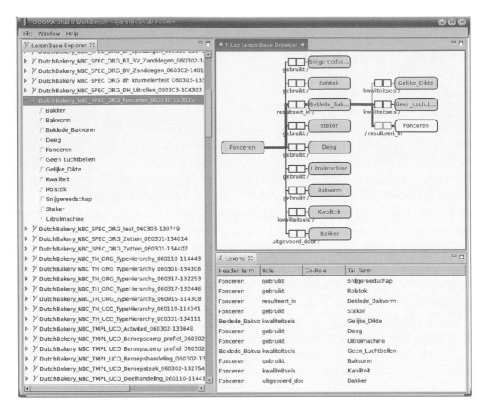

Figure 10-5. T-Lex, in-depth semantic functionality for the KE

3.2 Reusing existing consensus

In this section, we show how the DOGMA-MESS system handles previously existing consensus, and we take a look at the estimated cost of using the system.

3.2.1 Reusing consensus

By means of upward spiral knowledge creation, DOGMA-MESS aims to enhance the potential for relevant interorganisational knowledge creation in an efficient way through incentive templates. Consensus reuse is an essential criterion in order to realise the scalability of ontology engineering. We can define reuse as

the repeated use of an artefact in different situations, with or without making adaptations to it.

We discuss three prominent ways of knowledge reuse in DOGMA-MESS, viz. reuse of the lexon base, reuse of an existing upper ontology, and reuse of existing organisational schemas and organisational knowledge.

From the lexon base: In DOGMA, lexons are stored in an extensive lexon base, which is holds intuitive plausible conceptualisations of a domain. The lexon base is intended as a large collection of highly reusable pieces of knowledge (the lexons). These can be used (and reused) in any ontology and in any commitment to an ontology. These lexons can be collected from any input source, such as existing text documents or standards.

From the upper ontology: In the Meta-Ontology (MO) we identify two cases of reuse of existing consensus, viz. metaconcept types, and canonical relations. The MO contains domain-independent concepts, and is used to assist the CDE in a structural way of thinking about his type hierarchy and templates. The KE can use these to easily merge and map all collected concepts to external resources, such as Cyc's Upper Ontology (Lenat and Guha, 1990) and SUMO (Niles and Pease, 2001). At this stage, we opted for an extremely thin layer, containing only five types, namely "T" (the absurd type), with four subtypes "Actor," "Object," "Process" and "Quality." We found that for our case these four types are sufficient to guide the CDE. The canonical relations (e.g., agent of and instrument of) are based on those that Sowa (Sowa, 1999) identified in Fillmore's case grammar (Fillmore, 1968). In the Dutch bakery use case, we provided the CDE with five canonical relations (consists of, instrument of, quality of, results in, agent of). He translated these to his own (Dutch) terms and used only these translations in his templates. This approach forced (1) the KE to determine a relevant set of relations, (2) the CDE to construct his templates appropriately, and (3) all DEs to add their knowledge through semantics in concepts, instead of in a multitude of ad-hoc and ill-defined relations.

We found that it is very important to provide clear metatypes and relations. In the use case, we provided the CDE with a clear and well-formed natural language gloss *and* a few examples (instances) as well. Both glosses (Jarrar 2005; Jarrar 2006) and examples (Nijssen and Halpin 1989) have been proven to increase understanding for both KEs and (C)DEs.

From organisational knowledge: Second is the elicitation of organisational knowledge. Much of the existing consensus in the domain of our use case can only be found as tacit knowledge (Nonaka and Takeuchi, 1995). This will hold true in other domains as well. DOGMA-MESS provides the DEs with a structured approach to capture at least a relevant part of their tacit knowledge, and convert it into a formal (and thus reusable) representation. DOGMA-MESS can then identify how much of this knowledge is already agreed upon. Supported by the system (e.g., a discussion agenda of the most relevant differences), the DEs, supported by the CDE and if necessary the KE, can then perform meaning negotiation in order to reach consensus, where consensus is possible and necessary. The CDE also has to rely on his knowledge and experience, and try to get a mental view on the consensus in the sea of tacit knowledge in order to construct the appropriate templates and type hierarchy. In our use case, the initial UCO type hierarchy was actually reused from another nation-wide project in the Dutch bakery domain: Flexbase[10]. To our knowledge, there was no other (inter)national standard or shared resource available that could serve in our Dutch bakery use case. Through iteration and evolution of the templates, we predict that they will evolve into useful knowledge patterns for the domain. Under traditional circumstances, artefacts that are constructed as highly reusable tend to be difficult to actually *use* because of their generic level. We foresee that the evolved patterns could possible be used in other domains as well, either as a valid knowledge pattern (e.g., the subtask pattern might serve as a template in other domains as well), or as a good source of inspiration (e.g. bakery experts claim that bakery much resembles other process industries, such as the chemical industry, in many ways. Parts of the process patterns, for example, might be good starting points for domain ontologies of these other industries.)

3.2.2   Cost

It is difficult to provide exact details about cost or time spent in our approach. We did not yet perform measurements related to this issue. Based on user sessions held in the use case, we estimate that in general DEs can create the first version of a definition in about 10 to 15 minutes. This includes the accompanying changes they make to their type hierarchy as well. The templates are more difficult, as they require more abstract thinking, but this is offset by far fewer templates than domain definitions being necessary. The templates used in the Dutch bakery domain (five different ones) were crafted in an extensive afternoon session, and required a second such session to complete them. They will need several elicitation iterations before they evolve into actual knowledge patterns.

The process of negotiation in order to reach a common agreement is difficult to estimate, as it depends on a number of variables (the number of differences, the complexity of the differences, the people involved, etc.). We found that it is best to keep the discussion fixed on one difference at the time, and limited in time (e.g. by using a timer and an objective mediator). Any disagreement after that period must then first be solved at the organisational level, not at the common level. This disagreement can then be tackled in a next version (using an updated type hierarchy and templates).

---

[10] http://www.flexbase.nl/

The structured approach of DOGMA-MESS assists the (C)DEs in how to define their conceptualisations. It is not necessary to introduce a separate alignment process alongside the articulation, as any definition is inherently aligned with the template. The KE can perform mapping at the MO level and merging of OOs is done in the LCO through meaning negotiation.

3.3 Ontology evolution

The Dutch bakery vocational domain in our use case is only dynamic to a lesser degree. It does change, but not as fast as for instance the IT domain. On the other hand, many parties (e.g. educational institutes) are involved with a vested interest in their own organizational definitions, so many versions can be necessary before stable definitions have been obtained. Thus, in general it is very important to make sure that maintenance (and thus evolution) is manageable. This is a constraint for any system or methodology, and it should be a constraint from the start – not simply when evolution is noticed for the first time. We acknowledge that evolution is very important and continuously present in our (and any other) domain, especially when the domain is shaped (and formally described) by an interorganisational community of users.

In collaborative ontology engineering, multiple stakeholders have multiple views on multiple ontologies. Hence, a viable methodology requires supporting domain experts in *gradually* building and *managing* increasingly complex *versions* of ontological elements and their converging and diverging interrelationships. DOGMA-MESS adopts this principle by implementing the *upward spiral* model we discussed in Chapter 5. This naturally requires the appropriate versioning support. In this section, we discuss the evolution support in DOGMA-MESS in terms of the different activities from the single user and collaborative ontology evolution process model in Chapter 5.

Change representation: In (De Leenheer et al., 2007), we define a non-exhaustive list of change operators, hence a change (request) is represented by a sequence of change operations. Each user is granted change permissions based on his role profile, as we explained in De Leenheer and Meersman (2007). A user can also request a change to other artefacts, but these have to be validated by the authorised person. For instance, a domain expert is only responsible for an organisational definition that specialises the template provided by the CDE. However, at any time, he can submit and argue for a template change request to the CDE, based on his experiences with (trying to) specialise the template.

Prioritisation and change request types: The many dependencies between artefacts in the ontology require dependent artefacts to be updated in view of the changes in the artefacts they depend on. A prioritisation scheme for mapping the change requests, in order to decide which change should be implemented first, is based on the role of the change requester. For instance, the specialisation dependency states that an organisational definition (e.g., "Fonceren") must at all times be a specialisation of its template (e.g., subtask). A change (*on request*) made by the CDE in a template has priority over the specialisation by the DE. Hence, whenever a template changes, all the DEs are notified (*push-based*) that they have to change their specialisation dependent organisational definitions (*in response*).

Impact analysis: Currently, the impact of a change is analysed simply by counting the dependent artefacts using the context dependencies, and the current prioritisation schemes. Even if a change has severe consequences for some dependent artefact in the ontology, the priority of the change will influence this decision. We plan to extend this functionality.

Versioning support: In DOGMA-MESS, all versions of the ontologies are persistently stored in DOGMA Server, and tagged with appropriate meta-data for identification, and for describing the *how*, *who*, and *when* of the version. We learned that it is very important to provide (and encourage) the end-user with commenting functionality. A good description of *why* a new version was created avoids future insight questions, such as the familiar 'Why did we/they do this again?' Even if the new version is automatically generated (e.g., an automatically updated definition caused by a change in the template and the associated specialisation dependency), it is advisable to include a pre-defined system comment to assist the (C)DEs.

Through logging the change information (the dependencies and the operators), we avoided the difficult problem of having to induce them between versions. This kind of structured information allows highly granular version comparison and merging functionalities. At the time of the CODRIVE use case, comparison and merging functionalities for these processes were not yet available. Currently, we are extending the DOGMA-MESS interfaces in other real-world case studies to incorporate this convergence support.

An important experience was the difficulty that the DEs reported during version iteration. Our initial idea was to start a version iteration with the UCO type hierarchy and templates, and that these would be blocked during the entire iteration. They could only be updated in the next iteration. This resulted in the complaint that the DEs were not satisfied with certain parts of the UCO type hierarchy, but that they had to wait until the end of the version before something could be done. While this discrete versioning setup, including a negotiation phase at the end of every version in order to resolve the differences, was our goal, we concluded that it is important to provide more freedom for the (C)DEs. So, while the process itself is globally discrete (version iterations), the micro-processes (updating a definition, change to the UCO type hierarchy, etc.) should be perceived as continuous by the (C)DEs in order to obtain a stronger feeling of freedom.

3.4   Tool support

The DOGMA-MESS approach requires a lot of system support. Some of the necessary tools were available; others were built or adapted to fit in the scope of the use case. In the following subsections we present the used tools, and our lessons learnt.

3.4.1   Web application

For the general workflow of DOGMA-MESS, we opted for a zero-install approach in the form of a Web-based application (see figures 2, 3 and 4 for some examples). While this kind of platform used to provide rather limited client-side smoothness, the current trends with JavaScript (such as AJAX[11]) may allow a richer end-user experience. The zero-install was a necessity for us, as in many cases (C)DEs are limited in installation possibilities concerning their on-the-job computer systems. The Web-based approach avoids installation trouble and paves the way for low-complexity ontology engineering. In this Web-based application, we identified the different user roles (KE, CDE and DE) with a clear and continuously present icon in order to enhance recognition.

Our main reason to build this tool (supporting the DOGMA-MESS methodology) was the fact that there was no other proper workflow support available. However, in order to avoid too much development work, we decided to link the Web application with several other tools (for input, output, analysis and reasoning) to obtain the necessary functionalities.

3.4.2   Input

We initially chose the conceptual graph editor CharGer (Delugach, 2001) as an input tool for the CDE. Using this tool, the CDE could build the UCO type hierarchy and the necessary templates, and then upload them into DOGMA-MESS. At that time, CharGer did not have a proper layout algorithm integrated. It quickly became clear that the richly populated UCO type hierarchy was beyond proper manual management as Charger's visual representation looked like a jungle of concepts and line crossings. To solve

---

[11] http://en.wikipedia.org/wiki/AJAX_(programming)

this, we opted for an indented text format, in which the hierarchy depth is indicated by the indentation. Although this is a rather simple approach, it proved efficient and easy to use. As any text editor was sufficient for editing, this method was an advantage concerning client-side requirements as well. In the end, we incorporated this approach in the Web application.

3.4.3   Output

As the figures used in this chapter demonstrate, we also included a visualisation component in the Web application. The layout functionalities are provided by AT&T's GraphViz[12], a tool that provides several algorithms with numerous configuration parameters for graph lay outing. Thanks to the domain-specific terminology in the graphs, they are easily understood by (C)DEs. They also provide an immediate overview of the knowledge they represent, even for people who are not accustomed to working with graphs. In our use case, we did not encounter any direct opposition or difficulties in using them. However, we are also considering a more traditional (and omnipresent) spreadsheet-like approach as well as a natural language text representation as alternatives in the system. These will result in an even lower complexity, and a quicker way of capturing knowledge. We will keep the graph visualisation in future versions (because of its clarity and overview advantages), but we will add hide/show functionalities in order to provide (C)DEs with the freedom of choice.

3.4.4   Advanced

For the more advanced tasks of the Knowledge Engineer, there is a plethora of tools available (Gómez-Pérez et al., 2003), each one of them with its own strong advantages and theoretical backgrounds. Because of the DOGMA foundation of DOGMA-MESS, we incorporated the DOGMA Studio Workbench (see Figure 10-5). It provides the KE with advanced contextual browsing facilities (described in section 3.1.3), as well as support for detailed semantic constraints. It is based on the Eclipse Rich Client Platform[13], which provides a flexible plug-in architecture. A very important aspect is interoperability and grounding into formats and standards used by others. The DOGMA Studio Workbench can perform conversion to and from external formats, such as RDF (Miller and Manola, 2004) and OWL (van Harmelen and McGuinness, 2004) in order to provide proper operationalisation.

---

[12] http://www.graphviz.org/
[13] http://wiki.eclipse.org/index.php/Rich_Client_Platform

3.5 Storage and retrieval

The DOGMA-MESS methodology we applied in our use case imposes a number of requirements on the back-end. A first requirement is high scalability, as the method was developed with a large community of users in mind. A second requirement is the need for multi-synchronous collaborative editing, where multiple users can perform their part synchronously. The third (and last) requirement concerns the reasoner, which must be capable of handling all sorts of context dependencies.

DOGMA-MESS has been developed as an Apache Tapestry[14] Web application. It connects to the DOGMA Studio Server, which is a JBoss[15] J2EE application, backed by a PostgreSQL[16] relational database. The database hosts the relational model of the DOGMA framework, and the J2EE application layer provides the functional model. As one of the advantages of DOGMA is its scalability (Spyns et al 2002), we had to provide it with sufficient scalability support on the technical side. Relational databases have a long-proven track record to support this. Other storage approaches, such as XML databases and triple stores are currently growing in popularity and have proven to withstand large data sets as well (Lee 2004). At this point however, we chose the more traditional approach because of its longer history of scalability. The JBoss Application Server is widely used in industrial applications, and as such it has proven itself. Thanks to the J2EE aspect of the application, it is relatively easy to connect to the server (e.g., via Web services) and make use of the data. DOGMA-MESS stores and retrieves all its data using the DOGMA Studio Server and the DOGMA Studio Workbench provides KE access to the available content.

A very important aspect of using a client/server architecture is the scalable support for collaborative environments. Via this approach, we can avoid the problem of different users each having a different version of the ontology in some XML format. All content is captured on the server, properly versioned, *and* thoroughly described in terms of context and other dependencies. At all times, the server monitors all changes and updates in order to detect possible conflicts.

As a reasoner, we use the Prolog+CG engine[17]. This reasoner provides all the potential of Horn clause logic available in Prolog, and has incorporated conceptual graphs as first class citizens. We use this reasoner to validate the context dependencies using conceptual graphs operation. For instance, to check whether a specialisation is still in line with its template, we call

---

[14] http://tapestry.apache.org/

[15] http://labs.jboss.com/portal/jbossas

[16] http://www.postgresql.org/

[17] http://prologpluscg.sourceforge.net/

Prolog+CG and use its conceptual graph's projection operation. There are many other conceptual graph reasoners available, but we chose Prolog+CG (Christiaens and de Moor 2006) because (1) it allows easy integration in DOGMA Studio because of its Java implementation, (2) it includes Prolog, which provides a lot of logic processing power and (3) it includes the necessary conceptual graph operators (e.g., projection). In the use case setup, we had a single Prolog+CG engine, which required the relevant data in-memory. We did not experience performance issues, but we foresee that larger data sets might cause problems in large comparison operations (e.g., matching of a query against all graphs in the server). These can be tackled by using more than one engine (on different physical servers).

We tried to use as much open-source software as possible, both for legal reasons as well as integration aspects. In the case of Prolog+CG, this open-source aspect and good communication with the maintainer of the software resulted in an improved and faster implementation of the reasoner, which was a benefit for both parties.

4.   CONCLUSION

In this chapter we presented our experiences in the CODRIVE Dutch bakery domain. We described the additional difficulties that the interorganisational setting brings, such as the capturing of tacit knowledge, meaning divergence and context dependencies, and the need for co-evolution with the community of practice. We presented DOGMA-MESS, our answer to dealing with these kinds of complexity. We then described our experiences with this approach, related to the theoretical chapters in this book. These experiences show that it is difficult, but feasible to empower non-knowledge engineers in ontology management. A very important aspect is evolution, which needs to be thoroughly assisted by proper system support, especially in interorganisational settings, where the ontology needs to co-evolve with its community of practice.

We can conclude that there are two benefits to involving the community stakeholders in the ontology engineering: (1) the collected input represents correct and accepted knowledge and (2) the input results from and creates involvement and ownership of all stakeholders. An ontology that is created by a small group of knowledge engineers in splendid isolation and then forced into reality and implementation has little chance of acceptance.

ACKNOWLEDGEMENTS

We would like to thank Luk Vervenne (Synergetics) for the valuable discussions about theory and case, Hans Wentink (NBC) as the Core Domain Expert in our case, and all the helpful Domain Experts from the Netherlands. The research described in this chapter was partially sponsored by EU Leonardo da Vinci CODRIVE project B/04/B/F/PP-144.339, by the DIP EU-FP6 507483 project and by the Brussels-Capital Region (IWOIB PRB 2006).

REFERENCES

Banerjee, J., Kim, W. Kim, H., and Korth., H. (1987) Semantics and implementation of schema evolution in object-oriented databases. Proc. ACM SIGMOD Conf. Management of Data, 16(3), pp. 311–322

Christiaens S, de Moor A. (2006). Tool interoperability from the trenches: the case of DOGMA-MESS. In: Proc. of the 1st Conceptual Structures Tool Interoperability Workshop (CS-TIW 2006) at the 14th International Conference on Conceptual Structures, Aalborg, Denmark

Delugach H.S. (2001) CharGer: A Graphical Conceptual Graph Editor. Workshop on Conceptual Graphs Tools at the 9th International Conference on Conceptual Structures, 2001, Stanford University

De Leenheer P., de Moor A. (2005). Context-driven disambiguation in ontology elicitation. In P. Shvaiko and J. Euzenat (eds), Context and Ontologies: Theory, Practice, and Applications. Proc. of the 1st Context and Ontologies Workshop, AAAI/IAAI 2005, Pittsburgh, USA, pp 17–24

De Leenheer P., de Moor A., Meersman R. (2007). Context dependency management in ontology engineering: a formal approach. Journal on Data Semantics VIII, LNCS 4380, Springer pp 26–56

De Leenheer, P. and Meersman, R. (2007) Towards Community-based Evolution of Knowledge-intensive Systems. In Proc. of the 6th Int'l Conf. on Ontologies, DataBases, and Applications of Semantics (ODBASE 2007) (Vilamoura, Portugal), LNCS, Springer

de Moor A. (2005). Patterns for the Pragmatic Web. In Proc. Of the 13th International Conference on Conceptual Structures, Kassel, Germany, pp 1–18

de Moor A., De Leenheer P., Meersman R. (2006). DOGMA-MESS: A meaning evolution support system for interorganizational ontology engineering. In: Proc. of the 14th International Conference on Conceptual Structures, Aalborg, Denmark. LNCS 4068, pp 189–203

Diaz, A. (2005) Supporting Divergences in Knowledge Sharing Communities. PhD Thesis, Univesité Henry Poincarè, Nancy I, France

Edgington T, Choi B, Henson K, Raghu TS, Vinze A (2004). Adopting ontology to facilitate knowledge sharing. Communications of the ACM, 47(11), pp 217–222

Fellbaum C. (1998). Wordnet: An Electronic Lexical Database (Language, Speech and Communication). The MIT Press

Fillmore C.H. (1968). The case for case. In: Bach and Harms (eds), Universals in linguistic theory, Holt, Rinehart and Winston, New York

Gómez-Pérez A., Corcho O., Fernández-López M. (2003). Ontological Engineering. Springer-Verlag, New York, LLC

Jarrar, M., Demey, J., Meersman, R. (2003) On reusing conceptual data modeling for ontology engineering. Journal on Data Semantics 1(1):185–207

Jarrar M. (2005). Towards methodological principles for ontology engineering. PhD Thesis, Vrije Universiteit Brussel.

Jarrar M. (2006). Towards the notion of gloss, and the adoption of linguistic resources in formal ontology engineering. In: Proceedings of the 15th International World Wide Web Conference, WWW2006. Edinburgh, Scotland. May 2006. ACM, 2006

Lee R. (2004). Scalability report on triple store applications. http://simile.mit.edu/reports/stores/

Lenat D.B., Guha R.V. (1990). Building Large Knowledge-based Systems: Representation and Inference in the Cyc Project. Addison-Wesley, Boston, Massachusetts

Lenat D.B. (1998). The dimensions of context-space. Cycorp technical report (http://www.cyc.com/doc/context-space.pdf)

Meersman R. (2001). Ontologies and Databases: More than a Fleeting Resemblance. In: d'Atri, A., Missikoff M. (eds), *OES/SEO 2001 Rome Workshop*. Luiss Publications

Miller E., Manola F. (2004). RDF primer. W3C recommendation, http://www.w3.org/TR/2004/REC-rdf-primer-20040210/

Nijssen G.M., Halpin T.A. (1989). Conceptual schema and relational database design: a fact oriented approach. Prentice Hall, Australia

Niles I., Pease A. (2001). Origins of the Standard upper Merged Ontology. In: Working Notes of the IJCAI-2001 Workshop on the IEEE Standard Upper Ontology, Seattle, Washington, August 6

Nonaka I. and Takeuchi, H. (1995). The knowledge-creating company: how Japanese companies create the dynamics of innovation. Oxford University Press

Polanyi, M. (1967) The Tacit Dimension, Garden City, NY, Double Day

Reiter R. (1984). Towards a logical reconstruction of relational database theory. In: Brodie M., Mylopoulos J., Schmidt J. (eds) On conceptual modeling, pp 191–233

Sowa, J.F. (1984). Conceptual structures: information processing in mind and machine. Addison-Wesley, Reading, Massachusetts

Sowa J.F. (1999). Knowledge Representation: Logical, Philosophical, and Computational Foundations, Brooks Cole Publishing Co., Pacific Grove, CA, ©2000. Actual publication date, 16 August 1999.

Spyns P., Meersman R., Jarrar M. (2002). Data modeling versus ontology engineering. SIGMOD Record, 31(4), pp 12–17

Trog D., Vereecken J., Christiaens S., De Leenheer P., Meersman R.. T-Lex: A role-based ontology engineering tool. In: Meersman R, Zahir T, Herrero P (eds), On the move to meaningful internet systems 2006: OTM 2006 Workshops (ORM06), LNCS 4278, Springer-Verlag, pp 1191–1200

van Harmelen F., McGuinness D.L. (2004). OWL Web Ontology Language overview. W3C recommendation. http://www.w3.org/TR/2004/REC-owl-features-20040210

ABOUT THE EDITORS

Martin Hepp is a professor of computer science and a senior researcher at the Digital Enterprise Research Institute (DERI) at the University of Innsbruck in Innsbruck, Austria, where he leads the research group "Semantics in Business Information Systems." He created eClassOWL, the first industry-strength ontology for products and services and is currently working on using Semantic Web services technology for business process management. Before joining DERI, he was an assistant professor of computer information systems at Florida Gulf Coast University, Fort Myers (FL) and a visiting scientist with the e-Business Solutions Group at the IBM Zurich Research Laboratory. Martin holds a master's degree in business management and business information systems and a Ph.D. in business information systems from the University of Würzburg, Germany.

Pieter De Leenheer is a researcher at the Semantics Technology and Applications Research Laboratory (STARLab) at the Vrije Universiteit Brussel in Brussels, and holds a MSc degree in computer science from the the same university. At the time of writing, he is finishing his PhD on community-based evolution of knowledge-intensive systems, and is validating his work in the EU projects Prolix and CoDrive. As part of the European project DIP, he developed methods and tools for the management of ontologies supporting Semantic Web services. Pieter authored several publications in various international journals and conference proceedings. He is also teaching assistant of Robert Meersman, and a guest lecturer of database theory, (Web) information systems, and Semantic Web languages at the Vrije Universiteit Brussel and the University of Hasselt, Belgium.

Aldo de Moor is the owner of CommunitySense, a research consultancy firm in Tilburg, the Netherlands, which focuses on information and communication systems development for collaborative communities. Before starting CommunitySense, he was a senior researcher at the Semantics Technology and Applications Research Laboratory (STARLab), Vrije Universiteit Brussel, Belgium. Prior to that, he was an assistant professor at

Infolab, Dept. of Information Systems and Management, Tilburg University, the Netherlands. Aldo holds a Ph.D. in information management from Tilburg University. Aldo's research interests include the evolution of virtual communities, communicative workflow modeling, argumentation technologies, language/action theory, socio-technical systems design, and ontology-guided meaning negotiation. Aldo has been a visiting researcher at the University of Guelph, Canada, and the University of Technology, Sydney, Australia. Aldo has been program co-chair of the International Conference on Conceptual Structures, the Language/Action Perspective Working Conference on Communication Modeling, and the Pragmatic Web Conference. He has published widely and been involved in many projects related to the analysis and design of information systems for collaborative communities.

York Sure is a senior researcher at SAP Research in Karlsruhe, where he is working on the Internet of Services and semantic technologies. Before joining SAP, York was an assistant professor at the institute AIFB of the University of Karlsuhe, where he gave lectures on Semantic Web and computer science at both graduate and undergraduate level. While at the AIFB, he was project leader for the EU IST FP6 Integrated Project SEKT, the EU IST FP6 Thematic Network of Excellence Knowledge Web, and the international project "Halo — Towards a Digital Aristotle." York graduated in industrial engineering in 1999 and received his PhD in computer science in May 2003. From June to September 2006, he was a visiting assistant professor at Stanford University. In 2006, York was awarded the IBM UIMA Innovation Award and in 2007 the doIT Software Award.

INDEX

Abstract Mapping Language (AML), 193–195, 201, 203
Accessibility, 27, 29, 36, 152
Adaptive User Interface, 27
Algebraic operators, 43
Alignment, 18, 20, 77, 132, 156, 159–166, 177–204, 266, 272, 281
Analogy method, 210–213, 221–223

Business perspective, 207–224

Cognitive Studies, 49
Collaboration Support, 78, 167, 285
Collaborative ontology engineering, 60, 132, 152–161, 165, 169, 268, 281
Communities of use, 132–133, 139, 164–166, 170, 266, 269, 281, 285
Community, 6, 8, 60, 65, 68, 78, 132–138, 153–157, 160–169, 208, 212–213, 223–224, 266–269, 281
Conceptual dynamics, 8
Conceptual modeling, 5, 10–12, 15, 215, 217–218
Configurable User Interface, 41–42
Conflict management, 146, 151, 163–164
Consensus, ix, 5, 132, 156, 161, 164, 167, 233, 266–267, 278–280
Context matching, 181–182
Context, 133–135, 156–158, 166, 193–194, 269, 277
Contextual fringe, 47, 52
Contextualisations, 136, 161, 270, 277
Controlled vocabulary effect, 5, 7, 12–13
Correspondences, 179, 180, 184, 187–194, 201
Cost drivers, 145, 208–224
Cost estimation, 19–28, 98, 145, 210–213, 221–223
Cost models, costs. See ontology cost models.
Costs, costs and benefits , 11, 19, 145, 207–224

Customization, 25 28, 36, 41, 43, 49–55, 213, 222, 224, 235
Customizing ontologies, 51–54

Data individuals, 6
Data integration, 178, 181–182, 202
Data mediation, 190, 192, 198, 200–201
Data schema evolution, 132, 140, 141, 146, 148, 151, 164
Database mappings, 260–262
Database schema import, 259–260
Databases, 18, 90–106, 114–124, 140, 181–185, 259–262
Description logics, 76, 92, 100–107, 113, 149, 170
Disjunctive datalog programs, 101
DL reasoning, 18, 90, 103, 105, 113, 117
DOGMA, 268–269
DOGMA-MESS, 170, 268 273, 277–286

eClassOWL, 14–15, 289
Effects of ontologies, 10–16
Effort, 8–10, 15, 17, 19, 37–38, 48, 51, 137, 144–145, 211–212, 216–224
Entity-relationship model, 5, 16
Expressiveness, 8, 18, 45, 89, 115–118, 179, 262

Faceted navigation, 45–47
Filter operation, 52
F-Logic, 5, 62, 64, 72–76, 81–82, 85, 254, 257, 261, 263
Formal account, See semantic account.

Graph transformation, 163–164
Graphical user interface (GUI), 28, 35–37, 80, 84–85, 254
Grounding, 13, 81, 134–135, 138–139, 156, 238, 243, 273, 284

Human computer interaction (HCI), 16, 25–32, 41, 55

ICD-10, 17
Import function, 35
Incentive conflicts, 19
Individuals, 6, 8, 12, 15, 64, 100, 104–105, 179–180
Information integration, 258–262
Information sources, 215, 243, 246
Intellectual property rights, 19
Interaction, 25–31, 55, 114, 167
    user interaction, 38–46
    with human minds, 16–17

Knowledge base(s), 4, 6, 15, 37, 64, 100–105, 116–120, 257, 262
Knowledge organization system (KOS), 4, 6–8, 15, 17
Knowledge representation, 12, 31, 105, 123, 132, 164, 172, 248

Lexical disambiguation, 135–136, 273
Lexical enrichment, 10, 13
Linguistic grounding. *See* lexical enrichment.
Logical inconsistencies, 16

Mappings, 11, 39, 73, 77, 155, 179, 195
Meaning analysis, 277
Meaning conflicts, 137–139
Meaning consensus reuse, 278
Meaning negotiation, 132–133, 156, 166–167, 266–269, 272, 280–281, 290
Mediators, 106, 178, 189, 238–240

Natural language grounding, 135–136. *See also* lexical enrichment.
Network externalities, 19

OntoClean, 12
ONTOCOM, 208–210, 214–224
Ontological commitment, 5, 9–10, 18, 137–138, 277
Ontological individuals, 6. *See also* individuals.
Ontology alignment, 18, 20, 77, 132, 156, 159–161, 165–166, 177–204, 266, 272, 281
Ontology applications, 79, 136, 181, 233–243, 246
Ontology change management, 133, 152, 162
Ontology change operators, 139–148, 160–164, 281
Ontology cost models, ontology costs, 208–211. *See also* cost models.

Ontology debugging, 71–75, 149–150, 255–256
Ontology development tools, 60–74
Ontology divergence, 133–139, 155–156, 165–166, 281, 286
Ontology economics, 208–217. *See also* costs and benefits, incentive conflicts, resource consumption.
Ontology elicitation, 132–138, 155–158, 166, 266–273, 279–280
Ontology engineering costs, 209–214. *See also* costs and benefits, resource consumption.
Ontology evolution, 17–18, 77, 86, 132–134, 140–152, 163–170, 181–182, 216, 253–257, 281–283
Ontology learning, 17, 237
Ontology matching, 178–185, 193–197, 204
Ontology repositories , *See* repository.
Ontology reuse, 26, 31, 51, 168, 216, 220, 223
Ontology validation, 149–150, 193, 197, 255
Ontology versioning, *See* versioning.
OWL, 5–6, 18, 30–33, 37–40, 61–81, 90–123, 138, 149, 180, 237, 259, 284
OWL-DL, 61–62, 90, 99, 110–112, 123

Protégé, 30–32, 35–40, 63–68, 74–75, 167, 202, 237–238

Query answering, 61–62, 92, 95, 103–105, 118, 122, 181–182
Query processing scalability, 91, 116
Query rewriting, 198

RDBMS (relational database management systems), 18, 69, 74, 89, 93–95, 116, 120–123, 261
RDF stores, 62, 93–94, 116–117
Reasoner, 9, 14–15, 18, 59–75, 81–82, 90, 92, 95–96, 100–105, 109, 113, 117–120, 123, 262, 285–286
Relational databases, *See* RDBMS.
Repository, 18, 61–62, 69, 82–83, 90–94, 98–99, 114, 122–123
Resource consumption, 19

Scalability, 18, 43, 90–91, 116, 138, 267–268, 278, 285
Semantic account , 5–6, 10, 14–15
Semantic net(s), 5, 14, 47, 148
Semantic Web services, 90–91, 105, 123, 190–192, 231–232, 237–244, 289

SKOS, 17

Tacit knowledge, 133, 155, 158, 166, 266–267, 279–280, 286
Terminology representation, 248
Terminology research, 13–14
Thesauri, thesaurus, 17, 160, 183

UML, 5, 16, 68–70, 74, 84
UNSPSC, 11, 17
Usability, 29, 33, 36, 42
Use cases, 11, 19–20, 46, 54, 82, 90, 121–123, 170, 215, 246–249, 255, 261, 273, 279–286

Version, versioning, 9, 20, 37, 39, 64, 82, 133, 141, 146, 150–151,164–168, 281–282
Visualization, 16, 31–40, 47–49, 52–55, 65–75, 194, 255

Web Service Modeling Framework (WSMF), 238
Web Service Modeling Language (WSML), 5–6, 90, 104–119, 123–124, 127, 168, 203, 205, 238–240, 242–243
Web Service Modeling Ontology (WSMO), 105–106, 168–169, 232, 237–242

XML schema(s), 4, 6–7, 110, 119, 135, 167